INTRODUCTION TO PHILOSOPHY

*****

About the Author's Studies

ANTONIO ROSMINI

INTRODUCTION TO PHILOSOPHY

Volume 1

About the Author's Studies

Translated by
ROBERT A. MURPHY

ROSMINI HOUSE
DURHAM

Rosmini House, Woodbine Road
Durham DH1 5DR, U.K.

Website: rosmini-in-english.org

Translated from
Introduzione alla Filosofia
Città Nuova Edition, vol. 2, Rome, 1979

Typeset by Rosmini House, Durham
Printed by Bell & Bain Limited, Glasgow

ISBN 1 899093 02 8

Note

The many and long quotations given by the author in their original language have been translated. An *asterisk* indicates that the original language can be found in the section entitled 'Original Language References' (p. 211).

Square brackets [ ] indicate notes or additions by the translator.

References to this and other works of Rosmini are given by paragraph number unless otherwise stated.

Foreword

This work, offered as volume one of *Introduction to Philosophy*, is a translation of a part of Rosmini's single Italian volume, *Introduzione alla Filosofia*.

In the spring of 1850 Rosmini began preparing a complete edition of all the works he had published up to that time. He considered it opportune to begin the collection with an introductory volume which, as he himself tells us, is composed of various works 'written at different periods, on different occasions and in different circumstances'. These works, which include some letters he wrote on philosophy, were used as introductory material because they dealt with preliminary philosophical questions such as the characteristics of philosophy, a philosophical system and philosophical language. However he decided to precede these writings with an entirely new essay, a discourse, under the title *About the Author's Studies*, followed by a simple dedication 'To his friends and to all who wish him well'.

The dedication is significant because of the events that had recently preceded the writing of the discourse. Some of his teachings had been attacked, which resulted in a long drawn-out controversy, sometimes acrimonious on the part of his critics. Such was its vehemence and its relentlessness that the Pope eventually imposed silence on both parties. Finally, to add to his suffering, two of his (non-philosophical) books were condemned and placed on the *Index of Forbidden Books*. Added to these troubles was his reluctant involvement in the great political events of the time: in 1848 the Piedmontese government had persuaded him to accept an embassy to the Pope to persuade the papacy to support Piedmont in its struggle against Austria. The embassy failed, and when the Roman populace rose against the Pope, Rosmini had to flee with the Pontiff into exile at Gaeta, where Rosmini suffered continual harrassment and obstruction from the Neapolitan police and especially from the

Pope's Secretary of State. Aware that he could do nothing, he received permission from the Pope to leave, and late in 1849 reached his beloved Stresa where in the spring of 1850 he began *About the Author's Studies*, dedicated to those friends who, despite past events, still 'wished him well'.

The work is a kind of *Apologia*. In his mind, it would serve as a history of the deepest motives for his philosophy, and reveal the spirit which inspired his system and all his activity as thinker and author. He had reached the culmination of maturity and felt he should bring all his works together in an ordered collection. In this introductory work he speaks about the ends he proposed for himself in his philosophy: to reduce truth to a system and to form a philosophy which could serve as a solid basis for all the branches of knowledge and thus pervade all culture with a new spirit.

But, in his studies, Rosmini could not exclude religion and revealed truth, not only because of his own faith, but because reason, when enlightened and fortified by divine authority, can contribute to greater understanding of what is revealed and be a support, not an obstacle, to religious faith. Reason could therefore be an aid to theology, especially in its debate with the atheistic rationalism of the 18th century. Moreover, for him the human being is not complete if left solely in his natural state; the supernatural state was necessary if human beings were to be complete. This state, although essentially different from the natural state, was not entirely foreign to it. His studies therefore included those of man raised to the supernatural state, *Supernatural Philosophy* and *Supernatural Anthropology*, as he called them. Thus, the last part of the work deals with the role of religious belief and of its connection with reason.

TERENCE WATSON

Durham,
February, 2004

Contents

CONTENTS

PREFACE

The present collection consists of works on different subjects, written at different periods, on different occasions and in different circumstances. In some of these works, the approach I have adopted is based on natural reasoning. In this case, to ensure the results are true, I have constantly compared the conclusions with the traditions of mankind and with the common feeling of humanity, where such evidence is forthcoming. In others, I deal with issues on a higher plane to which reason can accede only when enlightened and fortified by divine authority. The entire collection, then, can be divided into two main parts under the headings:

1. *Philosophical* section: works dealing with natural reasoning.
2. *Theological* section: works dealing with supernatural teaching.

Although the first section is concerned with natural reasoning, I have not hesitated to make use of information from a higher source to supplement ordinary, dialectical reason where this was necessary. The use of such information is designed to ensure a fully rounded treatment, more useful to the reader — the works, after all, are written with the reader in mind. Similarly, in the case of the second section, the elevated nature of the subject does not prevent or rule out the use of natural reasoning which, in treating such subjects, is afforded unlimited scope for new and wonderful modes of expression. In this light, the two-fold subject and the single type of reasoning identical in each part enable us to call the first section *Natural Philosophy* and the second *Supernatural Philosophy*.

The first part, therefore, is to be the entrance, as it were, through which the well-disposed reader is led into the edifice of knowledge. I call it: *Introduction to Philosophy*.

An introduction to philosophy is not usually considered a

distinct branch of knowledge. It can include any items of knowledge which prepare and dispose the mind and spirit of the person who is thinking about studying the various branches of philosophy. The scope of such items is not strictly prescribed, and the different essays which make up the present volume would clearly seem to be relevant.

Nevertheless, these essays — some more than others — exhibit a more general purpose. They are intended to show the unity pervading the subsequent works, and the spirit animating them. This spirit, precisely because it is itself a unity, draws together the different members and forms them into a single body.

As I see it, prior knowledge of the overall pattern into which the essays fit and how they concur in a common aim can only make for an easier and sounder overall understanding.

[The following is a complete list of all the essays contained in *Introduction to Philosophy*. The volume numbers refer to the projected English translations.

Vol. 1. *About the Author's Studies*

Vol. 2. I. *Characteristics of Philosophy*
II. *The Philosophical System*
III. *On the Essence of Knowledge*
IV. *How to Forward Philosophical Studies*

Vol. 3. I. *The Classification of Philosophical Systems and the Necessary Dispositions for Finding the Truth*
II. *Philosophical Language and Some Objections to the Author's Philosophy*
III. *French Eclecticism*]

ABOUT THE AUTHOR'S STUDIES

It is hard to give
new life to what is old,
authority to what is new,
splendour to what has fallen out of use,
light to what is obscure,
grace to what is wearisome,
trust to what is doubtful.*

Pliny, *Natural History,* Preface

ABOUT THE AUTHOR'S STUDIES

To his friends and to all who wish him well

1. The public and authors have reciprocal duties which must be faithfully fulfilled if reading and writing are to achieve their purpose. Disregard for these duties makes it impossible for readers and writers to bind themselves in a truly human *society* formed on the basis of shared ideas and *affections*; they neither behold and seek the same truth nor desire the same good.

One of the duties readers have to themselves, if they wish to benefit by what they read, and to the author if they wish to judge him reasonably, is to take care to avoid misunderstanding. At the same time, authors have a duty, for their own sake and that of the public, to express themselves clearly, and above all to indicate the end they hope to achieve with their writings. They submit to examination the spirit and aim of the body of teachings and research with which they desire to communicate intellectually with their fellows.

1a. I have tried to do this — I'm not sure how successful I have been — in each of the works I have written and been bold enough to publish. Now, however, these treatises have been gathered together and the entire collection offered to the public under various headings. At this point, I need to fulfil another part of my duty as a writer. Each book, although sufficiently self-explanatory, cannot of itself indicate the general character and spirit which animates them all. It cannot show how they are *all* related, how they tend towards a single end, and how they attain unity as fragments, so to speak, of a single sphere of knowledge. This would be of considerable assistance, and is perhaps necessary, in uncovering the foundation of my thought and enabling readers with enough desire and patience to see for themselves that in all these works I have aimed at unity in

systematic knowledge. I am in fact persuaded that everything I
have written has been concerned with teaching a single, but
most fruitful and inexhaustible subject.

I cannot say that I have succeeded — it is up to others to
decide that — but I can say that that is what I intended.

I certainly hold that anyone who devotes himself to the study
and pursuit of truth must keep before his inward eye the image
of knowledge as one, simple and indivisible, applicable to all
individual entities yet remaining itself unfragmented. I would
go so far as to say that the human mind is naturally aware of this
image since it is nature itself which clearly exhibits perfect
unity; division and fragmentation are man-made. When human
art attains perfection it repents, as it were, of its initial
endeavours to decompartmentalisation; it is reconciled with
nature and, reassembling the fragments, gazes fondly and
calmly, with insatiable longing, on the restored and perfectly
united body of knowledge.

1b. When developing such a theme, I feel I am responding to
duty or something similar to duty. However, being obliged to
talk at length about myself and my studies makes me feel more
keenly than ever the need of special kindliness and indulgence
on the reader's part. It is to my friends, therefore, and all
well-disposed readers that my words are addressed.

Over the past thirty years during which this collection of
works was written, a good number of affectionate, wise and
loyal Italians have encouraged me in this arduous task, and
associated their thoughts, endeavours and concerns with mine.
They have shared my contradictions and disappointments, and
have always been responsive to my deepest feelings of sorrow
or hope for mankind with a warmth and generosity all their
own. Some of them have pressed me to undertake the following
work. As an expression of gratitude, I dedicate it to them all
and, although writing also for the public, speak to them
familiarly.

To give the argument some shape, I shall straightaway state
the particular aims I have pursued in my studies. Next, I shall
indicate how I achieved them. Finally, I shall sketch, albeit
crudely, the image of wisdom which, in my view, must regulate
all our thinking as well as all human actions. In this image, both
thought and action must come to that unique state of perfection

[1b]

for which every mind and heart has a natural yearning. As I said at the outset, prompted by nature, I hope to have kept my mental gaze fixed firmly upon that image as I wrote the different essays in the days of my youth when, under the guidance of excellent teachers, I first gazed upon it and tried the public's critical judgment with a few rough and ready essays.

PART ONE

THE PARTICULAR AIMS OF THE TEACHING IN THE VARIOUS WORKS OF THE AUTHOR

First Aim: To Combat Error

2. The human mind, although created for truth, is easily led astray by an alien, hostile principle which lures it into mistaking the outward show of truth for truth itself. In us the will, following the promptings of the mind, clutches at the empty, outward show of good rather than the true good for which it was created. This is the cause of error and guilt.

A primary, most useful task of the philosopher is to debate with this wily principle, to expose its insidious arguments and subtle errors, to confound it and thereby set minds free from its snares. This intellectual struggle in defence of the human mind exposed to deception and guile has been undertaken by scholars and philosophers imbued with love of their fellows. Following them, we find an abundance of arguments and dialectical weapons readily available for the fray.

These have been discovered and fashioned by a body of the finest, most sincere and charitable thinkers after deep reflection and long nights of self-sacrifice. With their arguments, they uncovered deceit, banished sophistry, confounded error. In the process, they unmasked that hidden deceiver of mankind who has always sought to cloak in darkness the light of truth — or rather to invest his darkness with deceptive light. The large, effective store of arguments built up by these scholars has been used by them to preserve for mankind the truth, our most precious heritage. Our forefathers have bequeathed to us such a large, abundant store of sound knowledge that every harmful error can, I am sure, be demolished and every fallacy can be exposed if only we use these weapons properly.

Each century has contributed to this inexhaustible store of wisdom, especially the nineteenth which has acquired a new and deeper understanding through the truth of the gospel. In spite of the wars of the present age and the changing fortunes of nations, writer after writer has embodied this wisdom in an impressively large series of volumes.

If only our contemporaries knew what riches they possessed! If only they were zealous enough in their love of knowledge and their passion for truth to devote themselves diligently to the study of learned works, they would discover the treasure they contain and use it to their advantage! Ours, however, is a thoroughly lax age in which substantial, impartial studies of this sort are rare; those who take pride in material, superficial things spurn the exertion involved in profound, spiritual matters. Ephemeral works are read, whilst those that have survived for centuries are ignored. This explains the naiveté and helplessness of our weak-minded age in the face of fallacies so often overcome by our predecessors. That is why new works are required to expound a more basic version of elementary truths vital to authentic, human living and revitalise arguments that protect truth from sophistry. Truths and reasoning are recorded in the archives of human knowledge but often lie forgotten, gathering dust. To present these truths to the reader was one of my aims when writing the essays in this collection.

3. The need to champion these precious truths will be better understood if we consider that error continually adopts new forms and puts out new shoots. The result is apparently new errors. Hence the need to devise and develop new arguments against them. Strictly speaking, it is not error that leads mankind astray; by his very essence, man is called to the truth. It is the form of error that tempts and deceives him by disguising falsehood and presenting it, dressed up as truth, to the unsophisticated mind. The real skill of the philosopher, then, as he seeks to protect the human mind from such deadly deception, consists in stripping error of its outward apparel. Everyone loathes error when it is revealed in its naked and disfigured state.

4. Side by side with the tradition of truth, an enduring tradition of error is handed down from age to age. 'Tradition' is, perhaps, slightly misleading here because there is continual

progression; not progression with regard to substance but to form, and more specifically, to dialectical form.

Psychology reduces to a single principle the shifting sands of these dialectical forms in which thought, whether true or not, enters the mind. This science tells us that the first and most universal law governing the gradual development of human intelligence moves intelligence from an initial, direct act of cognition to a first act of reflection, then to a second and a third and so on. The movement is gradual, without any sudden transition, towards an ever higher level of speculation. Consequently, the continuous intellectual activity of individuals, society and mankind (whether conscious or not) represents an unending attempt to transfer knowledge from a lower to a higher level of reflection. In other words, their dialectical and mental forms are changed. In fact, the various forms differ so markedly from one another that it is not easy to recall the exact scientific subject under scrutiny. Each order of reflection has a corresponding form of cognition requiring a new and distinctive type of language.

The disputes which arise between those who have reached one of these orders or spheres of cognition make no sense to those who have not yet reached such an order. Those whose thinking has progressed through further orders and have raised the debate to an even higher order of reflection find the issue changed; the questions seem different now because different language is being used.

Even if those involved were fully aware of the issue in dispute, they would not be satisfied with previous answers and solutions which they see as rough, crude or inadequate. When errors — even old ones — are preached in new forms, and solid truths are disputed in novel terms, people are tempted and easily led astray. It is as if these errors were being introduced for the first time and had never previously been eliminated. They have to be answered and dispelled once more, but through reasons advanced in a form corresponding to the order of reflection at which the conflicting ideas operate. It takes a while for the upholders of truth to exploit fully the numerous studies needed, and to find the appropriate form of replies by using corresponding terms to refute contrary views. This puts paid to deception and exposes error, and would signify the final defeat

[4]

of error but for the fact that, like Proteus in the legend, it casts about to find a new form within a new sphere of reflection and returns to the fray reinforced and revitalised. This explains why in history there are some ages in which error reigns supreme. At such times, deception and falsehood appear to be widespread, and minds irresolute. Unable to see the light within them, or so it would seem, they stagger and fall at every turn. These are periods when error, more active and restless than unruffled truth, has overtaken truth by even deeper reflection, assuming a further advanced form which truth with its tranquil approach has not attained.

4a. Error, it seems, has won the day and cannot find any new adversaries to take on. Conscious of the disastrous times, those totally dedicated to truth cannot bear to see mankind so bereft. They struggle to raise truth itself to the level of reflection attained by error where they seek the most effective types of argument in support of truth. They are then seen to have tackled the fallacies of error on its own ground and using its own terms. At this point, the intellectual and moral state of mankind improves, a new age dawns, men's minds recover their former vigour. They hold firmly to the truth and their spirits regain confidence. They are healed by new light and return through truth to virtue, truth's glorious offspring.

History reveals a pattern of alternating periods. In some, sophists are predominant, in others, philosophers. In some, a self-assured version of error usurps the name of philosophy; the average person, when confronted with the new type of argument, succumbs. In other periods, error is ignominiously stripped of its unmerited title, 'philosophy', and the great majority of people acknowledge that the work of these self-styled philosophers is in reality nothing but brashness and ignorance (which for a time had dishonoured the good names of philosophy and philosopher).

Divine Providence, as though by fixed laws, seems to regulate the rhythm and tempo of this ever-changing recurrent pattern of periods as error and truth predominate in turn. These laws control human history. The victory of good over evil transposes that history with its different notes into a harmony pleasing to God's ear.

4b. In the 18th century, sophists were in command of public

[4a–4b]

opinion. (*Sophist* is one of those titles originally used by the Greeks and later adopted universally. It lost its respectable meaning and took on a pejorative sense after the sham philosophers who had appropriated the title were vanquished by genuine thinkers). John Locke's work (1699) heralded the opening of this new age during which a campaign of crude yet effective deception was waged. From then on, humanity has been directed away from solid, established truths, and deceived by utilitarian considerations and wonderful promises of simple, previously unimagined knowledge. Minds were flattered into a docile acceptance of gratuitous opinions and gross errors in theology, ethics, politics, human sociability, and about all the most fundamental and most important questions relating to our life and salvation here below and in the world to come. Although some courageous writers did respond to these errors, the same mistakes are still leading people astray because they were not met head on in their own particular forms. These forms may be somewhat dated, but they still appear attractive, and it is essential to discover and make use of corresponding forms in defence of truth. That is what I have tried to do in the various essays making up this collection.

Second Aim: To Systematise Truth

5. I have already mentioned how Providence has so arranged things that from evil (that is, error) comes good (that is, the victory of truth). Long ago, St. Augustine remarked that heretics enabled the Church 'to defend the truths under attack by examining them more closely, by understanding them better, and preaching them with greater conviction'.[1] There are other ways

---

[1] 'The fact is that many aspects of the Catholic faith, whilst being vehemently disputed by heretics are examined more deeply, understood more clearly and preached more fervently so that they can be better defended'* (*The City of God*, bk. 16, c. 2). — 'It is indeed true that the refutation of heretics gives greater prominence to the Church's beliefs and the principles of sound doctrine'* (*Confessions*, bk. 7, c. 19).

in which teachers of error unwittingly assist in the spread of truth among the human race. As they are unable to pass on their errors to mankind without first disguising them as truth, they do not destroy the love of truth entirely but rather bear witness to it. Furthermore, they include within their falsehoods some fragments of truth which they use as signposts in their treatises and as the starting point in their reasoning. Usually, these fragments contain some aspects of truth which till then had perhaps been overlooked by genuine, sincere scholars. By passing these on with other newly discovered truths, sophists gain approval and enhance the reputation of their own philosophical school; in their efforts to propagate error, they bring to light a number of hidden truths. Thus every tiny aspect of truth has its appointed time to surface, find its true value and gain currency. In this task, even the enemies of truth have a part. Nevertheless, all those who swallow the bait are caught on the hook of falsehood.

5a. The harm such fraudulent scholars do is largely due to their display of worthiness. They are able to lead people astray only by transposing ancient, already refuted errors to a higher plane of reflection. The opposition is obliged to follow upwards and draw truth to this higher plane where its outward forms as perceived by the human intelligence are greatly extended. A person who reaches a higher plane of reflection is like someone who has moved from the valley to the mountain peaks where he looks out over an immensely vaster horizon.

At every order of true or false reflection the human mind discovers a new panorama of true or false knowledge. It is not surprising then that false scholars attract disciples by their use of original forms and language. Anything new is like a light; it dominates and appeals to minds avid for knowledge and always keen to go beyond long-established boundaries. Anything new appeals to them and elicits their admiration. Those who pass themselves off as teachers of mankind never fail to acquire in estimation the title and reputation of heralds of knowledge and progress. But we should give all their due, even the devil. So we have to admit that, in one sense, sophists are heralds of philosophical progress as they continually invent new absurdities which awaken from their lethargy true scholars who then feel impelled to rouse our minds into action. As a result, over the

[5a]

centuries, the human mind has been able to examine unchanging truth in all its beauty from all sides.

5b. However, truth reveals only one aspect at a time to the intellect, albeit under the most impressive forms. Experience shows only too well that scholars, unaware of the threat from apparent falsehoods to the satisfaction brought by truth, and oblivious of the risk to their fellows, who are easily ensnared by these falsehoods, may not be prompt enough to match the extraordinary activity arising in their captious and deceitful opponents from what Augustine calls 'their hot disquiet'.

But the children of this world, wiser than the children of light, cannot be given credit for any progress brought about by their errors, although the ingenuous crowd they deceive may consider they deserve it.

Any credit is due, not to man, but to the high designs of Providence which promotes and infallibly guides human development by either permitting evil to act as a kind of stimulus or by allowing good to prevail. Throughout its vast domain, in which every being is limited and none can accomplish anything on its own, Providence makes use of every kind of entia to contribute to the great work it has contemplated from all eternity. At one time it may permit wayward philosophers to introduce error into a new sphere of thought, at another it may assist sound and upright thinkers to introduce truth into the same sphere.

By means of these two operations, the human mind and the human heart make progress towards their goal. Furthermore, although the God of truth in his wisdom uses our potencies and will, whether good or bad, to hasten the accomplishment of the plan he had in mind when creating the universe, he does not employ duress. By exploiting the impatience and activity of some thinkers who continually abandon the truth to seek it amid falsehood, he obtains for true philosophers a further, most valuable advantage. Stirred to emulate false philosophers, they become ashamed of their own intellectual passivity which easily lapses into laxity and sloth when compared with the troublesome and ever-restless diligence of sophists. Honest thinkers feel ashamed when they see they have been left behind in their philosophical studies by thinkers whose aim is to obscure the primary, wholesome truths on which the intellectual and moral life of mankind depends. Such a feeling of shame was to be admired in earlier times; nowadays, the need for it is overwhelming and so pressing that, in my view, no honest, sensitive writer can avoid it.

5c. Over the centuries, there have been periods when mankind has suffered sudden and catastrophic harm as a result of the widespread dissemination of grave errors. Scholars who should have been ready and equipped to combat such errors as soon as they arose did not even recognise them at the time for what they were. Errors, which thus had time to take root in human minds, developed and flourished. Their eradication became immeasurably more arduous and protracted.

This stimulus, which Providence offers through experience on a natural plane to those who love truth and virtue, is that with which Christ urged his disciples to do good while emulating the astuteness of the children of darkness. Using the example of the unjust steward,[2] he taught them how to find something to imitate even in the wicked; indeed, using the examples of the unjust judge, the lukewarm friend and the cruel prince,[3] he pointed to a feature of their behaviour which was not intrinsically wicked and had some similarity to the laws by which God usually operates.

The finest scholars are stimulated by such encouragement and warnings. They are inspired not only to refute the specious arguments of the scholars who deprive mankind of truth, but also to forestall them. They experience a new and unbelievable longing to embody truth in its definitive, noblest form and expression, to gather together the different parts of truth and fit them into a single whole to form a noble, enlightened body of knowledge which, although not immune to assault by its detractors, will not be obscured by the kind of sophistry capable of winning certain minds.

5d. People only begin to experience this truly noble longing at a certain stage in history. It represents a new germination of the precious store of seed which lies hidden deep within the essence of human beings. We are not aware of it until the seeds ripen and become visible. It grows with the passing ages. Nowadays, almost everyone is aware of it. With so many noble, valuable,

2 Lk 16: [1].
3 Lk 18: [18]; Mt 25: [24].

fruitful truths available, already tried and tested by wise people and bequeathed to us over the centuries, could any honourable soul not wish to have them arranged in a great synthesis so that all of them can be apprehended almost at a glance, arranged to form a unity and given a new, greater life by showing clearly their ultimate principle?

It would seem that truth has now been beset by every sort of error in turn and that all its main aspects have been effectively defended, carefully catalogued and explained. Consequently, those who strove most insistently to obscure the truth and foolishly sought fame as its suppressors ushered in an age of great development. This inspired loyal, upright scholars some of whom (except for a few outstanding thinkers) were previously quite happy to hold on to the truth almost by habit or to come to its defence only when it was under attack. They now saw it to be so rich and various that they were fired to contemplate it in all its systematic integrity and to promote its study, not so much to refute errors as to express it in the most attractive form possible and consciously bask in the radiance of the new light in all its perfection.

5e. But even when the scattered aspects of truth have been woven into a single unified system, sophists may still not desist from their campaign to devise further new errors and use them to lead us astray. This thought must not reduce our mental effort to respond to the new requirements that Providence has instilled in our minds over the centuries, during which the individual elements of truth have been attacked and defended. After all, one should make a distinction between the individual parts and the overall system of truth. The orders of reflection which I have already mentioned when referring to the individual parts can be pursued indefinitely. This is not the case when the mind moves beyond the parts and has to address the whole. The whole does not admit of such indefinite orders. When the mind really apprehends the whole, further reflection cannot discover any new material (as there is nothing beyond the whole) but identifies itself with the previous reflection from which it cannot be distinguished. As a result, and on the assumption that the whole system of truth has been discovered and firmly established, the struggle can only continue against those who do not wish to acknowledge the system, or who have grasped the

[5e]

system and refused assent. Where this occurs, there remains a combat of wills, but not of understanding. This combat cannot be resolved by knowledge or human reasoning because we are free. Freedom may indeed be condemned by reason, but it can be overcome only by God. Let us hope that all scholars who study what is good and true may, as friends, make use of the materials which time has already generously donated, and devote their energies to setting up such a complete system of truth. I have done what I could to fulfil my part.

6. Later, I shall explain how I intended to set about this task. First, however, I wish to show how this second objective of my studies is related to the first. For the present, I wish to point out the close connection between this second objective of my studies [the systemisation of truth] and the first [the struggle against error]. In carrying out such a project, one comes across a new, more efficient and effective way of overcoming errors.

It is one thing to demonstrate that a teaching is false, quite another to show the right teaching with which to replace it. The former task is much easier than the second, but it does not fully satisfy the demands of our minds which naturally hunger for truth and require it to be expressly announced. Our mind has little liking for philosophers who will only combat errors (a negative process which is destructive, not constructive). Although errors have been dispelled we feel annoyed when we are kept in doubt and ignorance. We rally to any viewpoint which has the slightest probability or the least hint of fame. We are reluctant to sacrifice our erroneous ideas when we realise that such a sacrifice does not produce any alternative, positive knowledge.

6a. One of the tricks constantly used by false teachers to draw people into their own schools and ensnare them, is the promise of a positive, reliable body of teaching, superior to any other and capable of explaining everything. Their slogan is the ancient one: 'On the day on which you shall eat of this fruit, your eyes shall be open and you shall be as gods, knowing good and evil,' with which the oldest sophist of all invited Adam and Eve to judge the divine prohibition. This is an example of thought being raised to a higher order of reflection. Adam and Eve's judgment was the result of a higher type of reflection than that which involved mere knowledge of the matter to be judged.

[6–6a]

From that moment, true reflection had to be set against false. This was in fact God's judgment in the case of Adam's guilty judgment; consequently, the clash between truth and falsehood, between reason and sophistry became inevitable. True philosophers however are not as ready to make easy promises as false seducers, who are not concerned with solid knowledge but want to galvanise their momentary followers.

So the time has come perhaps to offer a positive, schematic exposition of truth in response to the heightened curiosity of a public avid for knowledge at this level of reflection. Indeed, without a sound, lucid set of ideas to counter mistaken teaching, false notions cannot be properly grasped or fully refuted. Their harmful effects are revealed and the absurdities they entail are pinpointed but their roots remain intact. Sometimes, a poisonous plant is unconsciously allowed to flourish. Even some of our own well-meaning authors have come to grief. Galluppi in Naples, Bonelli in Rome and a number of thinkers from Northern Italy thought that they had refuted empiricism and subjectivism, the twin sources of all our present philosophical aberrations. But neither they nor any other thinkers were able to put forward any positive system for establishing the nature and origin of knowledge in order to refute empiricism and subjectivism. True, they did expose some incidental shortcomings of these teachings, but without getting to their roots. In fact, they thinned out the shoots of error and made what remained even more resistant.

6b. It is extremely difficult to realise how poisonous such errors are, if all that can be done is to combat them without substituting the true system in their place. Not long ago Collizi, Mastrofini, Costa and others assured us that empiricism had been given a bad press; they were convinced that, by introducing a few changes, they had cleansed it of all taint. They even defended it!

I decided to take the opposite course. As a first step on any issue and in any inquiry, I seek the positive truth which I then describe and establish as best I can. It can then be used as a firm base for the refutation of error. I have judged the first step so important and helpful that I have not always dealt with the second. My view is that it is easy for anyone who has a firm grasp of the truth to provide his own refutation of error should he wish to do so, especially when we consider that truth is so fertile and powerful that it confounds a whole host of errors. To deal with each error individually would be a never-ending task. I feel that I have the answer for those who sense they have been led astray in some argument and who naturally ask, 'Tell us what system we should adopt when debating this topic?' I have tried to offer my inquirers the answer to which they are entitled.

7. People aspire to know and contemplate the truth, and want to do this reflectively and actually. This is particularly the case with our contemporaries who insist on an approach that provides the joy of conscious experience (but the human mind, shorn of its power of reflection, is unaware of what it knows). Moreover, truth does not present itself to the mind in its naked self but alongside and with the support of sensible things, amongst which only words stimulate long-term reflection. Thus it is truth as pondered and expressed in words that we clearly and consciously pursue. I hope, therefore, that I shall not need to justify my already stated intention of devoting my intellectual efforts, for what they are worth, to putting into scientific form and words the teaching which is or which I have thought to be THE SYSTEM OF TRUTH.

But even if such an intention needs no justification in itself, I realise that I may reasonably be asked how such an aim is possible, and how I could possibly get anywhere near it. Human knowledge is boundless and truths are without number. There are endless branches of knowledge today, each of which contains so many truths already known or knowable that they must overwhelm any single memory or mind. I have to answer these questions for the sake of friends who may agree with my aim but consider it impossible, useless and rash, until these difficulties are overcome. I have to clarify my views clearly enough for them to be understood, and fairly judged.

8. From a scientific point of view, human knowledge may be represented by a pyramid in the form of a tetrahedron. Its base is immense and made up of countless particular truths, like so many stones. On top of these is laid another row consisting of the universal truths closest to particular truths. There are a large number of them but not as many as in the first row. As one gradually ascends to the tiers above, each stratum has a smaller number of truths with ever greater potentiality and universality

until, at the summit, number itself disappears into unity. At this stage, universality has reached its full, infinite potential in the last tetrahedron at the summit of the pyramid.

This image conveys my meaning, but not entirely. Clearly, a material shape does not have the spiritual characteristics of ideas and cannot represent a higher order of truths which virtually contains the row immediately beneath it (the truths of the higher order are more universal than those of the lower order) from which Socratic minds can draw the lower order. Stones are not like that.

The characteristic of truth is to be intimately related with a supreme unity out of which it evolves into plurality. Each unit of this plurality also gives rise to a further plurality of more limited truths, which in turn produce an abundant crop of truths that germinate further rich crops. So the seed of immortal truths, which continues to extend ever more widely, is classified into species and genera and develops into various branches of knowledge, art forms and intellectual disciplines. The characteristic of truth, as I have already mentioned, is to flow into other truths, in which it is renewed and continually increases in number, without losing its primal unity and simplicity. It is so incorporeal and divine that, as I said, it finds no satisfactory likeness or representation anywhere amongst material, sensible beings.

This is not the place to inquire how a single truth becomes a plurality of truths, nor how, when these truths have been grasped by the human mind, the single truth which produced them remains quite unchanged, still bearing within it the same truths while retaining its original status. We do have to note, however, that truths generated from prior truths and contained in them receive the law and norm of their being from these truths and share their light. It is obvious that derived truths cannot contain more being or more light than the parent truth from which they were logically derived. Anything we may wish to posit in inferences, which is not contained in principles, is quite erroneous.

8a. We find, therefore, that truth has an extremely ordered constitution and an extraordinary nature. A series of more elevated truths carries in itself every lower series of truths. Moreover, the higher the level, the smaller the number of truths.

[8a]

Consequently, we find the pyramid of systematic knowledge has as many levels as there are human ways of conceiving and expressing the same truth; the pyramid contains the whole truth expressed in as many different forms as there are horizontal levels. However, the truths present in the lower orders are obscured if they are separated from the higher orders from which they derive. Without the light coming from their principles, we cannot use them to any great extent or apply them to our needs. On the other hand, if they are joined in the human mind with the higher truths which generate them, and are contemplated in these truths, they themselves reflect the light and become extremely malleable and useful.

Hence, although the truths belonging to the lower levels of the pyramid are immeasurably more numerous, and indeed countless, their multiplicity does not make them either more attractive or more valuable than the lesser number of truths belonging to the upper levels. In actual fact, their multiplicity has two disadvantages: a) because they cannot all be known and noted by the human mind, and b) because truth in fragmented form loses some of the eminence and splendour which it displays when entire. It is clear, of course, that truths from the upper levels are more used and have greater currency when we grasp them along with their derivative truths, that is, truths from the lower levels. However, as our intellectual and memory faculties do not extend infinitely, we cannot grasp all particular truths. It is, therefore, far preferable to know the few truths which comprise all the others than the many particular truths. From the few truths, we can deduce as many and as few of the other truths as we like, depending on the time and effort we spend in deducing them.

8b. The reader can now see what I mean by *the system of truth*. These considerations show that it is not impossible to discover this system, the noblest and highest objective of study, nor vain and foolhardy to attempt to do so. They also show that it is a necessary step for anyone wishing to set a fixed objective for philosophical thought. Finally, anyone who attempts to do this cannot be criticised if he succeeds only in part.

The system of truth, therefore, is simply the description of truth as contained in its principles, not in its particular truths; or, to put it another way, as it exists at the highest levels of the pyramid where it consists of a small number of great truths which contain potentially all the truths on the lower levels, and recapitulates truth in its entirety. The lesser truths do, in fact, reduce to a few principles upon which they depend for their pure, living light — a light in which all truths and all errors are discerned, recognised and distinguished. It is the task of PHILO-SOPHY to determine the principles or *first reasons* of all knowledge and to describe in precise language this high point of the huge pyramid of what is humanly knowable. Hence my application to philosophy, to which I have devoted my various works. Each of them deals with some aspect of philosophy.

Third Aim: To Present a Philosophy That Can Serve as a Basis for the Various Branches of Knowledge

9. I defined philosophy elsewhere as 'the study of the final reasons'.[4] Using this definition, it is easy to determine exactly which part of the above pyramid philosophy occupies.[5] In the first place, it is obvious that the tetrahedron at the peak of the pyramid which represents God, or systematic knowledge of God, has to be the main subject and principal branch of philosophy; God is the final and perfect reason of all that exists in the universe or can be thought.

Immediately beneath this divine, final tetrahedron comes the first order of truths which deal with creation. Philosophy cannot ignore these either, although they are not the absolutely final reason, which is God himself. They are, however, the final truths, the final reasons pertaining to the universe and in some way part of it. The universe has within itself the ultimate

[4]   *Final reasons* and *first reasons* are equivalent terms. Whatever is final for the mind in one direction is first in the opposite.

[5]   Modern philosophy, swamped by sensism and subjectivism, is no longer sure of its nature or its purpose. It cannot define itself and, according to some philosophers, cannot be defined. Others feel the need to apologise for using the term 'philosophy' precisely because they no longer consider it to have any meaning. See the *Preface* which Monsieur Prevost has written to Dugald Stewart's treatise on philosophy, p. xvii.

reasons relative to itself. These are the first created or co-created causes upon which all entia and laws naturally depend, and under whose direction entia move and operate and reach perfection — or partial decay, which also contributes to the perfection of the whole, a perfection which can never be thwarted. The ultimate reasons transcending this world, and the ultimate reasons in this world, are the object of philosophical study which thus deals with the two final and highest levels of the huge pyramid of systematic knowledge already described.

Philosophy, therefore, is clearly distinct from other branches of systematic knowledge and takes precedence over them as their common mother and guide. Other branches form the lower levels of the pyramid and depend upon the two highest levels for light and life. I could not even think about dealing with all branches of knowledge, but it was possible to study their common source, too often ignored and, in this arrogant age of mundane pleasure and preoccupation, wreathed in obscurity.

10. The subversion or rather the extinction of philosophy undertaken by sensists during the last century produced a hotchpotch of negation and ignorance. Taking the title of philosophy, empiricism swept through the whole of Europe inflicting greater damage upon sound knowledge than any barbarian invasion. This led to the radical corruption of ethics, law, politics, teaching, medicine, literature and of more or less all other disciplines. We are now witnessing and suffering its effects. This corruption has had an impact on the behaviour and the intellectual life of peoples and of human society itself; like a deadly poison, it continues to eat away at their vitals and threaten the very life of society.

In the field of ethics, it would seem that a great number of people now throw common sense to the winds. Minds are guided solely by human passions and the base calculation of material advantage. They are open to all kinds of prejudice and ready to give immediate assent to the wildest judgments, or withdraw their assent on the spur of the moment to the most solid of propositions, as the occasion offers. They pride themselves on submission to the most biased viewpoints and, precisely because of that, are squeamish about accepting the most rational suggestions. They are credulous to the point of absurdity,[6] incredulous of evidence, laying down the law for one and all, intolerant of any laws, over-zealous about their own rights, forgetful of their own responsibilities; they pay lip-service to altruism, but in fact practise deception and selfishness; they are irreligious, a disgrace in their wantonness, impudent, and seem to have lost any sense of virtue or truth, the very existence of which has become for them a problem or a vain illusion.

11. Such a state of affairs naturally gives rise to the determination and desire to look for a radical solution; it invites scholars to seek a sounder philosophy to replace a system which has caused such widespread harm. But other weighty inducements also steered my studies in this direction. My friends and well-wishers will not object if I tell them briefly about some personal experiences. This will also help to fend off the accusation, coming perhaps from other quarters, of excessive confidence in my own abilities.

What confirmed me in my present intention to attempt to restore philosophy, as far as my powers and opportunities would allow, was this. In 1829, I was in Rome, and Mauro Capellari, then a Cardinal of Holy Roman Catholic Church and a long-standing friend of mine, urged me to write and publish in that centre of Catholicism the *Nuovo saggio sull'origine delle idee* [*A New Essay concerning the Origin of Ideas*] which at that stage was merely an outline. I had sown its seeds in my *Opuscoli filosofici* [*Philosophical Booklets*] which had been published two years' previously at Milan. This *New Essay*, which I actually wrote and published in 1829 and in the spring of the following year, in the capital of the Catholic world, was approved by the Roman censors. The intention was to combat sensism, the source of so many errors and thus of all our evils. The purpose was not merely to combat the effects of sensism and to point out its erroneous principles but, as I have already mentioned, to confront it with the true system of thought regarding the nature and origin of knowledge. When falsehood comes up against the truth, it stands like a convicted criminal or a prisoner pleading guilty before the judge. It disperses automatically, as darkness is dispersed by daylight.

---

6 'Philosophers, that credulous tribe'* (Seneca, *Physical Investigations*, 5: 26).

11a. Another highly influential supporter persuaded me that the enterprise which I had begun with the *New Essay* was not so daunting, and that it was my duty to pursue it. At the very beginning of the following year, Pius VIII, now Pope, banished all my anxieties. These related not so much to the difficulties of the enterprise, as to uncertainty whether the time and energy I had to spend on it could not be more profitably spent for my neighbour in other ways. I still recall his fond, authoritative words which were more or less: 'It is God's will that you should write books; that is where your vocation lies. At the moment, the Church is greatly in need of writers; reliable writers are in very short supply. Nowadays, there is no other way to win people over than by the use of reason, and thereby lead them on to religion. You may be sure that you will do a great deal more for your neighbour by writing than by any other type of work in the sacred ministry.' That was how His Holiness of sacred memory showed me the path I should take and urged me to follow it. I shall never forget the words he used, nor the warmth and goodness he displayed as he insisted on the truth of his advice, and especially on the notion that people had to be led by reasoning. Pius, whose pontificate was short, was succeeded by Gregory XVI, the former Cardinal Capellari who first advised and supported me. During his long reign, he never ceased to encourage me in my aim, or to help me fulfil it with every demonstration of fatherly concern and constant protection.

This directed the course of my subsequent studies; the renewal of philosophy became the overall aim of the works I have published or promised so far. They will be followed naturally by the restoration of all other branches of knowledge which stem from philosophy, in particular the moral sciences, which constitute the genuine dignity and honour of mankind.

12. Sensism and subjectivism, which is not strictly speaking a philosophy, cannot have a moral system: we must not take as real the words which sophists toy with. The human subject is not the basis of any moral system, but someone subject to duty; he is not, nor can he be, one who imposes obligations. By transforming a person subject to obligation into one who imposes an obligation, by confusing passive and active, sophists have turned morals on its head. If this branch of philosophy is to be made upright once more (if it is not upright, it is not itself), we

have to show that it has an *object* worthy of respect and love. Establishing the dignity of the object, which implies a need for respect and love — failure to do this shows a truly reprehensible disorder — means rebuilding moral science on its original foundations. This object is BEING, in the fullest sense of the word; by its very nature, being possesses the form which enables us to call it *object*. It is OBJECT PER SE and can never not be object. If being cannot not be, and if its objective form is essential to it, because without such a form it would not fully be, it follows that objective being is necessary and hence that ethics also is necessary. Moral science could not be rebuilt on firm foundations nor properly protected from the assaults of its detractors unless the mind apprehended the theory of objective being. This obliged me to begin my series of works with ideology, the beginning of all human knowledge.

13. For the same reason and even more directly, sensism and subjectivism overturned the study of right which governs the relations both of human social living and of human societies. Right, in its material part, is a subjective faculty meant for the use of the persons who possess and exercise it. Morality is the opposite. It consists entirely in willed, respectful acknowledgement of the object; no eudaimonological consequences constitute or reinforce the binding character of obligation which, like truth, is absolute.

When morality is discarded, however, the subjective faculty (the matter, as it were, of right) remains, but deprived of morality (the form, as it were, of right itself) and consequently of the dignity and formal being proper to right. Moral dignity, which is not intrinsic to the subjective faculty of right, comes to the subject from without, from morality in fact, which confirms and protects this dignity, imposing upon all alike the obligation to leave it intact and free to act. With the restoration of ethics, the foundations are secured and right is rescued, together with the twofold ethical and jural excellence of human activity.

14. Sensism and subjectivism prevent the mind they control from apprehending the existence of duties or rights. With the elimination of the latter, the mind can only reduce politics to fraud and violence. Like Macchiavelli's ideal prince, it is biform, half-wolf and half-lion. The inevitable effect of this policy is to generate hatred of all government, a universal hatred, prevalent

[13–14]

throughout Europe, which makes all government intolerable; like a deluge, such hatred drowns rulers and all forms of government. Only when *morality* (which implies religion, the life-blood of morality) and *right* (not a deceptive shadow of Right) are restored will political science be possible. Such systematic knowledge will be the guardian of justice, defender of everyone's freedom, promoter of every good, creator of harmony among citizens, a resolute begetter of peace. Politics, which is merely *prudence* applied to lead civil societies towards their true ends, can have as its aim and effect only the utility of the governed. Nevertheless, after profound consideration and investigation into the long chain of all the causes and effects, and the connection between them, which enable civil society to achieve the prosperity proper to it, the mind comes to this most noble conclusion: 'Civil government, familiar with the three-fold teaching on justice (commutative, distributive and penal), and perfectly consistent in its reasoning, can and must deduce all the rules of political prudence from justice alone.'

An initial, superficial view would see this conclusion as paradoxical because it is so unconventional. There are very few people consistent enough in their thinking to see long-term conclusions in their principles. Unfortunately, the majority also lack deep moral feeling and high-minded, wise faith which expects the very best from justice, studies it incessantly, and looks forward in sure hope to ultimate success.

14a. Now the first lesson social justice teaches us — which governments nowadays have certainly not learnt nor seem to want to learn — is that civil government with its acts and ordinances must never transgress the natural bounds of its authority, which cannot be defined without prior definition of the type of institution proper to civil government. Unless and until the sovereign rule of justice is accepted, there are no limits a government will not transgress. Utility alone, such a vague and empty word, cannot prescribe any definite limits to it because it depends on the probable evaluation of circumstances. Utility which is of its nature variable, depends on the judgment of the person who carries out the evaluation.

Rulers guided solely by utility have no reason to put the welfare of others before their own if they believe they can get away with self-seeking. On the other hand, subjects will never foresee

[14a]

where government will stop, nor be able to prescribe a limit to its powers, nor reasonably insist on guarantees which, even if conceded, would be worth no more than the force subjects might previously have employed. If morality and justice are disregarded, binding agreements are an impossibility. When *verba ligant homines* [men are bound by their own words] no longer holds, all that survives is *taurorum cornua funes* [blind force].

The appeal of command and government, and the benefits to be gained from it, are so seductive that people are almost unaware of it. It seems incredible but it is a fact that no serious attempt was made to define civil power and describe it in detail, either before the time of Christ when seigniory and bond-service abounded, or even later when Christianity gave rise to civil society, the concept of which has been left vague and imprecise even though justice demands that the first question to be settled with the greatest precision by those who govern is about the exact nature of civil society and the purpose for which it is established. As long as this question is not resolved, government cannot be sure of remaining within its limits, nor can subjects make demands upon their rulers without incurring the same risk. Where the nature and purpose of civil government are obscure and vague, rulers think they can do as they please. This is highly favourable to them, but extremely harmful to the people as a whole.

14b. It is high time for us to realise that civil society is not a universal society in the sense that it embraces all other societies and their rights. It is a *particular* society which exists alongside others, as it does alongside everything individual which cannot be absorbed by civil society without losing individuality. Civil society, far from being able to appropriate or encroach upon the rights of other individuals or societies, is intended to protect them, not to destroy or weaken them, nor tie them down or harm them in any other way. This would be the very opposite of protection. It is a society based entirely on respect for others' rights, whatever they may be. Such respect is its primary, essential and universal obligation; all its other special duties stem from this. Its only right is to observe these duties. It is a society which, to protect rights, also modifies their *form*, and co-ordinates them so that they co-exist peacefully without impeding one another reciprocally, but develop and prosper. In

[14b]

short, it is a society instituted for the sole purpose of REGULATING THE MODALITY OF ALL ITS MEMBERS' RIGHTS without altering their status. This fundamental question of justice is more important by far than any question about forms of government and imposes on governments the same law of not disposing in any way of the *value* of rights, but of confining its efforts to regulating the modalities of all such rights so all can co-exist, develop unhindered and thrive. Civil society does not pronounce one form of government better than another unless, taking into account times and circumstances, one form of government is more likely to comply with the fundamental law in question.

14c. This precise determination of the sole universal function of civil society, when accepted or so obvious to all that those in office can no longer challenge it, proves to be the only radical and specific remedy against despotism which has appeared under all forms of government but is more cunning and more repellent in some than in others. This is the case with certain forms of despotism corrupted by deceitful passions from 1789 onwards. The caprices of parliaments appear before the public disguised by honest, gentle legality as though man-made law cannot be despotic and tyrannical but only a perfectly abstract idea, untainted by humanity and quite untouched by the self-will of its makers. The omnipotence foolishly attributed to people at large is transferred to deputies who — I am referring to the French and other corrupt constitutions — persuade themselves that laws are no longer to be made on the basis of justice but of omnipotence itself. Peoples everywhere revolt and struggle against such iniquitous laws but, with this corrupt principle fixed in men's minds, rebellion only serves to produce even worse lawgivers who impose worse laws on the people who elect them. How could it be otherwise when nobody, governors or governed, knows where they are going or how to get there? Nobody knows precisely why government exists or civil society was instituted. Nobody wishes to know this or to imagine that they know it; nobody takes the trouble to find out. Nobody — particularly careerists who undertake to guide the people — accepts the natural limits of such a society. The power-hungry see themselves as the people's defenders and trumpet aloud that the people's will, just or unjust, is

[14c]

paramount. In other words they create omnipotence to found an all-powerful civil society, with all-powerful administrative bodies and instruments which they themselves hope to take in hand. Such is the deceitful character of political egoism which decks itself out with the finest names, but above all with that of 'liberalism'. This form of liberalism consists in imposing on the bent backs of peoples an all-powerful government. Such despotism has not been seen on earth since Nimrod. And they have the impudence to call it freedom! The people's solace and consolation! Nations cannot throw off this noose unless they first break free of the trap of the sophism which has brought them to tear at and devour one another without knowing why. In other words, they have to reinstate the sanctity of right profaned by utilitarianism. This can be achieved only by offering right the protection of morality and religion — which is morality in action — and by recognising that neither nations nor individuals, parliaments nor monarchs, ministers nor any earthly authority can lay hands on right. It follows that a government's only task and remit is to ensure that the rights of all (which have not been created by governments as has foolishly been asserted), the rights of individuals and of all worthy societies are fully safeguarded *at their proper worth*. When this has been assured, the *modality* of rights can be regulated. Rights will no longer impede or fall victim to one another but rather co-exist, fulfil their roles and have full scope to develop. This is the only principle upon which a sound policy can be based to heal the ills of the nations and thereby save the society of mankind.

15. From the time that corporeal feeling, which cannot apprehend truth, has been taken as the only reliable tutor, the only trustworthy guide, people have taken refuge in this self-contradictory proposition. To such deluded visionaries, ethics, right and every other eternal feature have perished along with truth. Politics is seen as a gamble in which people are the stakes, and their most cherished possessions prizes in a game played with the dice of cunning and brute force. New generations have been reared on sensist teachings. Inevitably, gratification of the senses has become the end of knowledge and of pedagogy. To prevent sensual gratification from devouring goods too swiftly, political economy was put forward as a means of counterbalancing it. Another example of the corruption of a fine and useful

branch of knowledge! From Melchior Gioia, we in Italy learned that political economy and ethics were one and the same thing! I do not wish to inquire, however, why sensists feel they should take such great care to retain the term *ethics* when *political economy* would have been perfectly adequate. Two names are not necessary for a single science.

Truth, to be sure, stands upright and unshakeable amid the wild ravings of men. People who close their eyes and claim that truth does not exist because they do not see it cannot keep them unnaturally shut forever. Now and again, rays of light creep in and give rise to inconsistencies and indirect admissions of the truth that can be found if their statements are examined closely. If such rays of light are too bright for them, however, their inflamed eyes are driven mad with the pain. Hence the tremendous, never-ending and remorseless struggle on the part of many against the truth and those who uphold it. All other struggles come together in this one primary, essential struggle. Remove it, and all other strife either does not arise or is easily eliminated. But new human beings, like so many shoots, have to be consecrated to forming the 'wild, harsh and powerful forest' that will cover the entire civilised world. They are to devote their lives, according to these educators, to pleasure, to political economy upon which pleasure feeds, and to hatred of moral and religious truth.

15a. Such a system of thought, which denies any eternal and immutable principle, abandons mankind and its new offspring to the flux of the senses, and inevitably leads to such an outcome. On the other hand, experience shows that education, if it is not to represent a studied, systematic campaign to corrupt and debase the young, must itself be based on the eternal principle which constitutes human nobility and, by raising it above mineral, vegetable and merely sentient being, transforms us into kings of the earth and the ultimate purpose of creation. This principle, which is unrelated to and independent of the bodily senses, is indicated by epistemology in the *idea* apprehended by the mind as the first manifestation of necessary being. This idea shines upon the mind inextinguishably. Ethics indicates it in *law* which, as a second manifestation of being, has absolute authority over the will. Religion reveals God himself as the ultimate, perfect manifestation and

mysterious source both of this ideal light, and all legislation. .
is God who satisfies every desire of humanity, which is immor
talised, absorbed, enthralled and deified in infinite Being.

In us, mind, will and our very essence reach out to this sul
lime end, transcending the confines of created being. All th
resources of the science and art of education must therefore b
systematically and painstakingly devoted to it. All other aspec
of education, when reduced to this single, obvious principl
share in this infinite dignity and thus foster the true perfectio
and happiness of the educated.

16. On the other hand, once sensism has subverted the statu
and dignity of the intellect, there is no reason for not eliminatin
sentient nature also and settling for materialism. This has in fac
occurred. Anyone not bright enough to see the absurdity of th
claim that ideas are sensory phenomena cannot possibly se
the further absurdity of the notion that sensations are materi.
phenomena. A mind unable to perceive the first error is perhap
even less capable of detecting the second. The passage from ide
to sensation is greater than that from sensation to matter. Th
first leap involves plunging from the infinite to the finite, the sec
ond from one finite to another, although of an opposing natur
In fact, materialism has exercised its baneful influence not onl
in logic and ethics, which are concerned with the rational, mor.
spirit, but in all branches of knowledge and especially in med
cine and biology, which are concerned with the living bod
Sophistry in method, and errors in conclusions, are materialism
contribution to these sciences. Medicine, too, adopted materia
ism and arrogantly broke with tradition (I am referring here t
the study of medicine, not to its individual practitioners who, b
a happy inconsistency, can believe in the spiritual nature of th
soul while practising medicine as they find it; it is not given to a
to be reformers). Medicine thus refused the inheritance of i
forefathers. The father of medicine was no longer seen as
genius; the sage of Cos was merely a common, prejudiced mor
tal. Ancient medicine was wrong, they say, to acknowledge
spiritual principle in life and its functions, healthy or unhealth
Hippocrates recognised perfect unity of life and the living bein
and acknowledged even in diseases a hidden principle so alien t
matter that he had to call it divine. Consequently, it was imposs
ible to profess materialism without condemning what had bee

[16]

taught down the ages. The medical sophists thought it a magnificent triumph to stand alone and trample the centuries underfoot. These latter-day Hippocrates (if they will allow me that name) abound in every town now; medical research does not go beyond material considerations; thought and sensation are seen only as functions of the human fibrous system, on a par with mechanical and chemical activity; corpses are used to study life, and the microscope to explain vital phenomena.

But if we suppose that matter alone is the principle of life, we have to admit, whatever research we undertake, that we are in the presence of solely passive phenomena. The active principle, upon which all physiological or pathological functions depend for their cause, has been lost and with it the true principle of healing which will not be found until we retrace our steps and recognise once more that the *sentient principle*, far from being matter, is that which acts upon matter, enlivening and dominating it, just as the *rational principle* acts on the sentient principle which it modifies and rules to a great extent.

It follows that if medicine wishes to benefit the patient, it has to have recourse once more to these two principles (the sentient and the rational). The sickness or health of the patient depends upon their action. Medicine must also rely more upon such beneficial action than upon itself and channel all its efforts into furthering and reordering such action.

17. Passions, of course, are still present in the order of animal feeling to which sophists reduce all human faculties but they lack the guiding intellectual and moral norm which, sometimes calming or sometimes rousing them, always directs them towards the noble ends of human destiny which they must serve. When sensism exiled the intellect, the mistress and mentor of the passions, it bestowed upon them the longed-for gift of freedom (the kind of freedom which actually attracts larger and more clamorous numbers of followers). Passions, the raw materials for the literature of the age of sensism, from Lord Byron to Victor Hugo, were freed from the restraints of reason and pushed forward with all the vehemence, inconstancy and excess of which they are capable.

The spectacle of the passions taken to their wildest extreme in an orgy of scintillating dance and mortal combat is seen as the ultimate, sublime aesthetic expression worthy of the century's

literature. In fact, there is no other; sensism excluded every
thing else. But poor, exiled reason slips back furtively an
unexpectantly into the fray, because nature will out an
because, without reason, there is neither literature, science no
art. So sensism, condemned to inconsistency if it is to exist at all
ends in self-destruction. Reason, however, is allowed back int
their literature by these writers provided it remains incognit
— like an exile secretly called back to town by the police fo
some momentary service who comes and goes unnoticed
Undoubtedly, the passions need reason. Without it, som
would not survive; others cannot be aroused and stimulate
sufficiently to produce feelings of wonder. Literature welcome
reason for rendering such services, but only in the guise o
handmaid to sensuality; in her own garb as queen and mistres
of the passions, reason is abhorred.

17a. Again, no sublime pattern is discernible in historica
events unless they are considered from the viewpoint of th
reason and eternal wisdom which orders and directs then
towards their end. Remove the intellect from the equation, a
those do who count on sense alone, and history appears shabby
cold and entirely lacking in beauty. This is why sensists wer
obliged to tamper with history and re-shape it according t
their own views — all the historical accounts of the last centur
are being re-written not to take account of contemporar
records but to provide a vehicle for their authors' bias and pre
judice. Eventually, the *historical novel*, a genre which depict
passions being indulged to the full and disordered in a way tha
never occurs in history, was introduced as a vehicle for tota
arbitrariness. Like the crow in the fable, it wears a few feather
of real history in a vain attempt to be both history and story
Such contradictions do not bother those who expect literatur
to provide only the unbridled sensations and emotions whic
sensism teaches mankind while eliminating the desire for an
other form of beauty or sublime experience. But those wh
hold reason and love in high esteem, and are endowed with rea
sensitivity to moral values, feel that historical truth is profane
by such an approach. Indeed, historical truth transcribes, i
indelible characters, God's designs as implemented in th
sequence of events. Respect for such events and for huma
nature, which accomplishes them, wants factual truth to remai

[17a]

untainted. It is like a chest containing secrets of goodness and wisdom, which are non-existent for the sensist who views things materialistically. The author [Manzoni] of the most perfect and wonderful of historical novels (the plot of which was the product of his noble mind, not of vulgar sense-experience) was unhappy about his work [*I promessi sposi*]. Amid all the extraordinary fame that came his way, he alone reproved himself for creating fiction indistinguishable from true events. He took out the pen he had used to write his masterpiece and sharpened it to indicate the intrinsic flaw in the genre. Sensism robs literature, and the fine arts as a whole, of their ideal and divine dimensions. It either destroys them by restricting man to basic sense-experience or debases them by assigning them the role of merely imitating or representing the excesses of passion in a seductive light. The flame of genius can only be kindled in the fire of truth, morality and religion which are ignored by the senses, but kept alight in the inner sanctuary of the intelligence.[7]

Fourth Aim: Philosophy as an Aid to Theology

18. The three aims or at least the three desires which I have already mentioned explain on the whole why the various works in the present collection were written. But I was also stimulated by a further, modern requirement to which I wished to respond as best I could and which I took as a guide in my labours. I was only too aware that the light of the Gospel shone high above all human systems, like the sun which the clouds in the earth's atmosphere cannot reach. I also knew that 'heaven and earth will pass away but these words will not pass away'.[8] I was also

---

[7]   This is not the place to mention the assistance that mathematics and the physical sciences owe to philosophy. The discussion would exceed the inevitably narrow limits imposed by a mere introduction such as the present. Nevertheless, I intend to fill this gap with a short work *On the Philosophy of Mathematics* and with another which I shall develop under the title *Cosmology*. I abstain also from mentioning *critique* which, because it is the organ of history and belongs to logic, is itself a part of philosophy.

[8]   Mt 24: 35.

aware that divine wisdom, which is utterly perfect, has no need of any philosophical system to save mankind. But I also knew that there can be no conflict between revelation and true philosophy; truth cannot be contrary to truth. Truth, which is one and entirely simple in its origin, is always in harmony with itself. I also believed that philosophy, if it does not part company with the truth, assists the mind by giving it a natural orientation towards, and a remote preparation for faith, the need of which it arouses in man. Errors, prejudice and doubts which arise as a result of the shortcomings of reason, and which interpose obstacles to full assent to revelation, can and must be dispelled by reason itself. The Catholic Church (especially in the Fifth Lateran Council) invites and urges philosophers to render this service by their studies. It teaches that revealed doctrine cannot be expounded as a true science unless it presupposes truths demonstrated by philosophical reason. Religion does not destroy but perfects nature; divine revelation does not cancel but completes and ennobles reason. Nature and reason, then, are two postulates or rather two conditions and notions prior to the Gospel, and the basic foundations on which the structure of sacred theology is raised.[9]

18a. To avail themselves of such help, the early Fathers of the Church exploited their own amended version of the philosophy of Plato. In the mediaeval period, the philosophy of Aristotle amended by the schoolmen was preferred. In each of these two ages, the *philosophical teaching* favoured by theologians was universally accepted and agreed. Differences of opinion did not shake the edifice because they were few; nor did they extend to the whole of philosophy. The basic dialectic method and language were used by all and undisputed. This greatly facilitated the study of theology which towered like a temple, perfect in all its parts, extremely solid and august, for all to see. In the early centuries, this form of theology took on the appearance of a

---

[9]   Clement of Alexandria speaks of the relationship between philosophy and Christianity in the following terms: 'Our Saviour's teaching is perfect of itself, and requires nothing else. It is the faculty and power of God. Greek philosophy, as it draws near to this teaching, does not make truth stronger. But it weakens the assaults of sophistry against this teaching, and beats off treacherous plots against the truth. Philosophy provides a fitting hedge and wall around the vineyard'* (*Stromata*, 1).

[18a]

Greek or Roman temple, later, of a Gothic cathedral, but always perfect and magnificent. Recently, scholarship, criticism and classical literature have perfected the exposition of theology, making it clearer and enriching its dogmas with new, positive and well-founded proofs. However, with the collapse and abandonment of Scholastic philosophy which provided a foundation in nature, it lost its regular outlines and its wonderful intellectual unity. This unity was intimately linked to natural reason and the highest speculations; it shone forth as the supernatural fulfilment of human nature and human knowledge, the finishing touch, as it were, that God had put to his work.

At that time, man felt deeply that theology was not a remote study. Although, by its origin and subject matter, it transcended the limits of nature, it seemed to be a continuation of man. He moved, it seemed, from reason to revelation as though from a lower to a higher floor in the same palace of the mind designed by God on his behalf. In that age Christian theology was undoubtedly the mentor and guardian of all other branches of knowledge; it ruled all opinions. No-one would ever have thought that a time would come when some would believe that theology should be separated completely from philosophy. But such a thought did arise as soon as there was no commonly accepted philosophy, and no hope of discovering another that was sound and fully compatible with religion. But despair is no counsellor; it provides no reason. If theologians abandon philosophy, they will either have to disregard the most profound questions and settle for an inadequate theology[10] or, if they wish

---

[10] St. Thomas assigns two roles to the theologian: 1. *To refute* error. To do this it is sufficient to appeal to authorities that are considered undisputed by opponents. 'If, however, they will not accept any authority they have to be won over by the use of natural reasons.'* 2. *To impart necessary knowledge.* According to St. Thomas, this second task requires us to resort to reasons going to the very roots of truth. Here philosophy has tremendous scope. 'There is in fact a type of teaching in the schools the purpose of which is not the removal of error but the instruction of students SO THAT THEY MAY BE ABLE TO GRASP THE TRUTH WHICH IS PURSUED. In this case, the argument must be based on reasons going to the very roots of truth and explaining how affirmations are true.'* If this is not done, a person may well understand that *something is* but not *how it is*; as a result he will not know and understand the thing itself. 'In general, if the teacher confines the inquiry merely to authorities, the student will certainly know that the thing is what

[18a]

to deal with them, they will do so only partially or falsely. They will be criticised by real philosophers, despised by the rest; and sacred theology will be the loser. St. Augustine says:

> Let us imagine a man who, although living a chaste life, has no notion of nothingness, formless matter, inanimate form, the body, bodily species, space, time. Let us also imagine that he has no notion of presence in space and time, or motion in space and outside space, or stable motion or ages. He does not know what it means to exist without time, or not to be at any time, or never to be or never not to be (all of which are philosophical questions). This man, if he wishes to do research and argue not just about almighty God, who is better known through ignorance, but about his own soul, will commit untold, enormous errors.[11]

But philosophy, the natural friend and faithful servant of theology, still survives, especially today, despite its repudiation and rejection by theology. As Pius VIII said, men wish to be led towards goodness and to faith itself by their reason. However, its fate will be like that of a young girl, abandoned by her parents and guardians, who barters her good name and dignity for food. It is no surprise to see philosophy degenerating everywhere into arrogant *rationalism* which longs to stand alone, after sending all revealed theology into exile.

We need to reconstruct a philosophical system that is true, sound and thorough enough to be accepted by theology as its assistant. The two branches of knowledge may then be joined once more in the unity for which they were born, to their mutual help and assistance which allows them both to flourish and benefit mankind.[12]

it is BUT WILL NOT ACQUIRE ANY KNOWLEDGE OR UNDERSTANDING'* (*Quodlibetales* 4, q. 9, a. 18). — This teaching corresponds exactly to that which St. Augustine expounds so frequently. See, for example *The Trinity*, bk. 14, c. 3: *Ep.* 120; *Serm.* 15. — See Melchior Cano, *De locis theologis*, 9, 4.

11　St. Augustine, *De ordine*, 2, 44.

12　The inability of modern theologians to discover a solid philosophical system accepted in the Schools obliged them to confine their efforts as much as possible to proving dogmas. Here, argument from authority is sufficient for those who recognise authority. They ignored the arguments which, as St. Thomas says, examine the very root of truth and allow us to investigate the

PART TWO

HOW THE STATED AIMS WERE PURSUED

19. According to an age-old maxim, we should, before acting, select the loftiest aim to which our mind can aspire. Thus, by setting our sights on an ideal of beauty and perfection, we can discover sound and reliable rules of action for ourselves. From this ideal we can also draw the devotion, inspiration and strength we need so that, even if the noble ideal is not attained, we can at least get close enough to it to convey the intention behind our work. We are thus entitled to claim, without being boastful or ashamed, that *in magnis et voluisse sat est* [in great matters, even to have willed is sufficient]. On reading about the aims I had in view as a writer, my friends, realising what I had in mind, will either praise or excuse my enthusiasm. But I must now explain how I felt I could best achieve my purpose. I do not intend to talk about the means and kinds of assistance which proved invaluable — that would burden the narrative unnecessarily — nor justify in detail the method I adopted. I want to mention two points only: the freedom I have dared to show as a philosopher, and the conciliatory approach I have tried to display, as far as possible, towards the opinions of others.

relationships, knowledge and understanding it provides. Hence the need to defend the Fathers and St. Thomas from the accusation levelled against them (especially by heretics engaged in the total destruction of the Scholastic philosophy which they feared) of using such knowledge in their theological teaching. See Valfredi's booklet, *Commentarius apologeticus de usu Philosophiae in Theologicis D. Thomae Operibus*, Fr. Dom. Th. Valfredi O.P., Genoa 1777.

I

Freedom to Philosophise

20. True and false are qualities of human judgments and assent. If a person gives his assent to what is the case, his assent is truthful; if he gives his assent to what is not the case, his assent is untruthful. People regularly speak of ideas and cognitions as true or false. This is the kind of improper or unsound terminology which gives rise to irrelevant questions (questions which do not arise when the wording has been corrected), or which imply and unduly complicate straightforward questions. There is no doubt that a great number of mistakes would automatically disappear from our everyday language if we restricted the word 'knowledge' to what is acquired or appropriated by a true act of assent, and ignorance to all the rest. In the first place, a person's knowledge would correspond to the amount of pure truth they held. No account would be taken of the errors which frequently encumber the minds of so-called scholars, just as, for example, we find the net value of a family estate not by adding debits to credits, as though they were the same thing, but by subtracting one from the other. However, because a person who assents to many errors thinks he knows a good deal, 'knowledge' is normally a word applied to what is merely a false belief on the part of the deluded thinker. On this account alone, many would lose their reputations as learned scholars — reputations to which they have no title despite their extensive studies — and be judged ignorant. There would be a great fall in the number of pseudo-authorities who impose upon people and, instead of enabling them to arrive at the truth, keep them constantly hovering between true and false.

Likewise, we ought to say that people who doubt do not yet know; doubts are not cognitions. So, if we set on one side those who doubt about many truths and on the other those who give full assent to the same truths, we have to say that the second group has a greater store of knowledge than the first, even if those in the first group have taken longer to arrive at their doubts than the others at truth. Study is a means and not an end, and studies which result only in doubt about what is true are unproductive. The only type of study of real worth is that which provides us with truth, banishes error, or causes us to have misgivings about our errors — although creating misgivings about doubt can only be considered a benefit in the sense that a person up to his eyes in debt obtains the wherewithal to settle part of it.

Our assent to what is true puts us in possession of truth. Apart from this, all we have is *ignorance*, or *doubt* (which is greater ignorance), or finally *error*, the greatest ignorance. Assent implies knowledge of what is assented to, and of what is accepted as true in the act of assent. If something is true, therefore, every act of assent to it, no matter how it may be given, implies knowledge, information and the acquisition of truth.

20a. Assent, however, may be given for several reasons, which can be reduced to the following two: it is the result 1) of sheer will-power exercised on the faculty of assent, or 2) of some rational necessity perceived by the understanding which then triggers the faculty of assent. In the first instance, the assent is arbitrary, that is, it is intended for an *end* but not for a *reason*. In the second instance, assent is based on a reason, and springs from a faculty enlightened and also occasionally necessitated by evidence which in certain states of spirit determines a spontaneous movement of assent. An arbitrary assent not triggered by reasons which prove the truth of the matter, cannot strictly speaking be said to be based on reason. Nevertheless, it can be given to something which is (and therefore is true), or to something which is not (and is therefore untrue). If it is true, the person who assents, even in this way, participates and remains in the truth. At the same time, although he assents and knows what is true, he does not know why it is true. This is the aspect of truth of which he is still ignorant and still has to investigate.

This blind assent, which shows that we have the power to give or refuse assent, is a phenomenon deserving of philosophical study. It explains innumerable other frequently occurring facts which have a tremendous influence on human life. I mean all the rash judgments, prejudices, biased views, opinions, presumptions and convictions which sometimes play an important part in our spirit, though we are ignorant of their origin and unable to find any good reason for them. Indeed there may be no good reason for them, or at least no full and convincing reason.

Most of the acts we perform — I almost wrote all the

[20a]

necessary acts without which we could not live — are guided by prejudices and opinions which are at times completely unfounded. Their lack of any basis in reason is compensated by the power of the will to determine assent. I mean the will as influenced by inclinations, instincts, passions, needs. At times, such acts are based on purely conjectural, more or less probable reasons, or on real or imagined indications which are arbitrarily assumed to be signs and evidence of the truth. If we always needed to have before our mind evidence for truths which we presuppose when we act, and which incline us to take one course of action or another, we would never do anything. We would be statues, not human beings. The faculty of immediate persuasion, which depends on the will, is necessary and invaluable, and better able to lead us to act than demonstrative reason.

Nevertheless, although this faculty occasionally hits on the truth, it often falls into error. In fact, we can say, generally speaking, that man's tragic propensity to error stems from it. This is the real impediment to free, philosophical thought.

21. I shall now examine the role of philosophy relative to the many preconceptions which so easily lodge in people's minds.

Philosophy examines all such preconceptions, all more or less gratuitous acts of assent, and distinguishes those concerned with truth from those concerned with falsity. It remedies the shortcomings of the former group, that is, explains the reason justifying assent. When we grasp this explanation, we not only possess the truth which we already held without knowing why, but we also possess the additional truth which explains it all. Our knowledge is complete when we accept these two truths, and our conviction rational. Where assent has been based upon probable reasons, philosophy either attempts to convert probable reasons into demonstrations or, if this is outside its power, endeavours to show that in this instance certainty cannot be attained and to assess the relevant degree of probability.

When acts of assent have been given to error, either without any reason or for false reasons, that is, reasons based on previous errors from which present errors are derived either as logical inferences or as inferences mistakenly believed to be logical, it is the philosopher's duty to demonstrate: 1. the erroneous nature of what has received our assent; 2. the error of the mistaken reasons for the assent; 3. the erroneous nature of any

[21]

inferences leading from one error to another, if there were such inferences. In the last case, philosophy has to demonstrate at least three errors for each false assent.

Errors and erroneous preconceptions, however, often prove persistent. In fact, any persuasion, false or not, has a built-in instinct for survival — the very same power of self-preservation which is inherent in every ens, in every act of any ens whatsoever. Therefore, the philosopher, when he sets out to refute such convictions logically — which he is bound to do if he wishes to get anywhere — must engage in a more or less fierce, determined struggle with those who do not wish to give up their error immediately, as though doing so were cowardice. Philosophy does not encounter such resistance if the preconceptions which it comes up against in the human spirit, though gratuitous, are true. In this case, it needs to join forces with them, not combat them. Instead of overturning them, philosophy helps to reinforce, clarify, defend and perfect them by providing the missing foundation which explains them.

It is not preconceptions and prejudices in themselves, therefore, which create obstacles for philosophy (as is wrongly claimed) but only *erroneous* preconceptions and *prejudices*, that is, error lodged in human minds. Only the erroneous preconceptions and prejudices accepted by people make them totally unfit to philosophise freely. They first have to rid themselves of these convictions or at least adopt an attitude of spirit which enables them to consider the preconceptions as dubious and ready to discard or accept them with equanimity if philosophy, left free to operate as though these convictions did not exist, comes to some definitive conclusion.

22. This is the real cause of slow, difficult progress in philosophy. False preconceptions and convictions are the logical cause of its loss of freedom and its aberrations.

We can have no doubt that erroneous preconceptions and persuasions, especially amongst the masses, are responsible for the slow progress of philosophy if we bear in mind the following:

1. The philosophical system of truth cannot bear sound fruit in a nation unless it prevails in the minds and hearts of all. But the number of false preconceptions lodged in people's spirits is proportionate to the enemies philosophy has to

combat and overcome before it prevails. Where error abounds, those holding discordant opinions are more petulant and arrogant; nothing makes people more haughty and unruly than the tyranny imposed by error, which its slaves call *knowledge.*

2. Not only philosophy, granted that it has been found and systematised, but the person who seeks it thoughtfully, finds the false preconceptions of the society in which he lives a tremendous obstacle to reaching the truth. He has embraced these errors in part or wholly either because of his education and the pressure of his contemporaries, or because commonly-held views are put forward as authoritative — they may even seem to have the authority of the human race. People are reluctant to challenge this apparently commonsense view. They are diffident and loath openly to accept truth that is put to them which everybody else disagrees with and condemns, not with serious, well-founded arguments but often derisively.

At this point, philosophical *courage* and *zeal* are truly necessary despite their being taken so easily for presumption and rashness. These two sets of mutually hostile attitudes do at first appear similar. Error often resembles impostors who, upon the death of some emperor whose appearance and behaviour they imitate, act his part as though he were still alive.

23. This is real courage which frees philosophy from needless restrictions and bonds. It is enkindled in the mind of anyone who undertakes philosophy for *love of truth.* When this love is pure and vibrant; when the person devoted to philosophical investigation feels the incomparable goodness of truth (I am referring here to truth of a sublime and ethical order) and esteems it so highly that he is willing to jettison all else in order to acquire what he sees as a free gift; when he holds as vain everything except truth and everything opposed to truth, or indeed as worse than vain and vacuous because it actually obstructs the light of truth and its full and peaceful possession, as well as its expected harvest; when he submits to the powerful frailty which makes him incapable of resisting truth's immortal appeal and yields to it without any resistance or qualms: then the philosopher, captivated by truth — the master of his mind — is raised above himself, above his own and others' prejudices. He is prepared to sacrifice his own prejudices without demur, and combat others' prejudices fearlessly if, after impartial

[23]

inspection, they appear wrong. No longer can such a person lack the philosophic courage and zeal which go hand in hand with prudence and modesty. This is the basic freedom that philosophy claims as its own and, on that basis, proceeds to seek the truth, refusing to allow obstacles to halt its progress.

23a. I have always held that this magnanimous approach embodies the first, most important and inescapable duty of the philosopher. Persuaded of this, I endeavoured to push every investigation to its limits and accept the results, whatever they might be, with heartfelt joy; I tried to check whether such results were really final, why no more could possibly be forthcoming, and then finally to draw consequences from them. This represented the first phase of the work. Conclusions thus obtained do not yet deserve complete assent; they are to be viewed as possible or only slightly better than possible until the mental activity that produces them has been confirmed. Such confirmation is the second phase of the work. It consists in carefully examining whether the results, either in themselves or in their consequences, contradict some already established, certain truth or some probable opinion or even some gratuitous preconception. Granted the total self-consistency of truth, any conclusion or consequence which can be shown to contradict truth must be rejected as fallacious. The entire argument then has to be examined until the error is discovered. If the conclusion is at odds with a probable opinion, no progress can be made until the opinion is found to be false (in which case it can be ignored) or true (in which case the conclusion is at odds with truth). The same applies to universal preconceptions. They are not to be belittled, even if gratuitous, but examined to see if they can be underpinned by reason or shown to be groundless and erroneous. As a result of his research, the philosopher either changes them into established truths or finds them erroneous. Depending on the result, he uses them as sure signs of some slip or oversight in his earlier argument or, abandoning them, goes boldly on his way.

It is inadvisable, therefore, for a philosopher to give immediate assent to individual propositions which he thinks he has discovered as a result of his own thinking. First, he should be mistrustful of self and be thoroughly convinced that even the most attractive arguments may conceal some deceptive, hidden defect or jump (making mistakes is one of the most obvious limitations of human nature). To safeguard himself, he must test each individual proposition by comparing it with all the others and with certain truths, as though the proposition were an accused person faced with witnesses. If unable to stand up to this test, the proposition cannot be considered free from grave suspicion of error. However, if the proposition does stand up in all respects as consonant with all other truths, it can be accepted as true and admitted along with the others. In this case, it is not so much direct reasons which subjectively verify a proposition as its harmony with all other propositions. A system which displays such perfect harmony will appear to be, and in fact will be, true. All its parts, even the least, will proclaim with one voice the truth of each; the rays of them all will be focused on each, making each of them clearly visible. The primary requirements of truth are harmony, unity and perfect peace.

24. At this point, to forestall those who will certainly raise an objection of this kind, I must refer to a preconception or rather a most serious error which recurs in the work of a number of contemporary writers: the belief that freedom to philosophise is forbidden or blocked to Catholics. This is an odd view indeed, and odder still when one considers that such a restriction applicable to Catholics must for the same reason apply to every believer of any religion whatsoever. The bizarre conclusion would be that only an atheist can philosophise freely.

What principle warrants such a persuasion? Are we to claim that the possession of some truths is an obstacle to philosophical thought? If so, we would have to take the conclusion even further and maintain that the only person to enter the philosophical lists safely would be someone who does not know even a single truth. Fortunately, such a person, quite devoid of knowledge and devoid of any ray of truth, does not exist. If he did, he would not be human. We are given by nature an initial light, co-created with us, so to speak. This light is the first form which renders us intelligent, and grows with us in infancy, childhood, and youth. It continues to develop even when our bodily growth ceases, and remains with us throughout maturity, old age and death.

What do we expect of philosophy anyway? Those who know something about it will tell you that philosophy is the product of a reflective process of thought. But can there be a *process of reflection* if thought finds nothing to work on in the storeroom of the mind? Reflective knowledge in general and philosophical thinking more especially — a nobler form of reflection — implies a prior stage of *direct knowledge* as well as *popular knowledge of people and society*. In each of these types of knowledge, truth is to be found. In fact, without some portion of truth they could not be called knowledge.

My own definition of philosophy as that which examines the *final reasons* of human knowledge gives it precedence over all the other branches of knowledge. How then could this type of final inquiry be carried out if there were no prior store of knowledge in the various subjects and sciences? In fact, philosophers and philosophy, in the true sense of the word, appeared very late in human history; the materials on which to work had first to be collected. Only after numerous trials, and furnished with a rich store of facts, could the human spirit ascend to the sublime reflection from which it surveys the foundation of already known and assembled truths, passes judgment on itself, on its own path, and on the laws that guide it. It prescribes a method for itself and grasps the dialectical implications of such cognitions whose necessary reason it had previously been unable to express.

It is patently absurd therefore to maintain that truths previously held by a philosopher are an obstacle or fetter restricting his freedom to think. It is like saying that a bird's wings are an obstacle to flight.

24a. Truth is never a hindrance to thought. What does hamper thought and prevent it from free flight is error, due either to unsound reasoning or to gratuitous preconceptions. This is the true and only enemy of philosophical freedom. How strange and sad it is to see an author, when expounding the most outlandish and erroneous views in defiance of common sense — and priding himself on his irreverence for which he has no proof whatsoever — honoured with the title of free thinker by ignorant people. In fact, his thinking is so enslaved by error that he cannot make a single move towards truth. Worse still, by vainly opposing human nature, and turning his back on truth, he is dragged in the opposite direction. The attitude of those who rashly assail the most venerable, established truths is not

[24a]

the sure sign of a free philosopher, as ordinary people imagine; it is quite the opposite.

The word 'freedom' has been subject to so many interpretations, mistakes and disagreements! It has occasioned deceit and disagreement, hatred and turmoil, tears and blood amongst men who have used it as a standard in their fight against others who wanted freedom as much and more than they did — the freedom, I mean, that human nature cannot abolish. Either they did not understand what was meant by the word, and struck out at one another in the dark, or they did not want to understand, just as they still do not want to understand and continue to do all they can to oppress and crush one another.

All words which receive different meanings in philosophical arguments, and thus offer sophists of every profession the opportunity for guile and artifice, are eventually applied to the real world where they divide people into violent factions, each of which represents a different idea attributed to the same word. These ideas, incarnate as it were in their supporters, involve society in fearful strife to which there is no obvious end. Precisely because immortal ideas do not fall under the sword, dissension and civil wars cannot come to an end without returning to their starting point, that is, the region of the intelligence, where error first put on the mask of truth. When this mask is removed, the kingdom of peaceful truth is restored where all ideas return home. Erroneous assent and passions have no place here; they are not allowed entrance to the dwelling of divinely ordained and unified truths.

25. Freedom is an ambiguous, vague word with a number of meanings. The turmoil it causes, like a sea assailed by contrary winds, is witness to this. And the most abstract meaning of the word is the most ridiculous of all. For some people the concept of 'free person' implies the complete absence of any ties of subjection. They intend to free human beings from the yoke of truth and of error, and thereby create *free-thinkers*; they want to free us from the fetters of duty and virtue, and from those of vice, to create *free citizens*! This shows not only their ignorance of human nature, but their total loss of feeling for themselves. What is left of human beings deprived of both truth and falsehood, vice and virtue? All that remains is a brute animal incapable of freedom, whose actions are determined and dictated by

instinct. That is why Communists and Socialists who hold such a view of freedom begin by denying any free-will at all to man.[13]

In this way, excessive abstraction draws speculators away from the subject at issue, that is, away from man, whom they destroy. If we are not subject to truth, we are necessarily subject to error. A person who has cast off the weight of the moral law and of virtue, necessarily bears the weight of vice. Truth himself says: 'He who is not with me is against me.'[14] There is no *via media* between truth and error, just as there is none between uprightness and dishonour. The point at which they divide is the dead end of intelligence. We have to choose between them; we cannot simply cease from being human.

Let us grant that truth imposes some kind of subjection and yoke upon human beings. Truth in person did indeed say: 'My yoke is sweet and my burden light;'[15] he spoke of a yoke and a burden which he imposes upon us. One of the apostles of truth highlighted wonderfully the inescapable choice between the two forms of slavery when he wrote to the Christians of Rome: 'Do you not know that if you yield yourselves to any one as obedient slaves, you are the slaves of the one you obey, either of sin, which leads to death, or of obedience, which leads to righteousness? But thanks be to God, that you who were once slaves of sin have become obedient from the heart to the standard of teaching to which you were committed, and having been set free from sin, have become slaves of righteousness.'[16] Man, then, is always a slave, if I can speak like that: we cannot escape these two opposing forms of slavery. We can only choose between that which makes us bondservant to truth and justice and that which makes us bondservant to error and immorality. — Which shall we choose? — This is the only possible question; and God has given us freedom to resolve, or resolve once more, this very question. The choice cannot be deferred. Merely by wishing to defer it, we have already made our choice, and chosen evil. The moment of choice may indeed recur, but it is always a moment; it is not a state, not a permanent disposition. It is a point at

[13] Cf. *Il Comunismo ed il Socialismo*, Naples 1849.

[14] Mt 12: 30.

[15] Mt 11: 30.

[16] Rom 6: 16–18.

which human beings enter freely into one of their two states, or pass from one to the other; a point at which they enter or pass into the realm of truth or of error.

26. I can see, though, that those who have chosen truth as their mentor will complain about my using the term 'servitude' to describe their happy state. I apologise to them as Paul apologised to the Corinthians. Paul not only recognised two forms of *servitude*, one to righteousness and one to sin, but two forms of *freedom*: one which frees us from sin and the other which frees us from righteousness. He says: 'When you were slaves of sin, you were free in regard to righteousness.'[17] How does he justify this way of speaking? 'I am speaking in human terms, because of the infirmity of your flesh.'[18] Clearly, if man were not limited, weak, infirm, it would never occur to Paul that conformity to truth and corresponding righteousness could be a state of servitude. The normal concept of slavery contains something distasteful and involuntary. Would we ever, after all, call someone a bondservant who was able to do, and did, whatever he wanted? Who never encountered any obstacle to his will? Never came across anyone who obliged him to depart from the path he had chosen as the best of all and closest to his heart? No one would call this servitude, but total freedom. This would seem to be obvious. Let us see, therefore, how and to what extent, if we go by this same principle, we may use 'servitude' about man's subjection to truth and righteousness.

26a Human nature can be considered from three points of view; 1. in itself, without reference to the acts it has performed and the habits it has acquired; 2. in the state in which it has yielded to error and evil; and 3. in the state in which it has turned towards truth and goodness.

If we consider human nature purely in itself, we find it limited. But it was part of the divine plan that man should be able, through the opening provided by his intellect, to attain and win for himself by his efforts of will, the boundless realm of the infinite. Man, as a *subject*, with his limitations, has before him an unlimited and unlimitable *object*, that is, being itself in the form of idea, which is truth that we can pursue forever. Relying

17　Rom 6: 19.
18　Rom 6: 20.

upon it faithfully, as we would upon a guiding star, we can expand immeasurably. And we long for such expansion as our very own perfection. However, it is hard and wearisome for us to slough off our initial limitations and break out in pursuit of a fuller, nobler mode of existence. It seems to negate and almost shatter our whole being.

What happens is this. Human beings are endowed with a number of potencies, each of which has its own dynamic impelling it to function independently of the rest. The independent nature of these potencies and activity creates disorder and disharmony among the potencies themselves. Truth alone is ever present to keep the peace and ensure that all our potencies work together to improve their subject, from which they originate as from a single power, by guiding, restraining and urging us on from above. Truth, the great moderator of human potencies, has the authority to restrain them, but frequently encounters opposition from the clash between them as each goes its own way heedless of the others. However, it neither finds nor can find any opposition in the subject itself in whom all potencies are lodged. Truth controls them on the subject's behalf unless we willingly denature ourselves by abandoning our own unity and splitting ourselves in two. In this case, we seem to transform ourselves into one of these individual potencies to which we offer ourselves in sacrifice. When truth is in command, however, it is the individual potencies that are subjugated, not the power proper to human beings. In fact, far from being enslaved, we become 'the captain of our own soul', the master of all our individual powers.

27. However, when the human subject does not operate by his own proper instinct which fosters the overall good of the whole man, but allows himself to be led by the instinct of one of his unrestrained individual potencies and falls in with its promptings, we are dealing not with naked human nature bereft of modifications and alterations, but with a condition acquired as a result of the subject's acts and habits. He is already inclined towards error and evil. I mention error as well, although the human subject, if he does not abandon the truth, will not forget himself and lose his unity and totality to follow the exclusive caprices of some special potency by devoting and dedicating himself to this alone. Truth instructs him to do the opposite. It

empowers him to control his various activities and restrict them to their due sphere so that all concur in bringing about his over-all good, the good of the whole man. Man, considered in his integral unity, cannot, naturally speaking, desire other than his own good; he will not desire the good of one part to the detri-ment of the whole. Adherence to the norm of truth which instructs and empowers is in complete harmony with human nature. Indeed, the meeting between human nature and truth gives rise to the intellect, the greatest human power of all, and to the instinct for good, the most outstanding and characteristic of human instincts. It would be impossible to understand how man, who is beholden to truth for so much of his life as well as for the vital instinct which, strictly speaking, alone deserves the title *human*, could then turn his back on the light and act in a totally contrary manner unless we knew him to be endowed with free will — a potency unique in its kind, and absolutely distinct from all others. Other potencies tend to seek only their own good, and cannot do otherwise. But through free will we can choose between good and evil, and therefore work to achieve our own perfection or ruin. We can devote our efforts towards self-preservation or even to self-destruction (which cannot, however, be achieved completely). When we abuse this singular potency (a real stumbling block for philosophical investigation) and take our stand in the fight against truth, we necessarily consider the friendly light of truth as hostile. We see it only as an extremely stern law-giver, a cruel tyrant whose ser-vice is grievous and heavy to bear. We feel free only when we are relieved of its burden. But although we can fight against truth, it is not within our power to escape its servitude, which we have created for ourselves. The power of free will does not extend as far as that in us. It can determine our actions and impose on them a direction counter to truth, but it cannot in any way affect human nature which is guarded by the Creator. Truth lies within human nature, which is in the hands of the Almighty, and is there located as though founded on a heavily fortified, indestructible rock, unassailable by its enemies. There it reigns either by benefiting its followers — even consummat-ing its union with them — or by punishing rebels. Truth is indeed a form of servitude, but only for those who refuse to share its wedding feast and the kingdom to which all are invited.

[27]

No one capable of reigning with truth (which is much greater than being free), but choosing instead to be its condemned slave, can complain of such freely chosen servitude, or say that truth and its consequent justice eliminate freedom.

28. Summarising, we see that truth bestows light and intelligence upon us, considered in ourselves. In doing so, it restrains our individual potencies but not human nature itself. It grants us mastery over these potencies so that we can use them as we please for our own greatness. If we reject the gift of mastery which truth offers us, and prefer abasement and subjection to the capricious instinct of one of our potencies, the servitude proper to that power will be transferred to us as subjects, that is, to human nature; by yielding to that power, we become its willing bondservant. This abject servitude, however, does not come from truth, but from our own evil will. We prefer servitude to freedom. Acting in accordance with nature is not a form of servitude; it is spontaneous and highly delightful. The concept of servitude involves acting in a manner opposed to that intended by nature. Because intimate union between man and truth is natural, actions which respect such a union are consistent with human freedom. But *free will*, because it may act contrary to *human nature*, is the source of our voluntary servitude. Thus, because the person who acts in this way turns the awesome powers of his own freedom against himself, it can also be said with equal truth that this slavery springs both from the lordship proper to human nature and from the lordship proper to truth. The person endeavouring to throw off the lordship of his nature itself is trying (although in vain) to destroy nature; similarly, the person who decides to shake off the lordship of truth attempts the destruction of truth. Anyone not wishing to be the slave of human nature and truth may remain free and in control; it is in his power to do so. If he remains united with them, he may reign freely, in extreme happiness.

28a. The third viewpoint from which I intended to consider man is the situation in which he finds himself when he attunes himself fully to truth and goodness. Here, there is no slavery whatsoever, nothing to constrain or bind man to truth. It is impossible to speak of restrictions when we do whatever we wish. But this is precisely the case when a person wills only the truth and its consequences. For such a man, truth and goodness

[28–28a]

are not a yoke or burden; he cherishes, desires and wills them. With these as his object, he feels greater than himself; they give him a daily increasing potency, and an unending sense of delight which stills the longings of his soul. Such a person's free will is in perfect harmony with nature, or rather it is nature itself ennobled. As man's very own specific nature is characterised by proximity to and immanent vision of, truth, so his upright will does nothing more in all its actions than tighten, constantly perfect, and consummate this union in human beings on the path to perfection. The instinct of integral human nature and free will are no longer divided, opposed or at odds; they are united, and man is one and perfect.

This was St. Paul's meaning when he said with some force: 'The law is not laid down for the just but for the lawless.'[19] The law is not, in fact, opposed to the will of the just man; it merely expresses what that will wants. This explains why the Apostle says elsewhere that the man who seeks goodness is already a law unto himself.[20] The separate powers may in their blind way rise and put this peace at risk in their attempt to deceive and entice the will which, however, if it clings sufficiently hard to the truth, dominates them and remains untouched by their attacks. If the will surrenders through weakness, this is not the fault of truth from which all courage and strength derives.

The Creator provided a remedy for our weakness of will. He communicated his truth to man, more abundantly, more intimately and in a more sublime manner than when he first communicated it to human nature in general. God himself safeguarded and fortified man's freedom against the blind assaults of his individual, biased instincts. To those who love truth, God gave this promise: 'If you continue in my word, you are truly my disciples and you will know the truth, and the truth will make you free.'[21] Far from imposing a form of servitude on human beings, truth is the sole cause of their freedom. And they do not lose this truth unless they themselves reject it by rejecting its cause.

[19] 1 Tim 1: 9.

[20] 'For when the Gentiles who have not the law, do BY NATURE those things that are of the law, these, having not the law, are a law to themselves, who show the work of the law written in their hearts'* (Rom 2: 14–15).

[21] Jn 8: 31, 52.

[28a]

The whole thrust of philosophy is towards truth. What other aim is there for study and restless love of wisdom than to discover and contemplate truth and, contemplating it, penetrate ever further into its depths? The end is the ultimate recesses of truth which, when revealed, quenches the ardent thirst of human nature with waters from a purer and higher source. If truth involved servitude for thought, philosophising would be nothing more than a quest for ever increasing servitude; freedom of thought would be impossible for those who devote themselves to philosophy. What a contradiction when those who praise freedom of thought fear that truth and true religion may lead to its loss! Or consider as less free those who, possessing greater truth, are closer to achieving the end of philosophy! This strange contradiction is compounded when those who present themselves to the public as creators of the most grotesque, extravagant systems are acclaimed as free thinkers. Their systems are a jumble of absurd ravings, but their novelty and courage in dissenting from truths most readily accepted by mankind, and in moving out of the light as though escaping from some vile, vulgar form of servitude — the abject lot of ordinary folk — is taken as a sure sign of free thought! Thus, slaves of error are acclaimed as free thinkers while minds which truth has freed from error with its light and made lords over our dark passions are despised as slaves! Here, injustice lies in its teeth.

29. So far, so good. I think people will accept that the mind's acceptance of truths, even by way of preconceptions, prejudice or faith, is favourable, not unfavourable to true philosophising. Truth never imposes servitude but, as we saw, forms freedom itself in man. No one will object to this. Some may disagree, however, with my assertion that Catholic beliefs do not diminish the freedom of philosophical thought because, they say, I have assumed the truth of such beliefs. Those who disagree with this assumption will dispute the conclusion.

First, this objection grants that everything I said must be accepted without difficulty by those who profess the Catholic religion. This represents a large number of voices in favour of my argument. The Catholic Church reaches to the ends of the earth and embraces all or most civilised nations. Such a large, respectable and unanimous audience can indeed suffice on its own to convince a person prepared to reason.

[29]

To the rest, that is, to those lacking the gift of faith, or still doubting the truth of Catholic beliefs, let me say with all Catholic philosophers: 'Imagine that you go to a geometry class, and arrive while the teacher is proving the theorem of the square on the hypotenuse. You cannot understand this proof because it assumes prior knowledge and acceptance of a series of propositions which you have missed. You go to the teacher and say to him: "I can't assent to this proposition because you assume as true others which you have not proved. You are not thinking freely; you are constrained by gratuitous assumptions". The mathematician would immediately point out that it was you who were bound by false suppositions in assuming that his assertions were unproven simply because you were not present at previous lessons. He might even offer you geometry lessons proving his assertions and enabling you to catch up with the other students and work with them.'

29a. The person who chooses to think that Catholic philosophers assent gratuitously to their beliefs which, as false, prevent free philosophical argument, is like the man who judges mathematics on the basis of one lesson in the middle of a course, and accuses the teacher of being enslaved to prejudice. Catholic philosophers, on the other hand, are like the mathematician mentioned above. They consider themselves free to think, unlike others who, ignorant of Catholic truth, hold this truth as groundless. Such people are not only ignorant but in error, which is the opposite of truth and freedom. Our Catholic philosophers reply exactly as the mathematician did, and reduce the argument to an extremely important question of method. The teacher would have invited the would-be student to start from the beginning rather than from the middle. In the same way, Catholic philosophers invite persons who consider them to be 'unfree' thinkers because they subscribe to Catholic beliefs, to discuss the truth of these beliefs first, and then undertake further stages of the philosophical journey. In fact, the primary disagreement between Catholic and non-Catholic philosophers who mutually accuse one another of not being free to philosophise, is disagreement over method. The non-Catholic philosopher wishes to construct a philosophy *in toto* without ever inquiring whether Catholicism is true or false. He considers it false, or at least suspects it to be so, and wishes to philosophise

[29a]

without discussing this prejudice. The atheist goes further down the same road. He wishes to argue without reference to God, whom he assumes not to exist. Refusing to examine his presupposition, he uses it prejudicially as a preface and directive for all his philosophical arguments. Catholic philosophers first want to discuss religion itself with the person who does not have or doubts the true religion. They want to establish whether Catholicism is true or not. If found to be true, it is also shown to be no obstacle to freedom in philosophy. Indeed it facilitates and strengthens solutions to other philosophical problems. Catholic philosophers have as much right to this as the mathematician has to insist that people anxious to learn geometry start from the beginning. Non-Catholic philosophers have no right to accuse Catholics of holding a philosophical position obstructed by and captive to preconceived beliefs. They must either demonstrate the falsity of these beliefs or at least investigate whether or not acceptance of them is unreasonable. If true and reasonable, these beliefs will certainly not hamper human thought, but free man from error and help him greatly. This led Augustine, that sublime philosopher, to say: 'Study is not to be criticised in those who are consumed with love for proven truth. Rather, they should be encouraged to undertake study in an orderly manner (that is, with proper method) so that, beginning from faith and good living, it may achieve its aim,'[*22] that is, proven or scientific truth.

30. Non-Catholic philosophers are obviously relying on a false preconception when they claim that Christian faith is completely blind, like an act of belief made by a mob or when listening to glib quacks. These philosophers are so captivated by this rash judgment that they never feel the need to subject their prejudice to any serious examination. Consequently, it is based solely upon ignorance of religious doctrine and Christian faith.

It is reasonable, therefore, to invite them first of all to take part in such a discussion. Once they have honestly undertaken it, it will not be difficult to convince them initially that human understanding in Catholics precedes, accompanies and follows faith. Catholic faith is never bereft of intellectual light because

---

[22] *Against Faustus*, 22, 53.

faith, the more it is studied and penetrated, is seen as the better part of this light.

Indeed, the motives for belief are there for all to see; everyone has the right and sometimes the duty to subject them to examination and testing by reason. Under this careful scrutiny Catholic religion fears only one thing, namely, that the discussion may be too frivolous, superficial, imprecise, hasty and shallow. The longer the discussion is, the more rigorous, persevering and exact it becomes, the surer the Catholic faith emerges victorious. This always happens when truth is involved — the more it is put to the test, the more light it radiates. It is refused and rejected only when people despise it and, without looking at it squarely, pass it by with a smile of haughty contempt. Hence Bacon's almost proverbial saying: 'A little philosophy (never free from deception and error) inclines man's mind to atheism, but depth in philosophy brings men's minds to religion.' If the motives for belief successfully resist the test of philosophical reasoning, and demonstrate the truth of revelation and the validity of the Church's magisterium (which guards the deposit of truth and passes it on), can those who still refuse to accept this knowledge as true — whose source is not in any human school but in the mind of God — be called philosophers, or indeed reasonable? Thought in pursuit of truth cannot be afraid of losing its freedom when it finds truth at its highest level. Philosophy cannot cast doubts on such an acquisition after she herself has recognised its source and derivation, and ascertained its proofs. On the contrary, if philosophy has found the reasons for belief sound and conclusive, she has at the same time imposed on herself the obligation of accepting the articles of faith as true. Not to accept them would involve self-contradiction, which spells the end of philosophy. It is self-preservation which impels philosophy to accept faith, after examining the motives for it. In a similar vein, who can claim that thought, when functioning freely and naturally, and accepting the consequences, is thereby negating its own freedom? The very first law of thought is consistency: inconsistency as such is certainly not thought. Where thought, operating freely, has discovered the existence of some divine authority and an infallible magisterium, it has thereby incurred the obligation either of ceasing to be, or of assenting to everything affirmed by that authority. In other words, it must believe. Some kind of reason, therefore, does precede faith; belief is itself an act of thought which obeys reason, although it is also more than this. If it were otherwise, then and then alone would thought have lost all its freedom. Only an external cause could hamper its action, that is, prevent something to which it is determined by its own nature. Servitude is precisely this: the inability to function in accordance with nature when an agent encounters an external object to development.

31. But, you will say, not everybody subjects the motives of credibility to philosophical inquiry before making an act of faith. I grant that, but whether a large number of Christians do or do not examine the foundations of the gospel has nothing at all to do with the argument. We are referring to what philosophers can do, if they so wish. The fact that they can do so is sufficient to put paid to the accusation that Catholic philosophers cannot retain freedom of thought.

Nevertheless, allow me a few words on this matter. Here, too, I wish to put to the objector a preliminary question of method. Let us imagine that the motives of credibility are discussed first and proved valid. In other words, Catholic dogmas are shown to be true. At this point, another question arises, a genuinely philosophical one: 'How does man know truth? Is there only one way of knowing it? And is this sole way the result perhaps of philosophical discussion, of orderly, scientific inquiry? If so, are non-philosophers or non-scientists (the majority of mankind) denied access to truth? And, as an inevitable consequence, in the most important and necessary discussions in which human beings are involved, is almost the whole of mankind, except for a few scholars, condemned either to ignorance or to error? After all, with the removal of truth, only these two evils are left.'

In my view an affirmative answer to this question would mean a denial of philosophy because it implies the abandonment of common sense. Philosophy is no longer philosophy (I am referring to systematically thought-out knowledge) if it becomes so restricted and moves so far away from mankind that it considers itself the sole repository of truth and certitude, of which the great majority have not the least inkling. This is ignorant self-assurance dressed up as philosophy. Nevertheless, if there are such people, philosophers or not, who have blocked and bound thought to this extent with unjust preconceptions, it is possible to reason with them, provided they truly wish to follow the single slender thread of systematic knowledge which they accept, or rather say they accept. It is precisely by means of this systematic reasoning, which they take to be the heart of truth, that they will inevitably be led to a deeper understanding of the properties and operations of the mind, and be enabled to abandon their error. Such an erroneous, harmful belief does not originate in systematic knowledge, but in ignorance of the nature of human understanding and its hidden links with truth.

32. In fact a thorough investigation of the understanding leads to the indubitable recognition of an initial truth which communicates directly with all minds. This is *being* itself in its boundless essence and its ideal form. We have this knowledge through vision, not reasoning; it requires no intermediary. A careful analysis of the very nature of reasoning will convince any doubter that reasoning cannot exist purely on its own without proceeding from the *first truth* apprehended directly by intuition. Remove this truth, and reasoning is still-born. It is like positing the existence of colours after denying the existence of light.

Reasoning carries out its role and exercises its powers only by deducing one truth from a prior truth by means of an intermediate truth. The prior truth may originate, of course, from some previous reasoning. In this case, we deduce it from another truth. We can repeat the same argument about the origin of this truth also, and so on. But as we ascend from truth to truth and from syllogism to syllogism, we either never come to the end or have to rest in a first truth, not deducted by reasoning but known in itself as the direct light of the mind. Settling for the first alternative, or even attempting to do so, is absurd. If it were true, no reasoning would be possible and no certain truth attainable. Reasoning would be impossible because it would imply an infinite number of syllogisms before any final conclusion: the truth from which another truth was derived would itself be derived from another, and this from yet another, and so on *ad infinitum*. Now we are fully aware that none of the truths we know demands that kind of effort, and that none of the syllogisms which has enabled us to learn a particular truth is preceded by an infinite series of further syllogisms. Nor have we ever felt the need for such a series. Even if we were to spend our whole life in creating an intricate chain of syllogisms, the chain would snap and fall from our hands at death. It would not be infinite and a whole lifetime would have been spent without knowledge of the least truth. If, then, we assume that we are immortal, the absurdity of the hypothesis that truth can only be apprehended by reasoning becomes even more apparent. Imagine an immortal person who spends his whole lifetime stringing syllogisms together. Even he would never reach the end of his task by stringing together the infinite number of syllogisms required to produce a single truth. If he did, the series of arguments would come to an end; it would not be infinite.

It follows that if every truth has to be proved by argument, no truth can be proved because the first truth on which all subsequent truths rest is never found in such deduction.

Indeed, not only is it impossible to find; it does not even exist. For it to exist, the whole of eternity would have to unfold. But eternity cannot do this without ceasing to be eternal. In other words, the first link in the chain of truth would always be missing. Consequently, no truth could be known or demonstrated. Leading truth into such a maze we make a nonsense of it; truth, which is by nature necessary, becomes impossible. As I said, reasoning, without some prior, independently known truth, is either impossible or at least cannot provide any certain truth. It is impossible if the series of syllogisms is to be extended *ad infinitum*, as we have just shown. Nor can it provide any certain truth if it brings the ascending series of syllogisms to a close with a first proposition, and then denies either that this proposition shines before the intellect as a self-evident truth or maintains that the more or less remote proposition in which it is obliged to terminate has no authority whatsoever. In this case, the proposition is either an unfounded but necessary postulate, or a preconception whose worth cannot be assessed. Anyone who begins by declaring that reasoning is the only means of apprehending truth would, unwillingly and unconsciously, end as a sceptic. Entrusting freedom of thought solely to the custody of reasoning and refusing to accept any truth not demonstrated by reason means enslaving thought itself and rendering it incapable of knowledge. Thought has become both slave and dolt.

[32]

33. This is not just a dialectical consequence; it has actually happened. This is the history of modern philosophy, that is, of what our contemporaries insist on calling philosophy. We have seen German philosophers lead human thought triumphantly to extinction along a long and tortuous path. The conclusion they reached as a result of their tireless studies was that *theoretical reason* is powerless to know any truth whatsoever *in se*. With one stroke they have put an end to their philosophical revolution, and to philosophy itself. Subsequently, they attempted to resurrect it (for how could we settle for an existence without truth?) and resorted to *practical reason* (which assumes postulates without being able to demonstrate them) in order to have some foundation upon which human action rather than human thought may be based. In their view, they can dispense more easily with thought than action. They have resorted therefore to something unproven, rather than a truth; they have resorted to a type of reason that requires some qualification to be valid, in other words to an enthroned simulacrum of reason which, thanks to philosophers, may reign but not govern. After usurping the throne of truly free, royal reason, they have resorted to a man-made form of reason in bondage to the harshest necessity. This was inevitable once they had established the principle that thought is not free unless it relies completely upon reasoning devoid of any primal truth which may serve as a guide to every reasoning.

We have to recognise that these new mentors of mankind began their studies with an unwarranted, false preconception. They attributed greater powers to reasoning than it actually has. They themselves, therefore, were not free but truly prejudiced and captive thinkers. We have to acknowledge that reason is not the sole nor the primary means of knowing truth; if there is no means prior to reason, it follows that truth and certainty, and *a fortiori* philosophy, must be ruled out. We must resign ourselves to foregoing them forever.

34. Our conclusion about reason's inability *per se* to serve as a basis for human knowledge and certainty was inevitable. But we reach the same conclusion by carefully observing and investigating the nature and activity of human intelligence. A thorough analysis shows first of all that, prior to syllogisms (the form which all reasoning inevitably adopts), our understanding

makes judgments. Prior to judgments, it perceives ideas, without which judgments are impossible just as syllogisms cannot be formed without judgments. Composite ideas, however, are presented to us by judgments. We must conclude, therefore, that only simple ideas are present prior to first judgments. Trying to fathom what these are, we find there is only one, the idea of being. Analysing it, we see that it precedes all judgments, has need of none, and is so necessary to each and every judgment that none is possible or conceivable without it. This idea, therefore, is the first of all ideas; when seen by the subject, it enables him to judge and reason. In other words, it is the source of intelligence, the *light of reason*, the objective form of our understanding. We believe in this first truth; because it is pure light we cannot do other than believe in it. From this act of *rational belief*, all reasoning derives whatever value it has. Rational activity begins and ends here.

35. Let us apply this teaching to prove our claims. The Being who formed human nature by enabling it to intuit, though within certain limits, the light of truth, and thus rendering it intelligent, may wish to endow it with another element of truth, a further, specific degree of that light. There is no doubt that this Being, who knows his creature through and through, and wants to impart truth upon truth, would enlighten his creature in a way resembling and fully compatible with the way he adopted in creating him. So he would not assign to reasoning the new portion of truth with which he wished to enrich him but rather to that first faculty prior to reasoning and judgment, the faculty on which, as we have seen, judgment and reasoning are based. He could not, in fact, act otherwise. Reasoning does not create but deduces truth, just as judgment does not create truth but analyses and connects it. Consequently, no perfection added to judgment or reason would ever represent an increase in truth. It would merely provide a more reliable and swifter deduction of one truth from another; it would be the same truth seen in a wider context and its various relationships. Mankind would not acquire any new portion of truth as a result. As we have seen, judgment and reason are faculties which merely join us in new ways to the truth we already possess. They add nothing to truth, although by breaking it down into various parts and linking these parts in various ways, some are seen to be derived

from others. This gives us a more explicit, vigorous and effect-ive knowledge of truth, but does not alter the substance and ini-tial measure of truth that we have been allotted. It is clear, therefore, that God himself could not communicate any new, substantial part of truth to us without adding it to the part we naturally possess. He could not continue building where he broke off, unless he entrusted this new part of truth to the intellective intuition prior to every act of reason, prior to every judgment and prior to reasoning.

36. The grounds for belief of which I have spoken have enabled us to suppose what God might want to do. I now have to prove to philosophers that he has actually done it. At least, this is the method I have asked or invited our philosophers to adopt. I invited them first of all to discuss the grounds for belief. I showed that these do in fact demonstrate the existence of some divine revelation which contains a new portion of truth natur-ally invisible to man, and therefore called *supernatural*. It is accompanied by the existence of a visible, permanent magisterium which preserves undefiled the deposit of truth. I invited them to consider how God could bring human beings to accept the new truths contained in this revelation and assent to them spiritually. I concluded that God could do this only by illuminating the human spirit with a new light which would give rise to a new series of judgments, a new series of reasonings distinct from those based upon the first portion of truth bestowed upon human beings at the formation of their nature.

I must point out here that this is not simply my point of view. This is how the Christian religion explains itself. Christianity presents itself to man in the form of a basic, inner, new light which secretly illuminates the depths of the spirit in a way simi-lar to that used by the light of reason. Hence, from gospel times, Christians have proclaimed themselves as *enlightened*. Baptism, which Almighty God chose as the ordinary rite for imparting this light, was called *enlightenment*. This light, communicated at every stage of human life, was always seen as the origin of man's power to judge and reason soundly about things pertain-ing to eternal salvation, but beyond nature. No philosopher has ever thought like this; no religion has ever presented itself to mankind under the form of such a mysterious and such a ra-tional light. No other religion addressed the *essence of human*

[36]

nature and claimed it could exercise a power capable of ennobling and elevating it.

Every religion without exception, or rather all superstitions devised by human beings, have been intended for adults and not for children. They have directed their attention to our *potencies*, to our imagination and reasoning. None of them has ever dared or even thought of penetrating and setting its root in the intellective nature itself of human beings and from such depths, where only God can penetrate, of reigning over us and renewing, along with human nature, all our powers. Thus it is impossible to object that Christianity does not address itself exclusively and immediately to human reason, or to the more mysterious principle from which all reasoning arises and derives its light. In fact, this is a clear argument of its divinity. That other religions, on the contrary, are incapable of daring or promising or even thinking of doing this is a clear argument of their human origin.[23]

---

[23] This explains why the Apostles reproved those who rejected their preaching. People had been given another inner light (in addition to natural light). This endowed them, so to speak, with a new spiritual sense, enabling them to sense and discern what was true and false in the divine teaching preached to them. If they had to grasp it solely by the light of natural reason, they would have been blameless, even if they withheld their assent for a long period. On such matters natural reason either reaches no conclusion, or provides no firm persuasion, or offers an answer only after much hesitation and long investigation. People are not expected to do what is beyond them. As a result, the highly developed reasoning of scholars may delay, but never hasten the assent to faith, without perhaps any fault on their part. But where objections, put forward by reason, do not impede the assent to faith — this is where the simple have the advantage, as Christ notes — assent can only be delayed as a result of vice which prevents acceptance of the light of grace. This is the meaning of St. John's words: 'Whoever knows God listens to us, and whoever is not from God does not listen to us. From this we know the spirit of truth and the spirit of error.' (1 Jn 4: 6). The criterion the Evangelist gives for knowing the spirit of truth and the spirit of error lies in harkening or not to the Apostle's message because the person who listens, that is, who assents, shows he has accepted unreservedly the inner light which is the criterion and standard of truth applied to what comes from without. Anyone who does not listen shows that he has not accepted the inner light. That is why JESUS Christ prays for those who are to believe 'through the Apostles' teaching' (*per verbum eorum*) (Jn 17: [20]) since such persons who believe in their teaching, not as a result of natural reason but directly, show clearly that they have accepted without reservation the intimate light by which

[36]

37. Having reached this conclusion, philosophers will no longer ask: 'Why do many believe in Catholic teaching before examining the motives for credibility?' They will have found the answer for themselves. They will not even need to consider that certain miracles, prophecies and similar reasons can be recognised as legitimate and sufficiently persuasive arguments by the ordinary person without the need for lengthy inquiries. Nor do they have to understand that it was God's wish that such arguments should form part of his revelation to mankind precisely because they are more quickly grasped and more obvious. All this can be considered a bonus, or a confirmation of the more direct and intimate response which philosophers can provide to their questioning. We know, for example, that people begin almost from birth to make judgments about the existence of external things which affect their senses. They do so unerringly. They make these judgments, and assent to sense perceptions because they naturally intuit the light of being. They know being and, as a result, know that whatever acts upon them cannot be other than being; the various forms, the distinct and specific groups of new sensations which they experience, can only indicate other beings. Similarly, anyone who opens the eyes of his understanding to the gospel teaching can and must assent to it without resorting to any reasoning; he already possesses the criterion enabling him to distinguish true and false in the supernatural order. This criterion is the new vision of truth revealed by God to the intellect through grace. This vision, surpassing natural truth, is a new form of truth. It is what we call 'supernatural', the principle and foundation of a new type of reasoning. That is why, when appealing to this interior enlightenment of the Christian mind, St. Augustine is constantly saying that he cannot open up the secret of revealed truths unless God assists him from within.[24] Anyone wishing to investigate this additional element and form of truth overlaid on natural truth will not be far out in describing it as 'an intimate knowledge of God himself', who is subsistent truth. Just as we learn in the first instance by direct intuition what being is, and are enabled to judge the presence of beings, as well as what pertains

supernatural truth is recognised.

24 'Unless God assists me from within, I cannot do it'* (*Ep.* 120, n. 2).

to being, what is fitting to it, and what is repugnant to it (all natural judgments are reduced to these categories), so we are given, along with the intimate knowledge of God which we receive through direct, gracious perception, the power to judge where God's word is present, whether the message and preaching pertain to God, are fitting to God, or repugnant to God. All our supernatural judgments fall into these categories when we freely welcome gospel preaching and reject any other as superstitious or profane. If our philosopher pursues his studies in this direction and refuses to allow himself to be bound and hampered by false preconceptions about his imagined knowledge, he will pursue his inquiries more deeply into the mystery of human knowledge (a thoroughly philosophical topic), and accept that even the most uneducated person not only utters correct judgments, but does so as a consequence of interior, extremely rapid acts of reasoning. Thus the uneducated have a natural, individual way of reasoning, synthetical in form, which reaches conclusions as securely as, and sometimes more securely, than the scholar does. Learned people do not believe they are thinking unless they analyse and divide all their arguments into propositions which they spell out one by one. The ordinary person on the other hand, sees them at a glance and, unknown to others and himself, grasps the conclusion in a flash. This is all he does or can do. The philosopher who sees this will not be so sure that the majority of people usually assent to the gospel message without any reasons for belief or without resorting to reasoning. He will see that it is perfectly possible, and even certain, that people have resorted to reason, though not in the way the scholar does. They have their own, no less valid way, and no one can say they have not reasoned.

38. Thus, a person who philosophises in good faith will readily accept that Catholic beliefs do not undermine freedom to philosophise. This depends entirely on error, which places obstacles in the way of thought. If he then considers the motives for belief, which are subject to any reasonable inquiry, and finds them valid, he is obliged to conclude that these beliefs are not false but true. Nor could these truths act as obstacles to thought even if they were accepted by others as unjustified assumptions. They would not thereby cease to be true, and one truth, as I have said, cannot invalidate another. But treating these truths as

[38]

unjustified assumptions is itself a prejudice of many self-styled free philosophers who imagine these truths are accepted gratuitously. On the contrary, those who assent to gospel preaching have an inner light to guide them, as we said. This gives them a kind of intellectual feeling enabling them to perceive and savour the truth found in this preaching, and a faculty enabling them to utter true judgments as well as set out powerful, comprehensive reasons for assent.

Neither faith nor the Catholic Church which proposes faith has ever set limits to thought; it merely condemned its abuse, which is nothing more than an obstacle to thought itself. Indeed, the Fathers of the Church found in Christian faith a stimulus, and even an obligation driving them to develop the intelligence further than ever before. They were not afraid of any consequences that might ensue, as though these might contradict faith. They were convinced that all consequences would be consonant with that same faith, and that new evidence to support it would be discovered; light added to light to make the daylight even brighter. As evidence, I shall quote only the words of St. Augustine, the Eagle amongst the Latin Fathers. In one of his letters, he takes to task Consentius who wanted faith to be autonomous, divorced from reason. He writes:

> We cannot maintain that God is opposed to the faculty by which he makes us far superior to other animals. We cannot possibly maintain that the purpose of our belief is to dispense us from accepting rational arguments (from others) or from searching (of ourselves) for rational arguments, when we could not even begin to believe unless we had a rational soul.[25] Indeed reason itself tells us that there are certain cases involving the doctrine of salvation into which we cannot as yet penetrate by reason, although we shall do so one day. Here faith, which precedes reason, purifies our hearts and enables us to understand and bear the light of noble reason. Thus the message of the Prophet: 'If you do not believe, you will not understand', makes perfect sense. He clearly distinguishes these two powers and advises us to believe first so that we may be able to understand what we have believed. It is therefore reasonable to accept that faith precedes reason. If the prophet's

25 'We could not even believe unless we had rational souls'* (*Ep.* 120, n. 3).

precept is not rational, it must be irrational, which God forbid! If, then, it is reasonable to accept that faith *precedes reason* in certain important issues that are not yet understood, there is no doubt that reason itself, however feeble, also *precedes faith*.[26]

38a. Faith, which is light completing reason, cannot exist apart from reason, just as what is perfect cannot exist without its basic form, although reason, precisely because it acts as such a basic form to faith, can exist without faith. Consequently, the impact of the Christian faith on the world entailed an unexpected, wonderful and unlimited development of reason in man. Faith transformed the nations which embraced it, and entrusted to their keeping the sceptre of dominion over the whole world; not a material, easily broken sceptre, but a spiritual sceptre which controls matter, from which it has nothing to fear. What has mankind to be so proud of except the civilisation which is the permanent hallmark of Christian nations? Woe betide these nations if the light they owe to humble faith goes to their head. Pride draws ingratitude in its wake so that Christian nations, when they arrogantly display such failings, are

> like the lamb that spurns its mother's milk
> And guileless and wanton
> Goes its own way.[27]

They can lose their faith as a result of pride in its splendid effect. The perennial wellspring of civilisation itself and of light dries up in their midst.

Christian faith, far from depriving reason of its freedom and stunting its development, greatly stimulates us to use reason decently and lawfully, and adds a further obligation to trade more assiduously and carefully with such a talent. St. Augustine states that God, in bestowing his gift of reason, created man in his own image, far above the animals. The use of reason was to distinguish man from animals and draw him to what is divine, the cause of his dignity. From then on reason, because it was more robust, could function more reliably. Its infant steps became gigantic strides. The new light became the criterion, the

---

[26] *Ep.* 120, n. 3.
[27] [Dante], *Paradise,* 5, 82.

[38a]

paragon as it were, of the old which grew more courageous, more perceptive, more clear-sighted in such company. When faith appeared on the scene, the truths pertaining to natural reason became more luminous and sometimes so obvious that it was difficult for us to know why they had not already been seen or how they could have been found doubtful. It has often been remarked — it is a fairly obvious affirmation — that pagan ethical writers active after the coming of Christ had a huge advantage over their predecessors. Although without the faith, and thus blind to supernatural truths, they nevertheless shared in the glorious light which faith had shed over natural truths. Christianity embraces both natural and supernatural truths. Faith, which radiates its beams of supernatural truths, illuminates natural truths. Even today, pagan nations in closer contact with Christian nations, better reflect the light beamed to them by Christianity. In this way also Isaiah's prophecy is fulfilled: he invites the Saviour to rise like the sun upon Jerusalem and then adds that the Gentiles shall walk in its light, and kings in the splendour of its rising.[28]

39. Despite what has been said, someone may still suspect that faith places restrictions on the free exercise of reason. If so, I would maintain that faith obviously cannot constitute an obstacle to reason unless a principle or deduction of reason contradicts an article of faith. Where no contradiction is involved, it follows logically that either faith and reason are in agreement and reach the same truths or that they each follow different paths without clashing or obstructing each other. If they reach the same truths, they each benefit rather than thwart one another. If they operate separately so that each examines a separate order of truth, they fulfil free and independent roles without any possibility of conflict. Like two mathematicians confronted with two different problems, they cannot clash or contradict one another, although two mathematicians solving the same problem in different ways may well come into conflict.

The gospel has been preached to mankind for nineteen centuries now and during that time, when reason has been employed continuously, the branches of systematic knowledge

---

[28] Is 50, 1–3.

that have been founded and the discoveries made are as many as in the forty centuries before Christ. Nevertheless, throughout this entire period, when the Christian faith has had to combat all sorts of adversaries and all the equivocations raised by the spirit of unbelief, no one has shown a genuine contradiction between a truth of reason and a truth of faith. Apparent contradictions and conjectures have certainly been put forward but, when seriously examined, have proved unfounded and illusory. Not a single one of these alleged contradictions has been accepted by, or had the unanimous assent of, intelligent people. If such a contradiction did or could occur, is it likely, given the number and strength of anti-Christian objections, that over so many centuries not a single contradiction has been found or established in a clear and irrefutable manner? And this despite the fact that Christianity teaches unequivocally, and without any investigation, so many sublime doctrines that have never previously been expounded. It does not treat them as conjectures, as the more adventurous of the great philosophers did when they discussed such issues. Rather, it readily and frankly answers any questions regarding humanity's final destiny. It has been impossible to discover any internal contradiction within Christianity's own doctrines although it never changes its teachings and thus never retracts or hides any of its beliefs. Nor has it been possible to find any contradiction between faith and reason although, under the influence of Christianity, reason continuously develops, makes new discoveries and frequently needs to emend its results which thus change and increase over the centuries.

This is neither more nor less than the truth. The ceaseless efforts to catch Christianity out even in one self-contradiction, or in contradiction with the principles of reason or with their logical consequences, have foundered. They are simply clear proof of the ignorance and fallaciousness of the wise men of this world who are responsible for such endeavours.

39a. Although there will always be unbelievers — God has given us freedom to accept or to reject faith because he wants us to offer him our personal, spontaneous obedience — they no longer launch any sustained attack from this direction on Christian, Catholic faith nor attempt to show it to be in conflict with reason. In fact, they despair of their ability to find a single

[39a]

contradiction between it and the certain dictates of reason. Yet Christianity has always adopted an absolute stand before the world, implicitly saying to all: 'If you are able to discover a single real, apodictically proven contradiction, reject me'. This is the implicit agreement, so to speak, or rather the challenge, that all Catholic theologians issue to the philosophers and wise men of this world. The agreement has always been honoured and however hard these philosophers have racked their brains to catch the theologians out, they have never succeeded. The theologians have always seen off such changes.

This is what St. Thomas grants to reason. 'It is well known that things naturally implanted in reason are true in such a way that is it quite impossible to think of them as false.'[29]

As one commentator points out: 'The first principles virtually contain knowledge of everything else that can be known by natural inquiry.'[30]

It follows that Catholics accept that not contradicting reason is an indispensable and necessary condition for faith. If faith contradicted the basic principles of reason and their logical consequences, it could not be accepted as true. What more is required?

St. Thomas confirms this same condition by adding a further principle: 'Knowledge of principles naturally known is implanted in us by God who created us.' It would follow, therefore, that Christian faith would not come from God if it contradicted the principles of natural reason and their consequences. He also infers this from the absurdity that would arise if God, after giving us reason, were to impose upon us a faith in conflict with it. In this way God would ruin his own work by preventing our intellect from performing its natural operations, since, as St. Thomas never ceases to say: *intellectus noster ligatur, ut ad veri cognitionem procedere nequeat* [when faced with contradictory propositions our intellect is fettered, and prevented from attaining the knowledge of truth].

That is why, according to Catholics, total freedom for reason is a necessary condition of the truth of faith. If faith were considered divine, although in conflict with reason, it would

---

[29] *Catena aurea*, I, 7.

[30] Fran. da Ferrara, O.P.

impose an impossible obligation on us, and indeed totally inhibit our reasoning activity. We would be unable to give our assent to either reason or faith, and would thus remain deprived of truth. We could not assent to faith, because we cannot abandon rational principles; nor to reason because we cannot reject faith, which is assumed to be divine. We could not assent to both at the same time because they contradict one another: 'Contrary opinions about the same thing cannot be true at one and the same time.'*[31]

39b. Christianity itself professes first of all that it is not in contradiction with reason. It teaches us that any religion whatsoever, if shown to contradict the principles of reason and their legitimate consequences, would be false. It would not be religion, but superstition. Christianity provides us with this criterion to distinguish false religions from the true religion. It uses reason, and has always done so, to prove that other religions are false and to defend its own position with reason alone against sophists who have endeavoured to show that Christianity suffers from just such a contradiction. It shows convincingly that the so-called contradiction of which it was accused was not an actual contradiction at all. In fact, the need for harmony between reason and faith is taught by faith itself; it is an essential point of religion and is defined as such by the Catholic Church in the 5th Lateran Council. All those who believe in the Christian faith inevitably believe in reason also. While they know as convinced Christians that any statement contrary to faith is thereby false, they do not hesitate to say to unbelievers: 'If you succeed in demonstrating apodictically, by rational argument, any proposition whatsoever, you can be sure that Christian faith will not contradict it. You will have no opposition from faith because one of faith's initial claims is to accept as premises all rational truths whatever they may be.' If this is Christian teaching, how can anyone seriously claim that Catholics cannot philosophise freely, and that the Catholic religion is an obstacle or curb to the free development of human intelligence? Anyone maintaining such a thought would clearly show himself entrapped by error, and wholly ignorant of the Christian faith; he himself would certainly not be free to philosophise. Such

[31] *Ibid.*

[39b]

biased philosophers are in fact captives of error, and for the most part are ignorant of Christian doctrine. They envy us our freedom and, by a complete reversal of terminology, try to present as servitude the very faith which has brought freedom to thought.

40. I do not think it necessary to spend time dealing with the crude objection about mysteries. No philosopher would advance this in good faith. Anyway, it has been answered over and over again. The source of religious mysteries is to be found in the infinite, unfathomable nature of God. Simple reason states and demonstrates that God is infinite and therefore exceeds human intelligence. Religious mysteries therefore do not pertain to Christianity alone, but occur also in all systems of natural theology, a purely philosophical branch of knowledge. If all that was required to reject faith was to find that it contained mysteries, we would first have to reject reason, which goes on proposing them, telling us why they exist and why they have to exist. Confusing *mystery* with *contradiction* is a crude mistake which arises from mere ignorance, not from true philosophy.

A mystery is said to be involved when a given proposition contains something not understood, and impossible to be understood by limited reason. This does not mean that we do not understand many things in a proposition, but that one at least remains unintelligible. Arguments which prove the proposition true are produced either by reason or by authority. Thus, the proposition: 'God is infinite' is shown to be true with arguments provided by reason alone. Yet the *infinite* is incomprehensible, a mystery, the complex of all mysteries. The proposition 'One God in three persons' is shown to be true by arguing on the basis of the authority of God's revelation which itself is proved by the use of arguments provided by natural reason. *How* there is one God in three persons is incomprehensible; it is a mystery, though nature itself offers analogies of this mystery.

In these mysterious propositions, many other things are understood by reason besides the arguments proving their truth. For example, we understand, though not fully, what God is; we understand what is meant by 'infinite', 'one', 'triune', 'being'. But an incomprehensible element remains. For example, we do not grasp the connection between the terms, or *how* the thing is the way it is.[32] Even in the natural order, reason, while demonstrating that something exists, does not always show how it exists. Thus we see an event, or witness something happening without being able to explain it because we do not know what has caused it — a frequent occurrence. Human reason, therefore, ignores many things, but never contradicts itself. When one aspect of a given thing is known and another unknown, and cannot be known however hard we try, we say that it is a *mystery*, but not a contradiction. Unlike ignorance, a contradiction always implies an error. A person who does not know, does not err; he does not deny the truth as a person guilty of error does.

It is clearly a childish objection to put forward mysteries as an example of contradiction between faith and reason. If this were the case, it would not be faith which contradicted reason, but reason which contradicted itself. Ignorance is characteristic of reason; it is reason which is ignorant. Limitations are characteristics of the subject to whom they pertain, and ignorance is a limitation of reason. If human reason were not subject to limitations, it would not encounter mysteries in nature or in faith. Limitations, therefore, are not to be ascribed to nature or faith but to the limitation of human reason. Faith, in adding mysterious truths to those which reason discovers in nature, endows reason with new riches. Reason, therefore, always understands something, if not everything, in the truths of faith. When reason, assisted by divine light, is applied to such truths (a most noble and sublime subject), it can spring into action and penetrate understanding more deeply. In this way, the mysteries themselves are sources of inextinguishable light, although they can never be fully understood. Reason is aware of this beforehand and does not claim to understand completely. It knows its own limitations and the absolutely inexhaustible depths of its object.

Furthermore reason, which senses but does not understand the infinite for which it is created, does indeed plunge headlong

---

[32] As St. Augustine remarks in *On the Trinity*, 8, n. 7, there are always a number of things we know in the beliefs we hold. 'We believe,' he says, 'that JESUS Christ was born of the Virgin Mary. What a virgin is, however, what birth is and what a proper name is are not believed but known.'*

into the infinite to the best of its ability when unassisted by faith. But it does this to a far greater extent when faith presents the infinite. Reason knows that it cannot find true peace unless it plunges into that ocean of light, nor enjoy true fulfilment unless engulfed in those depths.[33]

41. It is not surprising that people who are prejudiced against the Christian faith and make no effort to understand or study it in depth, know nothing of this. They ignore and condemn Christianity without giving it a hearing. It is amazing, however, and lamentable that some Christians, and Catholics amongst them, who claim to be devout, are ignorant of this aspect of their faith. They do great harm to the faith, as well as to the truth, in which they show insufficient trust. These people are always so suspicious and afraid of natural reasoning, as though its legitimate use could ever endanger their faith. Such people hamper their own and others' thought; they are not the genuine Catholic philosophers or theologians I mentioned.[34] Nor is it right or reasonable that judgment about the relationship between the Catholic faith and philosophy should depend upon the fastidious ignorance of people totally lacking authority.

Excessively frightened by abuse of reason, they oppose its very use; others, impressed by the errors and wild ideas springing from such abuse, argue that natural reasoning cannot provide any certainty. They resurrect the system of Consentius to which I have already referred and which Augustine refuted. Monsieur Bautain, for example, despairing of finding truth in current philosophical systems, lost confidence in philosophy and resurrected this ancient system which isolated reason and posited all truth and certitude in revelation alone. It soon emerged, however, that he was in fact straying from Catholic teaching which he believed he was supporting. He retracted his error, and was led back by faith to reason. As a loyal disciple of the Church, Bautain the philosopher became once more a

---

[33] The more reasonable philosophers admit as much: as V. Cousin says: 'Like imagination, reason almost always pursues the unknown and the infinite'* (*Manuel de la Philosophie de Tennemann*, Preface).

[34] Anyone wishing to know the views of Catholic theologians on the subject should consult the fine treatise *De analogia rationis et fidei* by Giovanni Perrone S.J. *Praelectiones Theologicae etc.*, *Tract de locis th.* P. III.

[41]

disciple of reason as well. By contrast, the sixteenth-century promoters of Germany's false Reformation, as we see, rejected the magisterium of the Catholic Church and with it reason itself. Whatever interpretation is placed on Luther's theses, they devalue natural reason as something opposed to revelation.[35] It is equally certain that Daniel Hoffmann, who was a follower of that school, and his two disciples Johann Engel Werdenhagen and Wenceslas Schilling, openly rejected philosophy and the cultivation of natural reason. When the philosophy faculty of the University of Helmstadt rebelled against this, Hoffmann was obliged by a decree of Duke Heinrich Julius of Brunswick (16th February, 1601) to issue a public statement admitting his error.[36] Such was the contemptuous view of reason held by the early sectarians that they could not see, and went on to deny, the intrinsic difference between good and evil which they ascribed solely to positive revelation. Thus they removed the

---

[35] Cornelius Martinus of Antwerp and the Scot, Duncan Liddel, attempted to give Luther's fourth thesis, 'The same thing is not true in philosophy and theology'*, a favourable interpretation — as though he had intended to say that in philosophy supernatural truths cannot be affirmed as true or false because they are not matter for philosophy. Although this interpretation finds some support in the first thesis in which it is admitted 'that each individual truth is in accordance with truth,' Luther goes overboard completely in theses 2 and 3. One has only to consider the second thesis: 'In theology, "The Word was made flesh" is true; in philosophy, it is plainly impossible and absurd.'* Here Luther does not simply say that the Incarnation of the Word is a subject alien to philosophy, and that philosophy has nothing to say on the matter; he presents philosophy as stating the Incarnation is absurd. If this were true, there would be total contradiction between reason and faith. Whoever holds this, as Luther claimed to do, inevitably has to renounce reason. Luther's many followers included Chemnitz, who taught that in defending the Church's dogmas it was quite possible to fall into philosophical absurdities. *Examan Conc. Trid.*, P. I, p. 266. — See also Crusius, *Opusc. Philosophico-Theol.*, Leipzig 1750.

[36] On this controversy see: *Libellus de unica veritate scriptus ab Alberto Gravvero. Addita sunt nonnulla eiusdem argumenti Cornelii Martini et Duncani Lidellii. Recens accessit Jacobi Martini disputatio de vero uno et simplici opposita duplicistis ἀλὁγοις.* Third edition, *Vinariae*, Typ. Jo Weidner 1619, which contains the statement of Hoffmann's recantation. — *Corn. Martini scriptum de statibus controversis etc. agitatis inter Dan. Hoffmannum, et quatuor philosophos*, Leipzig 1620. — *Dan. Hoffmann, qui sit verae et sobriae philosophiae in Theologia usus.* Helmst. 1581.

[41]

primary foundation of ethics.[37] Breaking with the Catholic Church and rejecting reason went hand in hand. The Church could not refrain from issuing a rebuke but they would not listen to her voice nor the voice of reason which would have reconciled them to the authority of the Catholic Church.[38] But nature, put under pressure, reacted and exacted cruel revenge. Protestants who previously had downgraded reason in favour of faith, as they thought, later made the opposite mistake of downgrading faith in favour of reason. Disciples condemned their masters as masters had previously condemned this kind of disciple. Thus they invariably lapsed into extremes, displaying the exclusive attitude typical of all errors. Beginning their reform in a spirit of blind mysticism and *positivism*, they ended with an equally blind *rationalism*. They claimed to want no other guide but reason, but the reason they desired was their own version; naked, defenceless, and arbitrarily restricted to the type of matters they preferred to leave under its control, that is, natural truths, to the exclusion of supernatural truths. These rationalists thought they had thereby opened their eyes and become like gods. They soon received an unpleasant shock, however, when they were expelled from the earthly paradise. The more they exalted the status of human reason, the more they restricted it to itself (to the extent that they even wanted to fit everything in the universe into its inner world, and draw everything from it). Finally they realised that reason was dying before their eyes from overfeeding or, more accurately perhaps, from oppression, like the wife of the Levite from Ephraim. In fact, German philosophy, the direct offspring of Protestantism, having promised to work wonders in the world, expired in a desolate scepticism or at least fell into a pantheistic dream. Its last words were: 'I, Reason, can know only myself.' In other words (and here we can use another kind of metaphor), reason in the hands of those who left the Church was like a vestal virgin

[37] *Teodicea*, n. 40, footnote — Pufendorf, Selden and many others make natural right depend on revelation alone.

[38] The theses we have mentioned (11th January, 1539), which detract from reason while claiming to honour revelation, were upheld against the Sorbonne which put forward the Catholic Church's teaching and condemned Luther.

in the temple which they built to her; sterile, she could have no children without sacriligiously violating her own vows. This is certainly not free reason; it is not the free, fruitful reason of Catholicism. It is the reason called free by those who have left the Church. The choice between the two types of freedom and judgment about them lies with those who have not yet abandoned common sense.

42. Clearly, it is natural, even incumbent upon would-be students of European philosophy, when confronted by such a great and imposing body as the Catholic Church, whatever views and preconceptions they may have, to start by examining where philosophy stands, and what freedom human reason enjoys, in the Catholic Church. This Church is revered and obeyed by millions of disciples throughout the world. These include brilliant minds and outstanding experts in every discipline. She has been speaking definitively to all mankind for nineteen centuries, and has never lacked new disciples. Her persuasive voice is never old nor enfeebled whatever opposition and disagreement it encounters from those whom the world considers powerful, wise and shrewd. All agree that they owe to her the European civilisation in which they live and move and have their being.

If such philosophers examined the position of philosophy and the freedom that human reason enjoys in the Catholic Church, they would see, despite their opinions and prejudices, how freedom of thought is safeguarded and in many ways assisted. But without such investigation, and serious investigation at that, nothing remains except preconceptions which, however anti-philosophical, are met with so frequently and — I am really convinced of this — are so common in philosophers.

How do so many self-styled philosophers behave? Instead of investigating the Catholic Church's teaching on the use of reason, which is the only important question, they latch on to the opinion of some individual author who may indeed be a Catholic but does not represent the Catholic Church and does not convey its teaching accurately. They devise a system based on the opinions of this individual and themselves invent some ambiguous, unsuitable title for it. They then proceed to direct their attacks against this Aunt Sally of philosophy which they have created and deliberately turned into a terrifying spectre.

[42]

These attacks seem to be directed against the Catholic faith because her name is always omitted where it should be mentioned.

42a. I am sorry to have to make the same complaint against Victor Cousin, that elegant author who devoted such loving care and laborious effort to the task of fostering the study of philosophy in France. In the introduction to Tennemann's manual, he says nothing of the important problem of philosophical reasoning and faith, but instead refers to a *theocratic school*. By this he obviously means the thought of Bautain, that is, a set of beliefs which are not those of the Catholic Church and which Bautain later recanted because he admitted that they were contrary to that Church's beliefs. Cousin talks of the *secularisation* of thought, a partisan and foolish expression, unworthy of a philosopher. He creates a spectre of the theocratic school and sees it as an enemy trying to halt the march of civilisation and ruin philosophy.

This unsubstantiated opinion may be true or false but is in fact neither because it has no precise meaning. Cousin writes: 'Theocracy is the authentic cradle of emerging societies, but does not accompany them as they necessarily develop in the nature of things.'[39] If, by theocracy, he means divine authority, his statement is clearly false and contradictory unless, among such things, he wishes to deny the presence of God, the very first thing and nature. This is true even at a purely philosophical level and, it seems to me, even according to Cousin's own philosophy. What, then, is his problem? Why does he struggle with non-existent enemies? A better and more convincing answer to those who wish to isolate faith from reason by rejecting reason, would have been this: 'Why should I be afraid of you?. You have no support, neither from the philosophy you refute, nor from the Catholic faith to which you wish to adhere and by which you are rejected. The Church is the friend of reason and philosophy.'

43. I feel I must stress that any philosopher in our civilisation has first to settle the question of agreement between reason and faith, the two indivisible elements of civilised peoples. A philosopher who has not recognised this agreement from the

[39] Preface: p. vi.

[42a–43]

beginning will have no authority over his contemporaries. Either Christian civilisation, the only one that exists and has ever existed, will rightly suspect his pronouncements, or he will be unable to propound a philosophy in keeping with the aspirations of his age. This does not mean that philosophy is confused with faith or vice versa. Faith, which is quite distinct from philosophy is willing assent to the authority of God's revelation, however this authority is recognised. Philosophy is a branch of knowledge which investigates the reasons for things and, from these final reasons, deduces the consequences. Thus philosophy requires explicit reasoning which faith, as we have seen, does not need. Faith does indeed contain truths which can be imparted by philosophy and proved by natural reason, but it also contains other truths which, although not contradicting reason, are beyond its powers. Faith has only one reason, though an extremely powerful one, upon which it is based: God's authority in revelation. This, however, does not condemn or exclude other reasons but rather heightens their worth. Philosophy derives its reasons solely from the very nature of things and from the links between them. However, the subjects which philosophical reason discusses were not created by philosophy but come to it from an external source; they are given, and without them philosophy would have no material to work on; in fact, philosophy would not exist. The Creator provided material for philosophy when He made the universe but, in giving us faith, gave a new source of material for philosophical reasoning to work on. This new material does not destroy the first, but increases and completes it. So, as nature provides material for a first philosophy, faith provides material for another, more sublime, philosophy which does not destroy but extends and completes the first. Faith thus always remains independent of philosophy and self-sufficient, as well as sufficient for all human beings. This does not mean that it is hostile to philosophy, which is a treasure restricted to the few; rather, it takes its stance between natural philosophy which precedes it and supernatural philosophy which follows it. It is like a peacemaker between them, like an intermediary who joins their right hands. Only God, who created both nature and human reason, could communicate a sublime faith in harmony with them both.

44. But let us return to those Catholics who do not see how

faith presupposes reason (as Augustine says, we would not believe unless we had rational souls), and how faith and reason are mutually supportive. A foolish love of faith makes them hard on reason, but for different motives. One group is suspicious of the inferences of reason on the grounds that they might be contrary to the faith, and resents reason's progress. These, we may say, are *timid*. The other group has lost all confidence in reason which they do not consider capable of ascertaining the truth. This group whose system Cousin undeservedly calls *theocracy*, I would call *discouraged*. A third group, no better than the two main groups, is made up of the *indifferent*. According to them, we should not subscribe to any particular philosophical system. All systems that do not oppose faith are good, they say, and all should be used in the service of faith. But anyone analysing this statement must find it strange and absurd. It can only be accepted on one of the two following conditions: either the truth is to be found in different and contradictory systems, or truth and error are a matter of indifference. In the first case, there are not merely two types of truth, as certain Protestants absurdly maintain, but many contradictory truths, which is even more absurd; the second case is absurd, foolish and immoral. Equally extravagant is the view that, although there is only one truth and therefore only one true philosophical system, other systems, which are inevitably false, may nevertheless be compatible with faith and Christian theology and be of assistance to them.[40] As for me, I have always believed, or rather the whole of mankind has believed, that truth, which is

---

[40] Theologians sometimes have to resort to various philosophical systems, without accepting them as true (there can be only one true system and theologians are obliged to follow only the one they consider true). These systems have to be treated as concessions made to theologians by interlocutors whom they wish to convince. Theologians, like other thoughtful people, take *ad hominem* arguments from all systems and use them not to demonstrate the truth in a direct, totally convincing manner, but to win over adversaries who support such systems. This was frequently the practice of the Fathers and Doctors of the Church. However, a procedure which is valid in controversy, the aim of which is to persuade individuals or particular groups of persons by putting forward arguments from points which they accept, is not valid when it is a question of expounding the truth in an absolute manner. Only the truth — as I have already said — is suitable in this instance because it is one and agrees only with itself.

one, cannot contradict truth nor do it any harm. Error on the other hand contradicts and injures truth. That is why I have never understood how false philosophical systems can assist Catholic truth. Moreover, I have always believed that we have a moral duty to love the one truth, which can never be sufficiently loved. I would have felt I was going against my conscience by not adhering to a single system in which I considered all truth to be contained, although I am happy to allow others to do the opposite if for whatever reason they are unable to come to a firm decision — or even form a clear conception — about any one system. However, they must not insist on transforming their own intellectual uncertainty into a universally binding law, nor accuse of arrogance others who cannot live in the uncertainty which entraps the doubtful. Personally, I must admit that I was struck by the vivid, dazzling light of truth and could not have acted otherwise. I may be criticised, therefore, by the doubtful but I have no regrets about refusing to present truth as twofold. This is sufficient response to some who often accuse me of adopting a single system, as though to do so meant being arrogant and haughty. That is exactly the view of those critics who declared that in embracing a single system I was condemning every other system devised by thinkers of the highest calibre. I cannot and do not wish to deny this, but I can offer as my excuse that it was impossible to act otherwise. The truth, I have found, is so awkward and unyielding that it always seeks to stand alone, and refuses to be two-faced. But I cannot be held responsible for the way truth acts.

II

Reconciliation of opinions

45. Our limitations are such that when we are involved with some important issue, we can unwittingly be unjust with other, less important issues. If, therefore, we cannot praise the theologians we have mentioned (a small, unimportant minority) for their attitude, we can to some extent excuse them even though

they seem to belittle the importance of philosophical truth and, instead of trying to discover which system is true, prefer to switch from one to another, even when they are irreconcilable. For them, the thinker who is self-consistent and admits only a single system is too exclusive. One can see the reason for this but, on the other hand, it beggars belief that they find disciples among serious students of philosophy. Are there really philosophers unaware that there can be only one system of philosophical truth, and that other systems can only be false? Are there really people who intend to exalt philosophy even above religion, and yet maintain that the unicity of a system is the tomb of philosophy? Are there really thinkers who cannot distinguish philosophy itself from the history of philosophical systems which, for the most part, is a history of the aberrations of the human spirit? If so, philosophy for them is only a hand-to-hand struggle between infinite forms of error. Truth, which can be overcome, must never overcome error. If it were to do so, the show would be over and so-called philosophy would cease to entertain. Any philosopher holding such a view of his subject is like an historian who deplores ages without disasters, or a warlike ruler who thinks that his country is unhappy if it is at peace. It pains me when I come across statements such as these in the work of the famous representative of French eclecticism. Surely Cousin comes close to this view when he considers the history of philosophy as a perpetual illustration of the eclecticism which for him is the only philosophy possible for our time?[41]

He says:

> On the other hand, what is the history of philosophy except a perpetual lesson in eclecticism? What does it teach except that all systems are as old as philosophy itself and inherent in the human spirit which created them at the very beginning and endlessly recreates them. It is useless to attempt to establish one dominant system. Were this to succeed, it would be the death of philosophy. All we can do is honour the human spirit and respect its freedom by noting the laws regulating it and the fundamental systems that emerge from these laws. We must keep striving to

[41] *Manuel de l'Histoire de la Philosophie de Tennemann* etc. (Preface, p. xviii).

perfect these different systems by comparing one with another, but without trying to destroy any of them. We have to seek out and develop the immortal portion of truth contained in each of them. Each will then be related to the other and seen as legitimate offspring of the human spirit.

45a. However, when this *immortal portion* of truth which each system contains is found and removed, will these systems endure? Or does this portion of immortal truth, removed from the whole system, now become, according to Cousin, the entire system? Moreover, even if this particular portion is small, why doesn't he say whether this portion of truth, large or small, is the same in all systems? If he does not wish to say this (and it would be strange if he wanted to confuse with the whole system itself this portion of truth found within the system) why does he use the epithet *immortal* to describe the portion of truth that it contains? If this portion alone is immortal, he implicitly admits that the rest of the system is *mortal*. If what is left of the system is mortal (since it does not possess the immortality which is the divine prerogative of truth alone), why not let it die? It will still remain, dead though it is, in the history of the human spirit. Indeed, if he wants to admit the truth, he must do this — unless he claims the power to change what is mortal into what is immortal, and tries to act like a doctor who has found the elixir of life. In fact, he is endeavouring to keep alive errors, that is, systems from which, like a bee, he has extracted the honey of truth. And he wants us, and indeed everyone, to do the same! How can we? We simply do not have the power to follow his instructions and 'perfect the systems by comparing one with another but without trying to destroy any of them.' He must be careful, however, not to do unwittingly the very thing he forbids. So often philosophical systems are like those delicate insects which disintegrate as soon as they are touched. Despite his denials, it seems to me, he is attempting to ruin those systems not merely by venturing to touch them, but also by subjecting them to a very dangerous operation. He is removing from them the portion of truth which is their very soul. He admits as much when he says: 'The authority of these different systems is due to the fact that all contain some truth and some good.'[42] He also

[42] *Ibid.*, p. xvi.

[45a]

says that each system 'is related to all the others and, through the portion of truth it contains, is the true-born offspring of the human spirit.' It inevitably follows — he cannot deny it — that when he has extracted this portion of truth from the living body, which is what he proposes to do, what is left after the operation ceases to be related to the other systems, and is no longer the legitimate offspring of the human spirit. Another lawful conclusion from Cousin's teachings is that what remains of these systems may be buried in history. It is dead matter, killed by him, without any lack of respect for the freedom of the human spirit of which he rightly approves. Surely after these admissions of his, he cannot claim that freedom of the human spirit consists in allowing contradictory and erroneous philosophical systems to exist alongside one another, or the true system alongside systems with a mixture of true and false elements even when the truth they contain has been extracted? He hopes to retain them within your eclecticism. Like animals in Noah's ark, they will co-exist there and escape the flood. In fact, he makes the usual mistake of false liberals who exchange freedom for slavery. It is he who, in the name of freedom, imposes on the human spirit the most unreasonable, tyrannical captivity, when he says that there is no alternative to his eclecticism[43] which imposes on the human spirit the obligation (this is what he means by freedom) to preserve and perfect all systems. This is tantamount to saying that the human spirit is honoured when it is forbidden to exercise its right and fulfil its duty to reject false systems and adhere to the single true system! This is the view of freedom presented to human reason by liberal philosophers terrified of the looming spectre of the theocratic school, which haunts their imagination. And they assure you that this really is honouring the human spirit. They prove their argument in this way: 'All systems are as ancient as philosophy and inherent in the human spirit which initially creates them and continuously reproduces them. To attempt to destroy even one of these systems, which are all products of the human spirit, means dishonouring the human spirit; on the other hand, preserving them all means honouring each one.' What a pity that the philosopher who argues with

---

[43] 'I agree that it is a somewhat desperate resort but I must say that I can't see any other'* (Preface, p. xii).

[45a]

such subtlety lets slip the statement that systems of thought are legitimate offspring of the human spirit through the immortal element of truth that they contain. Having used the expression 'legitimate offspring', one must assume that there are also illegitimate offspring; and if truth is the legitimate offspring of the human spirit, it follows that error is the bastard offspring. If truth honours the human spirit, the same cannot be said of error, the illegitimate offspring. Thus our philosopher's concept of the honour due to the human spirit is no better than his concept of freedom. We would be crazy if we did not recognise that the human spirit is fallible and that the actions performed by it are not all true and pleasing. The person who truly honours the human spirit, who steers it towards the truth which endows it with honour and nobility, is not the superstitious person who worships it and makes a god of it. By doing so, he behaves like the courtiers who religiously collected and paid homage to their Emperor's excrement. We want nothing to do with such abject and servile behaviour. We wish to be free followers of the truth and we do not renounce for anyone's sake — even for eclecticism or syncretism which some wish to impose on us in the name of the freedom and honour that is due to the human spirit — our right to attempt the destruction of all erroneous systems and all erroneous elements we may discover in them. This is the concept I have formed of the freedom of the human spirit and of the way in which it is to be honoured. I feel that anyone who honours it otherwise dishonours it, although perhaps unwittingly.

46. A philosophical system is not a jumble of propositions without any interconnection nor are systems distinguished merely by the names of their authors, without consideration of their content. In my view, a system is neither a mere name nor fragments haphazardly taken from different philosophies; it is a noble principle with all its consequences. Thus, in the history of philosophy there are a number of so-called different systems, dependent upon different authors and a different arrangement of their contents. But in my view, they are not different if their philosophical corpus can be reduced to a single principle. Authors who accept a certain principle may indeed draw different and non-contradictory conclusions from it, or may endeavour to draw new conclusions, or may concentrate on

[46]

developing the principle by finding new applications that have previously been ignored. These authors, however, are not founders of new systems. They are working on the same system which they are all seeking to develop. Authentically different systems are not as numerous as people think, although so far the history of philosophy on which French eclecticism takes its stand presents them as multiple.

If a philosophical system is contained in this noble principle on which a thinker bases all his reasoning, the following will ensue: as the principle of the system, a single proposition, can only be either true or false (since there is no *via media* between truth and falsehood), so we have to say that different systems also can only be true or false and must, therefore, be either accepted or rejected. It is not sufficient to say that there is an element of truth in every system because, even if such a universal, unwarranted and antiphilosophical proposition were to be accepted, the element of truth will pertain either to the principle, if the principle is true, or to certain consequences, if such consequences are, taken by themselves, true propositions. If the portion of truth refers to the principle and the latter is therefore true, it follows that the system is true and that any false consequences can result only from wrong deductions. As such, they are to be eliminated as alien to the system and replaced by true consequences. But there can only be one true principle and one true system. If the element of truth pertains to the consequences in such a way that some consequences are in themselves true propositions but deduced (probably wrongly deduced) from a false principle, the entire system is false. Nor can it be saved by saving the true propositions, which do not truly belong to it. Rather, they have to be detached from this system by linking them up to the system to which they really belong, that is, to the system which has a true principle. To refrain from destroying any of the systems devised by the human spirit, which is what eclecticism peremptorily requires, is a vain, impossible procedure.

47. Eclecticism tells us that these systems are inherent in the human spirit, which discovered them at the very dawn of philosophy and continues to reproduce them. That may well be so, but are they true or false? This is the whole question for free philosophy, which does not accept the yoke formed by

aberrations of the human spirit, and refuses to stand surety and paymaster for the mind's errors and ravings. On the contrary, philosophy, that honourable lady, is rightly indignant with anyone who forcibly subjects her to such great humiliation and calls her 'scullion' and 'theocrat' because she refuses to pay the debts of prodigals and profligates. She protests indignantly, and states to eclecticism that if false systems are inherent in the human spirit which created them along with herself, it is the spirit which suffers. She did not give her consent. If the human spirit has used her name and forged her signature, she has only one recourse: to accuse the spirit of falsehood. Indeed, to claim that the human spirit, from the time it began to philosophise, produced all these systems, even the false ones, as Victor Cousin says, does not prove that the systems have to be accepted and piously preserved. Rather, it reveals the original sin of the human spirit, an inherent defect which weakens human reason and subjects it to the seduction of error. The defect cannot be due to God, who created the human spirit for truth. Nor can we wonder if the same systems keep reappearing when we know that the human inclinations and passions which bewitch and enslave mankind are always the same and governed by fixed laws. Mr. Cousin, by producing a *prescription* in favour of error which enslaves the human spirit, unintentionally behaves like a lawyer defending a debtor who refuses to pay his debts. He does not realise that prescription is valid in law for the external forum only; in philosophy it does not apply to either the external or internal forum.

48. Free reason, therefore, free philosophy, has the right to disdain all that is false and to ally itself with truth to destroy all false systems. No one can prevent it from exercising such a right of war; anyone can call it back into line if it does not adhere strictly to truth. Nevertheless, those who treat truth like a woman get angry and abusive when they find her disobliging and unwilling to comply with their vain, wilful opinions, and accuse her, 'rustic truth with dishevelled hair,'[*44] of uncouth behaviour. It is also true — we cannot deny it without prevarication — that all those who seek truth alone, take her alone to heart. Such people are easily considered arrogant because they

---

44 Martial 10, 72.

inevitably and unwillingly find themselves directly opposed to all others who do not follow them in their love of truth or who give precedence to other kinds of love. In every age, they have had to defend themselves against men whose wrath they have incurred. Even Socrates had to defend himself a few days before his death, which was caused by resentment on the part of those whose ignorance he showed up when he propounded the truth. He had to say to Theaetetus:

> Many persons, oh admirable young man, are now so ill-disposed towards me that they would like to tear me apart with their teeth if I were ever to rid them of their nonsensical ideas. They do not appreciate that I am acting out of kindness as they are quite unable to understand that the gods are not ill-disposed towards men. Nor do I act thus out of spite, but I do not feel it is right for me to accept what is untrue and reject what is true.[45]

49. It is precisely those who are accused of pride who are the most benevolent, indeed the only benevolent people, towards all other men. Although they are no respecters of persons or views, nevertheless, in their pre-philosophical studies, they do not reject history, and are perfectly willing to examine other systems of thought for whatever is true and sincere. However, they do not confuse history with philosophy, nor transform history into philosophy, nor believe that philosophy can be carried out historically. Philosophy is not based on divine authority and still less on human authority because philosophy is reasoning and nothing more. Infallible authority may prevent philosophical reasoning from error by indicating the way it should go, but it can never take its place. On the other hand, authority, even when fallible, can stimulate philosophical thinking but cannot take its place and remove it as though it were no longer necessary.

A constant source of amazement is the illogicality of those who harbour a deep suspicion of divine authority, which they view as a theocratic school, while exhibiting the most slavish respect for the opinions of the philosophers, or self-styled philosophers, mentioned in history. They scruple to destroy

[45] *Theaetetus*, p. 275 (London, 1826).

[49]

even one of their systems to avoid shaming, they say, the human spirit, which however is not always vigilant, but quite capable of dozing and dreaming. It is very odd to see the theme of respect for the human spirit being introduced into philosophy — it is the only example of respect they exhibit — as if this feeling or some other like it might be really important in deciding questions of truth and falsehood. Moreover, even if the history of systems of thought provides arguments together with statements, the arguments cannot be accepted by philosophy because they are historical, but only as true and in accordance with strict logic. In other words, arguments are valid not because they pertain to a given philosopher, but because they are proper to the mind and are thus common to all minds. Philosophy leaves completely to one side scholarly questions about who may have first grasped these truths intellectually and enunciated them correctly.

Just as Socrates maintained that no god was ill-disposed towards mankind, so I maintained that those who love and pursue truth — a divine gift that constitutes the glory of the human spirit not because the human spirit forms the truth but because the truth informs it — are the best disposed, indeed the only people well-disposed towards humankind and to the systems which others have thought out. They alone offer human nature the true good which stems from truth and is reduced to truth. Within their systems they willingly recognise, love and prize everything that is lovable and can be appreciated, that is, the immortal element of their systems, the truth on which the systems agree and unite. This is not the case with those who imagine that the human spirit itself deserves honour independently of any share in the truth. For them, the truth is honoured as a creation of the human spirit just as error is. And error, certainly, is an authentic creation of the human spirit.

49a. These pseudo-thinkers, who have no focal point for their sympathies, find philosophy's beauty, life and nobility in continuous change. For them, different and opposing systems rise and fall, reappear and jostle one another continuously in an unending struggle so that philosophy may thrive and flourish. They venture self-assuredly into the fray in search of war, not peace, and for the palm of victory. The best of them do not even resent the valour of their colleagues. Rather they exalt it as

[49a]

something which enhances and ennobles the battle for them.
The less refined and courteous, like Homer's heroes, simply
abuse one another before coming to blows. But all of them
really enjoy the idea of a continuous number of philosophical
systems. In that way, combat is more brilliant and spectacular
and offers a chance to a larger number of champions. This
explains why, up to now, the history of philosophy, instead of
telling the story of the Lady (Truth) who by herself overcame
many knights, is merely a continuous narrative of contests and
stubborn campaigns that have taken on the outward form of
systems. These systems skirmish most skilfully without understanding one another and without any outright victor because
both parties tilt with a lance made of truth and error.

Is there anyone who is unaware of the irascible, quarrelsome
nature of philosophers or who has not been bored by their perpetual disagreement and rivalries or not been scandalised by the
interminable tussle between ever new and conflicting views?
Views so confused that even the most far-sighted are unable to
discern the truth or even believe it exists when dense clouds of
Olympic dust obscure its light. But not everybody is aggressive
or enjoys the fray. As a result, in trying too hard to entertain
people, one finishes, unfortunately, by boring them. Nevertheless, people claim to restore philosophy in popular esteem by
using a new method (an old one, in fact) which consists in preventing the destruction of any system and in recommending
that they all be strengthened to fight even harder.[46] This is the
real reason for the low esteem or rather the contempt with
which philosophy is viewed, the reason why people will finish
by believing that philosophical truth is nowhere to be found.

---

[46] Referring to the sensualist school, Mr. Cousin writes as follows: 'Far
from weakening it I would, if I could, find for it a serious and worthy
representative. Because it embodies some great truths, it must occupy an
eminent position in Science and I consider as a real misfortune the pitiful
state into which it has lapsed in our present age'* (Preface, p. xiv, xv).
However, to give Mr. Cousin credit, I feel I must add that he is in large
measure responsible for the pitiful state into which the sensualist school in
France has fallen — a condition he so much deplores. If possible, he would
like to give this school a worthy champion; but how could he give someone
else a role which he himself refuses to accept? 'What you would not like
others to do to you, do not do to others.'*

[49a]

and that philosophy itself is a game played by certain crabbed, eccentric intellectuals who, unconcerned with the truth, without certainty, and of no benefit for mankind, love to show off and parade their talents by arrogant, fruitless quibbling! No wonder that when a new doctrine of a totally opposite type unexpectedly appeared on the scene, self-confident, as immutable as truth, as complete as wisdom — I refer to the Gospel — philosophy schools should be greatly shocked and become the object of treatises entitled: *Irrisio philosophorum*. Do people nowadays really want more treatises of this kind?

The Gospel produced them then and is now ready to do the same again if people return to sophistry, as Cousin's theocratic philosophy threatens to do. Only the Gospel was able gradually to rid philosophy of derision and mockery by giving back to people the confidence they had lost in reason and in truth. It imparted to them a great part of truth — the essential and necessary part — but it did much more than that. It ensured the perpetual survival of truth among men through the same power which commands the sun to rise each day and shine upon the earth. It strengthened the obligation to love truth whilst pouring infinite love into human spirits.

This was the achievement of Christianity which, along with all its other benefits, despatched false philosophy and saved true philosophy from its otherwise inevitable fall into Alexandrian eclecticism. To put it more accurately, such philosophy without Christianity would not have had even the time to flash its final ray of light before human eyes.

50. That is why I think it my duty to ensure that philosophy retains the honourable status assigned to it by Christianity. Such a status imposes upon philosophy the noble duty or, to put it another way, the happy obligation to act exclusively from then on as the teacher of truth. This is certainly not because those who philosophise have become infallible but because anything they think and say that contradicts truth cannot rightly be called philosophy. When the light of Christianity dawned, the following affirmation was made:

> I call philosophy not Stoic, or Platonic, or Epicurean, or Aristotelian thinking, but whatever has been well said by each of those sects, which teach justice along with science

pervaded by piety. But I would never call divine other conclusions of human reasonings which have been cut off from it and falsified.[47]

It follows logically that thinkers and writers are to be considered philosophers only in so far as their writings are true. If they have produced falsehood in abundance they should not be called philosophers [that is, lovers of wisdom] (such a name is intended for those who honour, preserve and advance the cause of philosophy). They should rather be called sophists, enemies of philosophy or, depending on their particular behaviour, *lovers of the flesh, lovers of wealth, lovers of disputes,* or generally speaking, as Plato called them, *lovers of opinion.*[48] Some tirelessly rack their brains, not to seek truth but where possible to destroy it, or deny some part of it; their laborious, contrived hair-splitting clouds men's minds; their behaviour is precisely the opposite of that demanded of a philosopher. Clearly, it is wrong and barbarous to give the same name to those who profess not only different, but contradictory roles, as though creating and destroying were one and the same operation. It is strange that people understand this when they assign names to other things (they would be misunderstood and ridiculed otherwise), but in this single field of philosophy, lapse into great linguistic confusion and contradiction without even being aware of doing so. Canova and anyone who delighted in scratching and drilling holes in his most accomplished statues would not both be called sculptors; Raphael and a desecrator of his painting would not both be called artists. It would never occur to anyone that such a contorted use of words could be justified by claiming that both Canova and the person who destroyed his statues, or Raphael and his assailant used the same implements.

50a. What is the system of truth but a kind of majestic statue or noble image of God himself, of much greater worth than anything produced by human hands. It is, after all, impressed upon immortal souls by the living image of eternal wisdom. The person who devotes himself to such a great work is called a

[47] Clement of Alexandria, *Stromata* 1, 7.
[48] *Phaedo.*

[50a]

philosopher and the subject he pursues is called philosophy. How, then, can such a name be profaned and abused by applying it to those who, although they too use their intellects, do so in such a shoddy way that their sole achievement is the demolition and disfigurement of the philosopher's work? Their sophistry obscures the light of truth revealed by true philosophy and daubs with falsehood the respectable limbs of the body of wisdom which the philosopher depicts in his writings.

This reprehensible and wayward attitude became the almost universal norm; during the last century, atheism was hailed as the sign of a philosophical mind! Yet we remain unmoved by the monstrosity of such a negation! Atheism, which wipes out truth altogether, is the greatest of all negations; common knowledge also recognises that it leads to great ignorance, great errors, great folly. How, then, could this kind of greatness be confused with the way 'greatness' is used in learning and philosophy? In fact the confusion between these contradictory views of greatness was explained thus: even the most barbaric, inhospitable people accepts some god which it worships; atheism, therefore, can be the only belief for learned men.[49] It is as if learning reaches its peak when it proves capable of ridding men's minds of those very truths which the most savage and wild barbarians were unable to stamp out.

50b. I know how odious it is — and always has been — to expel those who teach error from the company of philosophers. However, those who love truth must be prepared to apply to themselves the ancient proverb: 'Truth arouses hatred', as

---

[49] This argument, or rather this aberration, is found in the *Encyclopédie Méthodique* (Naigeon's *Philosophie Ancienne et Moderne*, Paris 1791, vol.1, p. 607). All those who have not abandoned common sense, even the gentiles, recognise in this limitless perversion of reason other features, such as ignorance, and a monstrous defilement of the human intellect which owes its origin to an inappropriate, persistent abuse of study and a constant endeavour to wrench thought from its natural course which, by comparison, makes barbarians appear real sages. Aelianus writes: 'We have to admire the wisdom of the barbarians. None of them has ever lapsed into atheism or questioned whether the gods exist or not and concern themselves with human affairs. No one, therefore, neither Indian, nor Celt, nor Egyptian ever thought of this. Only Evemerus Messenius, or Diogenes Phryse, Hippon, Diagoras, Sosius or Epicurus'* (*Varia Historia*, 2, 31) — 'All the barbarians believe in God'* (Maximus Tyrius, *Dissertations*, 38).

Socrates did when he had the courage to refuse the name of philosophers to the sophists of his day.[50] I shall therefore continue to maintain it is base flattery — because it is false — to bestow the noble title of philosophical system upon any jumble of true or false propositions produced by disordered reason and the ravings of a sick imagination and presented as a philosophical treatise. To consider as authoritative something based on titles of books and authors' names could spring from weakness of character and intellect, but wanting to maintain such imprecise terms for the sake of some mutual advantage amounts to flagrant collusion. How can we consider philosophical systems based on false principles as true on the pretext that they nevertheless contain some particle of truth? This truth is an alien element which has to be removed from these systems and reinserted into the system of truth in which it is at home. Otherwise, we are providing an unfair, unjustified and lavish award to an undeserving system. Other forms are the refusal, or diminution, of the honour due to truth by unjustly designating all systems in the same terms, lumping them together, whether they are based on a true or a false principle. This reduces truth to the same ignominious level as error, and humiliates the human spirit.

How do you know, we may ask, that all systems are a jumble of truth and error? Do you claim that as a philosopher you should be taken at your word and that your judgement is sufficient authority? Is it jealousy, therefore, that makes you so afraid of theocracy? Yet it does not require much intelligence to grasp that, where the fundamental principle of a system is true, the entire system must be accepted as true and conclusions rectified only if they are illogically deduced. Then indeed other deductions are to be drawn in order to develop and complete the principle. If, however, the fundamental principle of a system is false, the entire system is to be considered as false. Any truths contained in it are there by chance; they neither belong to the system nor make it true. Accepting all systems without

---

[50] At the end of the fifth dialogue of the *Republic*, where Plato defines true philosophers as 'those who are eager to discover truth' and calls those who enjoy arguing over different opinions not philosophers, but 'philodoxers', that is, not lovers of wisdom but worshippers of opinion, Socrates adds: 'Although we would arouse their anger if we were to say so.'*

discrimination means wishing to be a philosopher as Homer was; as Seneca observes, Homer embraces all philosophies in his poetry but in fact has none himself.[51] Strictly speaking, it must be said that no system is a mixture of truth and falsehood (although truth and falsehood may co-exist in books containing different systems). All systems are either true or false. True systems[52] are further from false systems than the earth is from the heavens, and cannot, therefore, be lumped into the same category nor judged *en bloc*. Moreover, false systems are erroneous and, as such, cannot strictly speaking be called 'philosophical', but 'anti-philosophical.'

We should indeed pay tribute to the human spirit — on this point I am in agreement with Mr Cousin — but there are different ways of interpreting 'tribute'. As I see it, 'tribute' cannot be given to the zeal and persistence displayed by the human spirit when it contradicts and tears itself apart, nor when it harkens back to a pagan way of life which has vanished forever. A new and powerful voice has been heard rising above the disgraceful clamour of philosophers: 'Philosophy has no place among those who waste their time in quarrelling and heated words.'[53] This message was heard by the best philosophers,[54] but more readily

---

[51] 'Unless perhaps they persuade you that Homer was a philosopher, although the very passages they use to prove it contradict what they say. At one time, they show him as a Stoic, approving of virtue alone, rejecting pleasures and refusing even immortality if the price were dishonourable. At other times, they show him as an Epicurean, lauding a peaceful State which spends its days in banqueting and song. Sometimes he is a Peripatetic, affirming three kinds of good, sometimes an Academic, stating that nothing is certain. It is quite clear that none of these doctrines is homer's because they all appear in his works and are mutually incompatible'* (*Ep*. 88).

[52] In using the plural form *true systems*, I do not wish to suggest that there can be more than one true, complete system. However, there can be a number of incomplete, true systems depending on the level at which philosophers deal with the principle. Moreover, all true but incomplete systems are merely elements of the single, complete, true system, the ideal to which philosophers must aspire in their aim and meditation.

[53] 'Philosophy is not produced by those who spend their efforts on verbal skirmishes and contests'* (St. Isidore of Pelusium., *Ep*. 220).

[54] Seneca on several occasions condemns the philosophers' ambitious and noisy disputes and refuses to accept that they constitute *philosophy*. See *Ep*. 1, 20.

heard by the whole world which clearly sees through the vanity of scholars who pursued their philosophical studies in the way that mediaeval *condottieri* waged war. I must repeat that in my view the nobility of the human spirit consists solely in the truth in which it can, and actually does, participate. Truth leads to peace and harmony just as error and perpetual uncertainty create dissension and bring dishonour to the human spirit. There are two equal ways of debasing and sorely injuring the human spirit; first, by dishonouring the truth — which the human spirit does not create but sees, and by which it is enlightened and ennobled — and second, honouring error, the unfortunate creation of the human spirit, which blinds and dethrones its creator. Both of these ways operate simultaneously when Mr Cousin's opinion, which is merciful rather than fair, is applied to true and false systems in an endeavour to preserve and strengthen each in the same measure.

51. The effect of this opinion is to satisfy all the makers and followers of false systems. On the one hand, the would-be peacemaker's opinion will be opposed by all the makers and followers of true systems whose complaints will be heard and attended to by the sense and conscience of mankind, a much more authoritative and indeed theocratic court of appeal. It is clear, therefore, that eclecticism's promise to reconcile all systems, philosophical and antiphilosophical, without distinction is impossible. For my part, I intend to please the founders of true systems, and have grave doubts whether Mr Cousin will ever manage to pacify his followers.[55] On the other hand, I am confident that I can be at peace with my own people because we consider the system of truth as the basis of the only peace possible among human minds, and the cause of all other peace.

How can peace be achieved when it is located in combat, in a conflict between systems? How can we speak of reconciliation, show its importance and condemn those who reject it when we are compelled to preserve and consequently strengthen all opposing systems and, at the same time, affirm on Cousin's word that all of them, without exception, contain some

---

[55] Even Mr Cousin seems to despair of it. See page 13 of the long passage which begins: 'Eclecticism! I am fully aware that the mere name rouses the exclusive systems to revolt.'*

falsehood? It is typical of errors, which are by nature multiple, to be mutually exclusive and hostile, and above all to wage war against truth. If, therefore, all systems contain truth and error[56] (eclecticism is built on this postulate which fortunately is not irrefutable as a mathematical postulate is), we shall have many conflicting systems, each of which will contain the seeds of conflict. We should also note that, on their own admission, each of these systems tends to be exclusive and indeed the only system. It is this desire for exclusivity that makes the systems distinct. If there were no exclusivity, all these systems would merge. This, too, is recognised as a defect so intrinsic to each system that, without it, the system cannot survive and certainly cannot be strengthened. Nevertheless, each system desires to survive and strengthen its position provided that none dominates the others. In other words, they are not exclusive! I have to apologise here for the patent contradiction which has as it were cut my argument in two. I cannot ask whether a contradiction is possible because that would be the same as asking how an impossibility were possible. For the moment, therefore, we shall simply have to hide the contradiction under the veil of the vague, nebulous word used by the founder of eclecticism. In other words, I shall substitute 'contradiction' with 'conciliation', and ask how the promised conciliation is possible.

51a. The answer we are given is *tolerance*,[57] a fine and very acceptable word to human ears. But do we give any serious thought to what it means? Certainly tolerance is a precious virtue if by it we mean mistrusting our judgment and respecting that of others within the limits of prudence, as well as being considerate about even the obvious mistakes and malicious frailties of others and not using them as a pretext for encroaching upon others' rights, refraining from any rash judgment and being kindly and well-disposed towards all. But we practise tolerance towards persons, not systems. Precisely because tolerance is a virtue, it is a habit proper to the human will, not a

---

[56] 'All of these systems have had to withstand overwhelming attack. All of them in some measure have been exposed, accused and convicted of containing unacceptably wild notions'* (Preface, p. ix–x).

[57] 'The history of philosophy would alone have been sufficient to produce eclecticism, that is, philosophical tolerance'* (Preface, p. xviii).

[51a]

branch of knowledge. At the moment, however, we are discussing the intellect, not the will; we are speaking of the mind, talking of philosophy, of philosophical systems, of error and truth. We must not forget this.

Surely it is a great fallacy to apply the laws proper to the will to the intellect and to claim that the intellect obeys laws other than its own? Everyone knows that the mind is incapable of tolerance, and is by nature intolerant (if I may be allowed to speak in this way). The self-denial entailed in the tolerance of known contradiction and falsehood would bring about its own extinction. To oblige the mind to be tolerant means, therefore, obliging it to seek its own destruction. This is certainly not a philosophical stance. On the contrary, it can rightly be considered 'intolerance', a form of intolerance so monstrous that human beings no longer tolerate the very existence of their mind and certainly not the existence of philosophy. The mind, however, is not to blame if it does not comply with laws which are not designed for it. The blame, if there is any blame in this case, is entirely due to the extreme intolerance of truth, of an inexorable logic. We do not make ideas, we receive them ready made; nor can they be remade. Moreover, ideas are not persons towards whom one can exercise the virtue of tolerance, courtesy and such like. The reconciliation of different systems achieved through tolerance, as it is proposed by French Eclecticism, is exactly like the union of the seven Protestant sects initiated in the duchy of Nassau in 1817 and subsequently extended to other states, especially to Prussia by the late King. This is an odd grouping in which each sect retains its beliefs. Nevertheless, despite such different, contradictory beliefs, each of which condemns the others, the intention was to form a single, so-called *evangelical* Church, as if the Gospel were a mass of contradictions, a monstrous syncretism composed of all the Protestant sects! In order to create a single Church, such believers were quite happy with a common *name* and a few external forms. They were indifferent to the realities, to dogmas professed by individual believers and yet they assure us that they closely resemble the Christian Church of the early centuries! French Eclecticism is modelled on a similar example. It offers philosophers a union, or a settlement on the same scale in which a common name, a few vague expressions and a few gibes against theocracy excuse and cover up the essential difference of views which separates the Eclectics, who protest that they are retaining and strengthening all the opposing systems for the sake of honouring the human spirit. There is one reservation: another special condition is added to this proposal of reconciliation; the exclusive systems are to make mutual concessions,[58] as though systems founded on such different principles could be so accommodating or make such concessions without mutual destruction. Indeed, they would apparently even survive and grow stronger. Such unions and settlements, however, are not philosophical, nor can they be put forward or accepted by philosophers. We shall leave them, therefore, to politicians, comperes and Protestants. I make a distinction between the law governing the intellect and that governing the will. Imposing the latter on the former would be a gross mistake. Such confusion will never advance the cause of philosophy nor enable us to distinguish between what can and cannot be reconciled in the intellectual order.

52. Truth always agrees with truth, error rarely agrees with error, and never agrees with the truth. Granting oneself such a tremendous right as to impose arbitrarily upon the mind a law alien to it is a greater absurdity than that of demagogues who exercise the vilest form of tyranny and call it freedom. It means assuming one can impose one's own intellectual despotism with impunity upon human nature and upon truth which is the sole lawgiver and ruler of human nature. Truth therefore represents the only possible point of agreement — there is no other — and it has always been my focus in philosophical discussions. I hope my friends will bear with me if, once again, I recall my early studies and describe how the desire and determination to effect such agreement grew up in me.

In my youth, when I knew nothing of what had been thought and written, I plunged enthusiastically — the way the young do — into philosophical questions. I was introduced to them by Pietro Orsi, whose name is virtually unknown but whom I shall never forget. Night and day, my mind ranged to and fro over the vast field of philosophy — it was like wandering in a garden. I experienced the delight that comes with one's first scientific glimpse of truth. I was full of almost arrogant self-assurance and

[58] 'I offered them a peace treaty on the basis of mutual concessions'*
(Preface, p. xvi).

the limitless hopes so characteristic of the young when, nobly and in full awareness, they apply their minds to the universe and its Creator and seem to take them in as easily as breathing. I was not awed by any difficulty I encountered, but stimulated. I considered every difficulty to be a mystery designed to awaken my curiosity, a treasure to unearth. Each day I wrote down the results of this ingenuous and still amateurish philosophical freedom, aware that I was sowing the seeds for the life's work which God had assigned to me. In fact, all the works published when I was older sprang from those seeds.

52a. After these initial efforts, I compared, one by one, all the teachings of the philosophers with my own spontaneous, imperfect thoughts. Whenever I found agreement, I cherished these teachings as though I had met a friend and triumphed while he looked on. I was well aware of the fallaciousness of a lone mind, my own in particular. I realised, too, that to be absolutely sure of the truth, I needed some authority on divine issues which the rational mind cannot address. Moreover, authority or, to be more precise, the assent of other minds is required to confirm the correctness of even natural reasoning which, of course, is the basis of the science called philosophy where argument, not authority, holds sway. Authority, however, always steps in at the appropriate moment to review and confirm with its own witness the arguments put forward by philosophy. This is highly useful. At this point, I grasped ever more firmly and approved what Seneca wrote: 'I revere philosophical discoveries and those who are responsible for them. It is a pleasure to be the heir to so many bequests. Those discoveries were made for me and worked on for me. However, we should act like real fathers and add to the family inheritance. The legacy must be increased and passed on to our descendants. Nevertheless, much remains to be done. Work will never cease. All will have their chance to add something, even in a thousand centuries' time. Let us grant that the Ancients have discovered everything; even so, the use, knowledge and arrangement of their discoveries will never cease.'[59] Seneca, one of the soundest philosophers, is not afraid that the adoption of the one, true system will signal the demise of philosophy. When Cousin, the

[59] *Ep.* 69.

[52a]

founder of French eclecticism, is troubled and intellectually disturbed over what he takes to be a turn for the worse, he reminds me of Alexander the Great who grieved that a victory of his father might have left no lands to conquer. I believe, on the contrary, that the right of conquest is now discredited in this old world of ours which has seen so much and experienced so many disappointments. Just as this right, when applied to politics, may easily be considered a form of tyranny, so, when applied to philosophy, it can easily be considered a form of deception. In any case, I believe that the truth already discovered is preferable to the noble rivalry between minds aspiring to discover truth. Even after some truth has been discovered, much work remains to be done by intelligent people who are willing to undertake the task of making it clearer and easier to grasp. I am convinced that truth can shed its light ever further into our intelligences. I hold that, as every system is based on a single principle from which it develops, so the principle of what I call the system of truth constantly gives rise to new conclusions, and fresh, unexpected and vital applications. This goes on whatever the energy expended on it. The task of associating all the different branches of knowledge and all the corresponding facts of nature and history with this single principle, and of drawing from it all human knowledge organised in a single, magnificent corpus is inexhaustible and almost infinite. In my view, even when this enormous task has been finally completed, another would remain. This task, always new, ever recurring and equally valuable, would allow no respite because we would still have to preserve the great store of systematic teaching, impart it to all, adapt it to all purposes, hand it down intact to successive generations, defend and protect it from the ever-active, restless, quibbling principle of evil and error which never dies and is always disruptive. Finally, I believe that intellects exert a great and thorough influence even when they merely abide in the truth, enjoy it, and share this enjoyment with their will which alone activates and implements truth, and bears it to the highest point of the mind where it is suspended and truly available to us. Philosophers should not be frightened by the spectre of the death which eclecticism predicts for philosophy, nor abandon or moderate their pursuit of the one system, the highest idea of all, on which to concentrate their

[52a]

philosophical inquiries. Nothing dies as a result of attaining perfection, and it is unlikely that such a fate would be visited upon philosophy when it reaches its perfect, systematic form. Rather the arduousness and enormity of the enterprise suggest that we should prepare ourselves for the task. In this case, the first thing is to remove the obstacles raised by disagreements which prevent the true union of minds in truth.

This is why the unveiling of false systems and the merciless dispersal of their shadows in the light of truth is always a step towards the goal we have in mind. Such systems should have the same markings in history as reefs and sand banks on navigation charts.

53. I mentioned that it is possible and extremely desirable to reconcile true systems. First, we should do our utmost to avoid injustice by wrongly including any system in the class of false systems. If some tiny, erroneous element appears in invalid conclusions drawn from a true principle, these should be corrected; the system itself should not be rejected. We must also assess the importance of each of the principles which constitute the base of the systems. The less important are to be subordinated to the more important, and all of them to the highest principle of all from which the others are derived as conclusions. This first stage of operations sees one system fitting snugly into another at the right place like a branch on its trunk. Consequently, a number of partial systems produce a single or complete system, or at least one that is less partial.

Next, it is necessary to distinguish truth from the various forms it may take, from the varied ways in which it may be conceived and from the different aspects or viewpoints by which it is revealed to our minds. These 'various ways' are merely parts of the same truth. None of them excludes the other, none contradicts the other, each one adds a new ray of light. Scholars moved by the spirit of conciliation will discover behind so many different expressions and wide range of philosophical views, the beautiful unity of truth, unlimited in its multiplicity of appearances, but always in accord with its own nature. This is the second task by which correct reconciliation can be reached by all sound philosophers.

A powerful aid to bringing about this philosophical conciliation is the generous interpretation we give to others' views. As a matter of fact, it is just as hard to express ourselves correctly as it is to think correctly. Consequently, we often fail to express our entire thought adequately. Fairness therefore dictates that the listener or reader should interpret it and tease it out, so to speak, from its enigmatic, inadequate expression which covers it like a veil over a portrait. In such a case, we should seek out the spirit of the writer rather than cling to the letter. We should bear in mind the context of words, sentences and arguments but, above all, concentrate on the coherence that doubtful conclusions must have with established principles and the clearly expressed intentions of the thinker.

54. By applying these rules, I enjoyed success well beyond my expectations. I came to the conclusion that on important issues necessary to human beings, all the great philosophers differed from each other in appearance rather than in substance. Although they clothe the truth in different forms, which are sometimes unsuitable or deficient, they stumble upon it unaware of their basic agreement. If we ignore the 'minuscule philosophers' (*minuti philosophi*), as Cicero calls them[60] — the Roman orator's distinction between 'minuscule' and 'great philosophers' corresponds to the distinction I felt obliged to make between the founders of false and true systems of thought — their judgments coincide remarkably about the noblest, supreme truths and with the beliefs and conscience of mankind. Such 'minuscule' philosophers, who are not philosophers but sophists, dissent from these truths and, in their foolish vanity, think that they are erudite. They misuse their talents, whatever illusions they harbour that fence them off from truth. Whatever the depths in which they founder as a result, they never manage to eradicate completely from their souls the indelible stamp left upon them by nature. They cannot entirely extinguish the unquenchable flame which enlightens the intelligence, nor stifle completely and permanently human feeling which, like the pupils of a dying man, seeks the light so cleverly removed from it. These people, too, can offer witness to truth, not because they are philosophers but because they are human beings. They do this either in their occasional, unguarded admissions, when they are least vigilant, or in the contradictions by which they

---

[60] *On Divination*, 1, 30.

[54]

betray themselves and destroy their own errors, or in the qualifications which they diffidently append to their own teachings — teachings which, by their plain absurdity, would be too offensive and would rouse common sense to the defence of truth. Such people inevitably feel a fortunate obligation to add some scrap of truth to error. Just as 'nothing' cannot be conceived without the concept of being, error requires the notion of truth. Our mind would instantly reject error if it did not exhibit the appeal it usurps from truth, with which it so cunningly associates and for which it is mistaken.

54a. There is another way in which true and false philosophers indirectly witness to the truth and advance its cause. Their intellectual efforts identify the crux of the problem, that is, the awkward knot which they have vainly tried to untie, and which caused many of them, despite their utmost endeavours, to fall into error. Knowing where the problem lies represents an important stage on the way to the attainment of truth, which cannot be assailed in its hidden stronghold unless the fortress defending it has been inspected from all sides. One example of this would be the numerous disputes and philosophical systems arising from the fundamental question of the origin of ideas. All philosophers have come face to face with this problem, although they have encountered it in different ways and helped to make it clearer and visible from a number of viewpoints. In this way, they made access to the problem easier, and prepared the groundwork for its solution.

This explains why I think it worthwhile justifying the arguments I put forward by relying in most cases upon the expert opinions of others and especially on the judgments of great philosophers. These views, honestly interpreted, can serve as comparisons and confirmation of my own views. I do not intend to substitute authority for argument in philosophy, but to offer some guarantee to the mind and comfort to the human spirit. Philosophy needs such harmony between human intelligences as it goes on its arduous journey.

But reconciliation and agreement can only be found in unity. To find it among the multiplicity of philosophical systems which eclecticism tries at all costs to preserve in the hope of pleasing its followers seems to me the height of absurdity. As I have already pointed out, this means looking for harmony in

[54a]

philosophy outside the mind, where philosophy does not exist. At the same time the clash of opinions and ideas is allowed to smoulder — or even stirred up. But if intellectual reconciliation, and philosophical perfection and harmony, are to be found solely in the unity of a philosophical system it follows that they are to be found in truth. Truth alone is one; error is manifold.

55. Certainly, such reconciliation and unity may seem unimportant to those accustomed to an academic life, whose thoughts extend no further than the walls of the university and whose joy lies in disputation and the sight of young, abrasive minds producing unexpected sparks of light. My own opinion is quite different: philosophical studies should concentrate seriously on such points. Moreover, if minds and hearts are permitted to break out of their philosophical stockade, they will realise that the consequences of the proposed reconciliation are of immense importance to mankind. They will also see that the idea of preserving a multiplicity of systems as fuel for academic questions is culpable rather than childish. And, as we saw, there is no fear that questions will be lacking.

The evidence that such reconciliation is desirable is apparent in the disagreements which rend and disrupt human society: dissension, hatred, war, threats of war, and groups which, as an ancient writer said, are like bulls prodding empty air with their horns. In Europe, where culture flourishes and science advances, intellectual divisions, the many factions which seek mutual destruction, and the arousal of passions (which scandalise still uncultured nations) are not due to the multiplicity of ideas. Divisions of opinion arise, not because there are many ideas and opinions but because these ideas are so divergent. There is no doubt that the real basis of agreement in human society, as well as that of discord, must be sought in harmonious or contrasting ideas or opinions. It is always an idea which presides over, guides and marks, so to speak, all of our acts. And it is not only individual acts which are based upon an idea. Among ideas themselves, some are so general in their application that they constitute a type, and stamp their impression on the long sequence of actions which are the warp and woof of an individual's whole life.

Similarly, one of these basic ideas, acting as a kind of a secret standard, imprints its own unique stamp on the complex mass of actions which in every age produces the moral, civic and political state of nations. As we have seen, a few ideas keep recurring in the very depths of the historical process and through all the vicissitudes which mankind traverses in its development and decline here below. These ideas become laws which regulate the extremely complex and apparently casual sequence of events which, however, regularly break up into set periods. Each of these ages is regulated not by the influence or ascendancy of a star but by the ascendancy of an idea then dominant in human minds, and gradually replaced when another idea takes its place. Consequently, if ideas and opinions clash in our minds, the affections proper to our spirit and the actions of the exterior life are inevitably at odds. On the other hand, when human minds agree both in their ideas and opinions, the resulting mental consensus produces its effect on everyday living in mutual good will and the kind of union which establishes peace and social power.

This is known only too well in Italy where the dire effects of disharmony have been felt longer and more keenly than in any other region. Poor Italy! I believe that the spirit of evil, fearing more from her than from any other nation, has thrust the torch of discord into her every nook and cranny. Evil has set the torch alight so that Italy, at odds with herself, should be divided, and divided remain weak. Weakness would develop into cowardice and sloth. Prostrate in her sloth, she would be incapable of grasping the real reason for her disunity. This is the cause: her lack of any firm opinion, combined with the presence of any number of feeble, conflicting opinions. In her laxity, in her superficial studies, she is like an immature child reciting the lessons learned in someone else's school, and unable to produce a philosophy or teaching of her own nor any overall nation-wide view. Let her awake and seek the intellectual unity she needs. She has only to desire it, and she will have it; her ill-starred beauty would recover all its strength and glory.

56. Here I would like to thank those noble souls who held out the hand of friendship when I attempted to set out a philosophy which would realise the aims I outlined in the first part of this work, and obtain the advantages accruing from the reconciliation of opposing views. Many of them were fellow-citizens; it would be impossible to name all of them, though my thanks go

out to them all. I must not, however, fail to mention first of all the professors at the University of Turin, Giuseppe Andrea Sciolla, Pietro Corte and Michele Tarditi, who were the first to discuss, defend and introduce in their lectures, in a rare display of unity of intention, the very teaching that I was offering. Alas, two of these distinguished scholars, whose love of the same truth and whose exposure to similar philosophical labours had made them like brothers to me, were soon snatched away by death, a great loss to scholarship and their native land. Sciolla, a perfect example of integrity and friendship, was already in late middle-age; the other, Tarditi, was at the peak of his powers with a rich future ahead of him. Leaving behind a fine group of talented followers, they are now where 'they keep watch with endless gaze in sacred love.'[61] And this is our consolation.

Gustavo di Cavour, with whom I have shared a special bond over the years through feelings of affection and esteem mingled with religious faith, was perhaps the first who presented these teachings in French. Alessandro Pestalozza, lecturer in Philosophy in the Archiepiscopal Seminary of Monza, was the first to publish in Italian a complete, substantial course, and wrote a number of works ably defending it against objections put forward and eloquently developed by a celebrated mind [Gioberti]. Finally, I must mention the writer [Manzoni] who captivated the whole of Italy with his volumes of a new type of heavenly lyric, and threw himself into historical studies with a zeal not often found among us and with a critical insight rarely found anywhere. His novel [*I promessi sposi*], a highly skilful portrayal of the human spirit, offered stern yet sensitive lectures on moral matters. In adopting new principles governing language and literature, he succeeded in showing how language could be made more homogeneous and precise, and literature more virile and sincere. Both language and literature were thus made more conducive to peace in Italy. After successfully undertaking such diverse studies, he found rest as it were in philosophy, which was wonderfully suited to his age and erudition. His recent work, a dialogue entitled *Dell'Invenzione*, is noted for the admirable subtlety and perceptiveness of his intellect and the equally admirable culture and polish of his style.

---

[61] Dante, *Paradise*, 15: 64–65.

Finally, I must also express my gratitude to my loyal opponents.

PART THREE

THE CONCEPT OF WISDOM

Κυρία — ἡ σοφία τῆς φιλοσοφίας
[Our mistress is the wisdom of philosophy]
Clement of Alexandria, *Stromata*, 1, 5.

57. In the two previous parts, I dealt with what I have done or what I have intended to do. To complete what I have to say, I still have to describe what I have not done and what cannot in fact be achieved by literary effort and studies. These studies, of which I spoke to my friends and to all those kind well-wishers who deserve my gratitude, were the source of the essays which I have published and here gathered together. But books deal exclusively with systematic knowledge which represents neither the whole man, nor what is best in him. Books have as their subject either things which we have not brought about but merely contemplated, or things which we not only contemplate but actually bring about. But the power we have to do things and the actions with which we carry them out, along with all the other realities we perceive, are not systematic knowledge, nor can they be dealt with in books. Nature itself excludes them in written form and places them outside systematic knowledge to which books, like signposts, refer and direct the attention.

Everyone accepts this but few realise how important it is to bear it in mind. For this is one of those singular truths which are extremely easy to admit yet very difficult to grasp. A clear proof of this is the way in which even scholars frequently view systematic knowledge as all-important and seem to believe that through it anyone may become a wise and perfect human being. As a result, they repeatedly confuse *goodness of life* with *systematic knowledge*. But knowledge in this sense belongs to the order of ideas, whereas goodness pertains to the order of actions and real things. Goodness, which certainly touches

[57]

upon systematic knowledge, goes far, far beyond it. Evidence for this can be seen in thinkers who concentrated on ethical issues. Their opinions rarely agree, but are for the most part totally inconsistent, and affirm now one thing and now another. Sometimes they differentiate between virtue and philosophy; sometimes they fuse them; sometimes they end by differentiating between them but always leaving them inseparable. This type of inconsistency may be found in Seneca's letters.

In a number of places, Seneca assigns to philosophy the task of *teaching* virtue. Moreover, just as earlier I ruled out from the category of philosophers those who do not profess the truth, Seneca refuses the title 'philosopher' to those who do not expound the doctrine of virtue: 'Do these people teach virtue or not; if so, they are philosophers.'*[62] In this proposition, which is fairly close to my view and is likewise intended to restore words to their true meaning, a distinction is made between *virtue* and *teaching virtue*. The philosopher's role is confined to the teaching of virtue.

In another letter, however, having forgotten what he said about philosophy as systematic knowledge (which consists wholly of ideas) and teaching (which involves the use of words) — although each of these may have virtue as their object — he no longer locates philosophy in ideas or in words expressing ideas, but in realities conveyed to the mind through ideas, or taught to others. He tells his correspondent: 'Philosophy deals not with words but with things.'*[63] Thus, despite his earlier, clear distinction between *systematic knowledge* and *action*, he later lost sight of the wide gulf between them. Although systematic knowledge can never be stripped of its status as information without losing its nature, and action must refer to real things, Seneca maintained that philosophical science involved things themselves, things whose link with philosophy is solely for instructional or explanatory purposes.

But in a third place, he later came round to admitting that the two things, which here he took to be one, really were two, and even as contrary to one another as active and passive. When expounding another's view, which he does not deny, he

[62] *Ep* 88.
[63] *Ep* 16.

maintains that they are distinct though indivisible. He states:

> Although philosophy is the study of virtue, which it seeks, some amongst us have concluded that they cannot be separated. They say that philosophy cannot exist without virtue nor virtue without philosophy. Philosophy is the study of virtue carried out by means of virtue, although virtue cannot exist without its being studied. It is not as though a person wished to hit an object at a distance (with the person who sees in one place and what is seen in another), nor like roads outside a town leading into the town. Virtue is attained with the aid of virtue itself. Consequently, philosophy and virtue go together.[64]

Although, in the above passage, the study of philosophy is distinguished from its object, virtue, they are not recognised as two categorically distinct forms, but rather as two grades of the same thing. As far as I can see, the notion expressed in the text quoted above can only be interpreted in this sense: philosophy is an incipient stage of virtue which grows to perfection as it develops, or philosophy is a special virtue which guides us towards the acquisition of other virtues, to universal virtue. In each of these two forms, philosophy has lost its character as pure, systematic knowledge.

58. The view held by the two sophists of Chios, Euthydemus and Dionysiodorus, whom Plato introduces as disputants in the dialogue named after the former, that they 'had discovered the art of converting evil men into good' by an easy and thorough method, relying solely upon certain of their arguments, is substantially the same as that promised by all pre-Christian pagan philosophers to mankind. Many modern philosophers offer as much, implicitly at least, but often not explicitly, because they would not be believed. But in doing this, they cannot avoid one of two errors: 1. goodness and moral virtue consist solely in systematic knowledge (which confuses disparate things), or 2. knowledge of what is good immediately brings us the will and the strength to apply it as we should. Both conclusions are equally refuted by experience and close observation of human nature. For example, one frequently comes across books in

---

[64] *Ep.* 89.

which *art*, which is a habit reduced to the category of action,[65] is confused with *systematic knowledge*, which pertains to the category of *contemplation*.

I have already noted the impropriety of the word *practical* applied to what is merely speculative information. Thus, the term *practical philosophy* is used to describe the type of philosophy which considers practical issues, such as human actions and the definition of moral conscience as a practical judgment, despite the fact that conscience is merely a speculative judgment on the honesty or dishonesty of one's own individual actions, that is, in practice.[66]

59. It is therefore extremely easy to give an answer to someone who asks bluntly and peremptorily: 'Is *knowledge* of something real, or knowledge of one's own action or that of another, the same as the *thing*, or the action itself'?' Everyone (if we exclude a few philosophers who lose their way in speculation) becomes aware very quickly of the difference, acknowledges that these are two distinct things, and affirms that knowing and acting are worlds apart. Why is it then that such an obvious difference, which everybody accepts when it is considered directly, should be forgotten when it appears as part of a discussion? Why do we keep coming across examples of really fine passages in the greatest writers where the two are reduced to one, or each is confused with, or converted into, the other?

This contradiction, to which people inadvertently succumb, must have some reason which is worthwhile pursuing. We certainly need to seek it if we are going to set out the idea of

---

[65] Seneca himself falls into this error when he calls philosophy 'skill in living' (*artificem vitae*) (*Ep*. 90). Philosophy is 'systematic knowledge of the art of living'; it is not the art itself, and even less, skill in living.

[66] Systematic knowledge can properly be considered as a habit, that is, as a faculty acquired by an intelligent being to recall swiftly and reason about what is already known. This use of the phrase '*systematic knowledge*', which I am not against, is very different from a system of information received by the mind in any way whatsoever. The understanding receives the information, a reception which may indeed be called an act of the understanding. However, we must be extremely careful to keep the concept of this kind of operation, which we call *reception* or *possession*, separate from the other kind which we call *action*. Indeed, it is often necessary for clarity to distinguish this concept from that normally expressed with the word *suffer*.

wisdom, which is the aim of this discussion. It stems from the fact that there are two kinds of information: in the first, only the intellect is involved; in the second, the activity of the subject unfolds. As a result of the intervention of this subjective activity, the second kind of information becomes operative. In fact, we can say both that the second kind comes into action through the will, and that the will comes into action through it. Everyone agrees, of course, that human actions have their origin in the will. But what is the will? Could this power exist without information? It could not, because the term *will* is not bestowed upon operating principles which function without the light of knowledge. Will is a rational principle; hence the well-known axiom that the will is never moved by the unknown. Some information, therefore, is necessary and essential to the will, that is, it is the objective form of the will itself. The subject's activity, when all informational content is discounted, is only the constitutive matter of the will, if I may put it that way. But this activity, when informed by knowledge of what is good, becomes will. It is no longer a mere material rudiment of will, but fully developed will. It is not the will on its way to being — will described by an ancient term of the Italic school as *non-ens* — but will which has attained its complete being.

This, then, is the intrinsic order by which will attains its nature. The first stage is objective information in the intellect, followed by assent on the part of the associated subjective activity; subjective activity thus joined to the object has become an active principle called *will*. This juncture, this capacity of will, is the source of human activity. Its power is proportional to the extent of its adhesion to the intellective object. We can say, therefore, that knowledge in the intellect becomes operative as a result of the subject's adhesion to it. This information acts through the will of which it has become the formal part. We can also say that the will acts through the information which is its form. To sum up: there are two types of information, one speculative, the other practical or operative. The former constitutes *systematic knowledge*, the latter the real principle of human *actions*. Here we need to note (because this is the origin of the equivocation and confusion I am trying to explain) that science may *speculate* on anything, even on the will, the principle of our actions, on practical information and even on itself. However, speculation on an object does not mean that we make the real thing speculative, or absorb it into speculation. Speculation, far from changing and assimilating real things and actions into itself, informs us that these things and actions possess and retain a nature different and opposite to the nature of systematic knowledge whose objects they become. The *practical* information of which I am speaking is not systematic knowledge and cannot be written down in books. If it could, it would no longer be *practical.* When an attempt is made to write it down (and this is where the mistake occurs), or when a person thinks he has written it down, he has merely written about the *teaching* related to the *practical information.* He has not written the information itself in so far as it is practical, that is, in so far as it is the root of real actions. Man's transitory actions cannot be frozen within the pages of a book, although a book can contain a scientific treatise on such actions. Ideas are not transitory, even though the things of which they are ideas are transitory.

60. What gives rise to this hallucination, which leads to confusion between two such distinct orders as that of *ideas* and that of *things*, categories which we frequently need to distinguish and which are in fact frequently distinguished in everyday language? The first reason that comes to mind depends upon vocabulary. The same terms are indeed used to mean both the ideas of things, and things themselves, and thus to mean possible as well as real things. When, for example, we say: 'Man is a rational being', the word 'man' does not refer to any actual man but man in his essence and possibility. When we say: 'The man you see is Peter' the same word 'man' is used to refer not only to the mere idea of 'man' but also a real man. Now, the use of words applied to a number of different entities sometimes results in the entities themselves, which are confused in everyday language, becoming confused in the mind and spoken of as though they were interchangeable.

This, however, is not the final reason. We still need to know why we apply the same words to ideas and things, to purely ideal beings and to the real beings which correspond to them. The theory dealing with human knowledge provides us with this further reason: there is no doubt that we can apply a noun, a vocal sign, to something we know. But we could not know what happens in our feeling unless we referred what is sensible to the *idea*, and thus rendered it *intelligible*. On the other hand, the idea, in order to be understood, does not need the presence of what is sensible. Clear proof of this is the fact that the idea remains in the mind without the reality. In other words, although the idea is intelligible *per se*, what is sensible is intelligible only through the idea, and the continual presence of the idea. The idea, therefore, is *ens* in so far as it is *per se* knowable; it is the knowableness of things or entities which are not ideas, that is, entia in so far as they are real and sensible.

60a. There is a logical order in knowledge whereby ideas are known first, then those things which are known through ideas. It is fitting, therefore, that the words we discover should mirror this order. Hence we have two classes of words: words which stand for ideas, and words which put the mind in touch with reality. The first category includes *common nouns* (and almost all are common); the second are *proper nouns* and all the grammatical particles (pronouns, adverbs, and so on) which are used to lead the mind from general, universal ideas to what is particular and real. Thus, when I wish to use the common noun *man* to mean not just the idea but a specific, real human being, I cannot use that noun on its own. Otherwise my interlocutor would think merely of universal man, that is, the idea. I need to add some other word which makes it indicate a particular man. For instance, I add the proper name *Peter*, or 'whom you see'. I can also add specific terms which indicate the man's presence to the senses, such as 'who is here' or other phrases which recall a man who was present to our own or others' senses on other occasions, or a particular man who has been determined in some way. These additional words restrict the meaning of the common noun and convey to the interlocutor that the *idea* refers in this case and on this occasion to a given sensible reality and nothing else. Consequently, the idea is taken as the knowability of the sensible reality, although *per se* it signifies universal knowability. Common nouns, therefore (to which verbal infinitives, participles and all types of adjectives are reduced) do not refer to real things; this reference is made through additions in conversation. Common nouns, however, are necessary because ideas are necessary to indicate what is real which, when detached from ideas, is vague and basically unknown.

60b. But if what is ideal and what is real are so utterly different

[60a–60b]

how can the latter be known in and through the former?[67] The answer lies in close observation of knowledge and the way in which we know.

Such observation shows us that the case is as we have stated it, and this should be sufficient. It is never reasonable to deny a firmly established fact, as any reasonable man would agree. Moreover, the same observation, if suitably acute, not only testifies to but explains the fact because this fact is one which contains its own explanation. When, therefore, we think very carefully about this fact, we find that what is ideal and what is real, although very different, possess an identical element, *ens*. The same identical *ens* exists in both but under differing conditions and in a different form. Under one form, we find ens as ideality, or knowability, or objectivity (terms which substantially express the same thing); under the other form, we find the same ens as reality, sensibility, activity (these, too, are terms which are substantially the same). Thus despite the *greatest difference* in form, there is complete *identity* of content, which is *ens* itself. *Ens* as purely knowable is ideal; ens as sensible is real. When what is sensible is made knowable, that is, when the two forms are drawn together, we have intellective perception and knowledge of what is real.

After this, we should not be surprised if philosophers occasionally confuse the two forms. This happens whenever they forget that their argument revolves around *forms* and imagine that they are discussing *ens*. They take the two forms as one, or confuse one with the other, precisely because *ens* which they think they are discussing is one under two forms. On the other hand, when they fully realise that their argument revolves around forms and not around ens — as for instance when they go directly to the question involving forms and ask 'whether the idea and the thing are one and the same' — they never confuse them.

61. There is a further step to take, however. Why does it often happen that, when an argument is dealing with forms, philosophers forget about this and refer what is said to an argument about ens? Why is it so difficult to distinguish when the object under discussion is *ens* and when it is *forms*?

---

[67] This is one of the objections Aristotle raised against Plato. It has also been raised repeatedly against me.

Obviously the average person unfamiliar with abstract, scientific concepts, never focuses his intellective attention on either the real object unaccompanied by the idea (because the real object cannot be known without the idea), or on the idea alone (he certainly knows how to use it to know what is real, but cannot deal with it on its own). Thus, our natural attention is always on what is real and on the idea to which the real is united. This union enables the formation of the term of perception. However, when we rise to scientific abstractions, we become aware of this duality in the entia we have perceived and distinguish the matter and form of cognition (or whatever we call these two elements). At this point, the idea acquires a new relationship with the human mind. It is no longer merely the object of intuition and a means of knowing realities, but has become once more an *object of reflection* and systematic knowledge.

But what is real, when unaccompanied by the idea and deprived of its light, is altogether unknown. In other words, it has ceased to exist for the mind. The mind, however, which has previously known what is real, does not wish to see it disappear; consequently, the mind, albeit unconsciously, restores the idea to what is real. The idea, which the mind has consciously removed, is now unwittingly restored. This first illusion to which the mind falls victim is then dragged along by the mind which becomes rather like a pen with a hair on its tip; as it writes, all the beautifully formed letters are spoiled. In our case, the mind bases philosophy on two elements, that is, on the idea detached from the real and on the real reunited with the idea. But this involves considering the idea twice instead of once. A further spontaneous reflection on the incorrect conclusion derived from the previous reflection inevitably lures the philosopher into another error. He now finds the idea on every side: he finds it in the element which he thought he had stripped of any idea, because unknown to him (as I have said), it has returned there. Or rather, he has reinstated it through an intellective instinct, without reflection and therefore unconsciously. Then, finding the idea where he thought he would find only reality, he inevitably confuses the idea with reality itself. This, I believe, is the true origin and development of the error made by a famous Italian [Gioberti] who, upon this error, erected a Germanic type of philosophical system. The German philosophers who had fallen into this error, to which so many others succumb, were as delighted with it as if they had found a treasure. On it, with their usual diligence and sense of wonder, they erected a gigantic or rather a grotesque system.

On the other hand, those who confuse systematic knowledge with real action do so unconsciously and without attaching any importance to it. Nevertheless, even they still manage to posit the full reality of human nature in systematic knowledge, and reduce man simply to what is known systematically. We should not be surprised, therefore, if they easily persuade themselves that a person who possesses systematic knowledge also possesses virtue, and that such virtue is the gift that they alone proffer in their academies where they expound their theories. In other words, because it is impossible to think directly of what is real, and even more to consider it totally unaccompanied by the idea, the thinker who does not exercise the utmost caution, is led through a series of delusions. He reduces everything to *systematic knowledge*, outside of which he sees nothing, or at least considers systematic knowledge as moral virtue. This, however, consists of real actions which in order to be virtuous, have to relate and conform to the idea, or rather to that philosophy which Seneca, when not confusing the two things, defines (still too narrowly) as 'the law of life' (*lex vitae*).[68]

62. Beyond systematic knowledge lies a real world which frequently eludes the gaze of scholars and philosophers. Man, who does not live by systematic knowledge alone, lives to a great extent in this world. If we look for what is perfect in man — which may properly be termed *wisdom* — we should not settle for the first item, that is, systematic knowledge or more generally, *knowledge*. This has to be united to the second item, *real action*, that is, moral goodness.

Even pagan philosophers, in some of their more lucid moments, thoroughly grasped this truth. They speak of wisdom as something complete, something which necessarily comprises all *human perfection*. Wisdom originates in the mind,

---

[68] *Ep*. 94. In its abstract form, the law is always an *idea* or concept, as I have already said in the *Principles of Ethics*; virtue, by contrast, is not an idea but a reality, the realisation of an idea.

but then goes on to impose order upon the affections and to render even the least of its actions virtuous and harmonious. In this connection, Seneca wrote: 'The greatest role and sign of wisdom is that actions and words go together, and that man be always self-consistent and the same.'✢69 Here Seneca does not overlook the distinction between philosophy as systematic knowledge, which can be expressed in speech or writing, and the fullness of wisdom, which cannot be imparted in its entirety either in speech or writing. According to Seneca, such wisdom is only achieved when systematic knowledge passes into human action, reforming passions, affections and actions. 'I beg and exhort you, dear Lucilius, to allow philosophy to sink deep into your heart. Note what progress you have made, not in speaking or writing but in strength of mind and the reduction of covetousness.'70

Here we can see the distinction between philosophy and the use of philosophy. *Using* philosophy, we carry out what philosophy teaches in speech and in writing. We operate not by argument and in a literary fashion, but by facts and deeds which lie altogether outside systematic knowledge and book-learning. We convert philosophy's maxims into feelings; we allow them, so to speak, to sink into the heart, which the ancients considered the seat of the passions.

62a. Plato describes wisdom in a similar way in the dialogue he named after young Theaetetus. In it he attempts without success to arrive at a definition of systematic knowledge; at least he did not succeed in specifically expressing it. The problem perhaps, which may also account for the length and complexity of the dialogue, was the failure to distinguish between the concept of art and *life*, and that of *systematic knowledge*. *Wisdom*, however, unhesitatingly takes her stand on 'the perfect conjunction of justice, holiness and prudence.'71

Socrates, having said that it was impossible to eradicate all evil

---

69 Seneca, *Ep.* 20. In this letter, he gives his reasons for defining wisdom as the consistency of a man's inner life with actions that are coherent and constant: *Non potest cuiquam semper idem placere nisi rectum* [That which is always the same can only please a person if it is upright].

70 *Ibid.*

71 *Theaetetus.* See: *Alcinous ad Platonis doctrinam institutio*, Chapter 1.

from human affairs, added: 'However, it can find no place with the gods.' He went on:

> It follows that we should strive to hasten there (where the gods are) as soon as we can. Such a flight involves our doing our utmost to become like God. Justice together with prudence and sanctity makes us like God. Moreover, O best of men, you will find it difficult to convince people that they must indeed seek after virtue and flee from vice, but not on account of public opinion, that is, to appear good, not wicked. That I consider as mere old women's talk. The truth is: God is in no way unjust, but just beyond limit. He envelops everything to which justice extends, and nothing is more like him than the just man. In such a reckoning, man's industry and fortitude, along with his idleness and foolishness, need to be taken into account. Knowing this is indeed true virtue and true wisdom; ignoring it, on the other hand, is non-knowledge and patent dishonesty.[72]

62b. Thus, in the fuller, purer sense which the ancients ascribed to it, wisdom has two parts which are joined within it. The first is in the mind, and is called *systematic knowledge* when it is isolated, studied and arranged in due order. This knowledge can be taught and written down. The other aspect is not taught in academies, and cannot be written down in books. Its sole, individual locus is in the heart and will, and in all our affections and actions. Nevertheless, it is, as it were, the very same systematic knowledge. It has moved down from the mind and been distilled into the reality of feeling, finding its way into everyday life where its domination is total yet beneficent. Can we ever really put action, human action I mean, into writing at any of its three or four levels which consist of practical knowledge, feeling, decision and external action? The distinction cannot be overstressed. When we have written the word *action*, we have written only an idea. But the idea of an action is not the same as the occurrence of an action. If, instead of merely writing *action* we added: 'this real action' or 'this practical knowledge, this feeling we experience, this decision of our will which imparts movement to the hand which is now playing with a sword,' we

---

[72] *Theaetetus.*

would indeed have written about real actions but this does not mean that we take the actions themselves, put them down on paper and insert them in a document. It merely means making signs on paper which remind us of the actions. When our understanding receives these signs, what action does it take to direct its attention from such signs to the actions referred to? It certainly does not insert real actions themselves into our thought as into a bag, as though the knowledge we acquire were to become those actions. What we know as we think is that these actions could have existed before we thought, and will exist when we stop thinking. We also know that they have a cause, which may indeed be unknown to us, but which is definitely different from our thought. We will certainly not believe, as long as we are sane, that we produce them by thinking about them. Consequently, neither the written document nor thoughts about these actions are the actual actions of writing and thinking. They are thought in their ideal being by simple intuition, or in their real being by apprehension and affirmation. Beyond theoretical knowledge, beyond systematic knowledge, there is always something further — real action. The subject in its fullness remains outside ideas.

63. However, the laws of the soul are such that in acting exclusively through one of its chief operating principles, it becomes the very principle into which it has poured all its actuality. At least, it seems to be so because its other principles are not actuated at this moment. Now the scholar's, or rather the thinker's, life is bound up with thinking, so that he is actually thought itself, and is in great danger of imagining himself as though he were thought and nothing else. But, I have already said, those things which are not actually being thought are *non-existent* to thought. Consequently, immediate thought declares them to be *nothing*. Here, once again, we have the origin of Hegelian *nihilism* which is basically identical to the nihilism I mentioned earlier although here it is expressed in different terms. The *nothing* from which Hegel derives all that exists in the universe, and into which he later consigns it, is basically no different from the nihilism which has not yet become the object of thought. It is, therefore, *non-existent for human thought*, and reverts to its primal nothingness when thinking ceases. This phenomenon, to which thinkers can be prone, deluded Hegel — as it did the

thinkers of ancient India — who posited *nothing* as the original source of things (because entia are not initially thought and are nothing to the thinker; at a later stage, they are the objects of thought and are therefore existent to the mind). Something therefore which was a mere appearance to immediate, perceptive thought or even to conscious thought, and dependent on a subjective law of thought itself, became absolute for Hegel, entrapped in his own thought. To be sure, the soul which engages in systematic knowledge is not and cannot be, in that process, other than thought because the soul is actuated only in thought. Even if the soul were actuated in some other act, this act would not produce systematic knowledge for the soul and would not therefore re-present it.

If we add that the basic foundation on which German philosophy was built was a universal prejudice originating with Locke ('cognitions are a mere product of the mind' and hence of the human subject), we have an obvious explanation for Hegel's system. In its aberration, it reveals the inventor's powerful dialectic. The system is directly derived from the following two propositions, both of which are false: 1. the thinker as such does not recognise as existent anything that is not yet the object of his thought, and thus declares it to be NOTHING ; 2. cognitions are a mere product of the understanding. Consequently the objects of thought are produced and created by the understanding. Thought causes them to be transferred from NOTHING to BEING.

I stated that the first of these two propositions was also false (the falsehood contained in the second one I exposed at length in the *New Essay*) because as a proposition it is not derived from thought taken in its entirety, but from a particular act of thought, the act of *perception*, which the Germans extended unduly.[73] *Reasoning*, which is subsequent to perception and certainly is thought, although in a more advanced form, leads us to admit also the actual existence of entia which do not fall under acts of perception, or under conscious thought, provided they are related to things which do fall under that form of thought.

However, Hegel's illusion is not an isolated fact; it is similar to the illusion to which humans succumb when they abandon

[73] Cf. *Sistema filosofico*, 74, 77.

themselves to sensual pleasure. People of this kind are always inclined to believe that such pleasure is everything. They think that man's soul, like that of the animals, is purely sense-oriented, precisely because their own souls are so actuated and almost absorbed by sensations that they know themselves only as sentient souls. They are aware of nothing else. But the illusion of Prussian philosophy has a characteristic feature distinguishing it from that of the sensual man, and making it more arrogant. This characteristic derives from the fact that philosophy is effectively an operation of thought alone, not of sense. Consequently, the philosopher who is reduced, as it were, to pure thought, very easily falls into knowing and admitting thought alone. He takes the facts of thought as ontological facts. This happened in the Indian Schools and even in the Eleatic School. The sensualist, however, if he begins to philosophise, is therefore obliged to ascend to thought and, as he cannot disregard it, is happy to attribute it to sense, which he takes as the bedrock of reality.

64. After human beings were reduced by these philosophers to pure thought, and ideas reduced to mere products and modes of thought, and inevitably confused with things (nothing outside of thought was recognised), we were then forced by philosophers into a state of objectivity and impassability that necessarily cut us off from human feelings and from moral duties. I leave aside the other grave consequences, such as pantheism, which follow from the principles of the Hegelian school, along with all the wild, horrendous and profane doctrines of Germanic thought. I wish merely to point out that despite our own deification in this philosophy, our nature lies withered and shorn of all noble, human emotions, which are only noble when ennobled by moral duty. When we confine ourselves to feelings and duties — religious, paternal, filial, marital or any other — we have not yet become God, according to these scholars, because we are not yet consumed in the objectivity of our thought. To use an expression familiar to such sophists: 'Our consciousness is still involved in the pangs of our own creation.' When consciousness subsequently emerges fully developed from its 'creative immediacy', like the butterfly from the cocoon, it becomes objective thought and looks down from its lofty throne of abstract thought upon everything else that

[64]

pertains to human beings, that is, feelings and duties. Such things, it believes, are far inferior to itself. They no longer belong to consciousness but appear before it like a play in which the spectator takes no active part. The EGO , then, is free, they say, because morality itself lies beneath it. Consciousness gazes upon morality with a spirit of total independence and alienation. It is like a rich painter whose earnings have raised him to the point where he can sit back and look with disdain on the work of others.

64a. This monstrous doctrine was to have an impact on politics, on the family, on German literature, of which Goethe was the most admired representative. The main feature of Goethe's writing is precisely *objectivity* in the sense given it by German philosophy. This is not the objectivity which we recognise as superior to ourselves, to which we submit humbly and reverently, but the objectivity which we overcome and displace. We rule from its throne (that is, we imagine we rule) and no longer need to recognise anything above ourselves. Everything is beneath us. In other words, we aspire to the impossible. All feelings, all duties lie under our feet. 'Goethe', says one of his ardent admirers[74] 'is a deep and vigorous thinker; he never

[74] It is odd how this admirer justifies the proverbial egoism of the poet of Weimar. After speaking of the women who yielded to him, and of their illusions about being loved by him, he says: 'It is as if the morning lily were to ask the bee for love. In fact, the lily lives its life and dies exhausted, the bee uses the lily to make its honey, and along we come to feed on the honey.' He goes on to talk of the unhappy Frederica and says: 'With the divine spark snatched from the maiden's heart, this strange Pygmalion brought to life the beautiful marble statues in his garden, Clare, Margaret, Adelaide, Mignon. Realising she had been cruelly deceived, Frederica cursed her rival, poetry, and died. Poor Frederica! Her brow was broken upon bronze-like selfishness when she asked GENIUS to act with humanity. Yes, indeed, who could read Goethe's soul? Who would dare to make a final judgment on certain actions of such a calm and profound life? Everything is mystery about men like him until it is looked at from the point of view of the work they have to accomplish. Only then does some ray of light break through, and doubt begin to clear. At this point, we can see that wanting to anathematise Goethe for what has been called in Germany his egoism, or claiming to denounce the author of *Faust* to posterity because he immured himself IN THE WORSHIP OF HIS OWN THOUGHT (doubtless finding it more sacred than all the uproar about him), is neither a crime of *lèse majesté* nor a sacrilege; it is simply an infantile revolt against the finest poet of our age'

[64a]

confronts any dogma unless he can subdue it.'[75] Faust is the kind of person who cannot bear to feel confined by human limits. He wishes to break away from them and tries everything to do so. He immerses himself in natural sciences, but in vain; he appeals to magic, but in vain; he throws himself into a life of pleasure, he complains against God who has imprisoned him in human nature, he sells himself to the devil — all in vain. Eventually, after hoping in vain to discover the ALL in the NOTHING-NESS of Mephistopheles,[76] he is overtaken by death and in its presence, exclaims: 'O Nature, let me be merely a man in your presence!' He would then endure the torment of being a man! This is copied from Aeschylus' *Prometheus*, except that the character of Aeschylus' demigod is conceived on a grandiose and pure scale. Faust is a little 18th century Titan, a genuine German university professor, without any solid learning, endowed with a vast yet wayward imagination, credulous, pleasure-loving, ambitious, visionary, mad. No doubt, from this point of view, Faust is the most bitter satire on the philosophy from which Goethe seeks life. Such is the masterpiece of the poet who was a product of German pantheism. It is worthwhile here adding Herder's judgment of Goethe:

> It remains to be seen whether a man has the right to aspire to such heights where all suffering, whether true or false, real or merely imagined, becomes the same for him; where, though he does not cease to be an artist, he ceases to be a man; where the light, though still shining, no longer fosters any growth. We have yet to see if this maxim does not imply the total abnegation of the human character. No one bothers to contend with the gods over their everlasting stillness; let them look upon everything here below as a game, and arrange the results in accordance with their own designs. We humans, however, who are subject to every human need, should not allow ourselves to be amused by theatrical attitudes; let us remain serious, with that sacred earnestness without which all art, of whatever kind, degenerates into farce. Comedy, o comedy! Sophocles, however, was not a comic dramatist, Aeschylus even less.

(Henri Blaze, *Essai sur Goethe et le second Faust*, p. 8, 9).

[75] *Ibid.*, p. 38.

[76] *Faust*, Act 1, Part 2 — Scene of the Dark Gallery.

All of this is the invention of our age. David sang his
hymns with greater earnestness than Pinder, and David
still ruled his kingdom. What do you rule over, then? You
study nature in all its manifestations from the slender
hyssop to the cedar of Lebanon. Nature! You absorb it
into yourselves, as you go on saying. And that is well put,
but I would not want you as a result to rob me of man in
his natural, moral grandeur, the finest of all these phenomena.

65. I have felt it worth while expatiating somewhat upon the
consequences of an error into which — if the question is put
bluntly — human beings never fall and into which it seems
impossible for anyone to fall; mistaking the idea for reality, and
absorbing everything into knowledge and the thought which
produces knowledge.

Neglect of this distinction, which may perhaps seem useless
metaphysical sophistry, gives rise to all the consequences I have
mentioned. This neglect was the forge in which were made the
weapons used by certain German professors, envious as it were
of the reputation of the giants who moan beneath the waves. The
average man, who instinctively adopts a logical approach quite
adequate for the sphere in which he acts, is not subject to such
strange delusions. For the aim upon which his thinking focuses is
always association of idea and real, which his perceptions
encounter. He does not separate the two elements; he does not
pause to consider the idea as distinct from the thing, and even less
the thing as separate from the idea. He distinguishes them but he
does not separate them: he sees one over against the other. Consequently he finds nothing mysterious or surprising in reality.
Any thing which retains its links with the idea is illuminated by
it and is knowable. However, if something is separated from the
idea by a constant process of abstraction — which is how the
philosopher operates — it suddenly becomes an enigma for him:
an indefinable entity which he cannot deny because he can still
remember the concept he had when he considered it in association with the idea; on the other hand, he cannot accept it because
he no longer knows what in fact it is when separated from its
prior form or shorn of the idea. It seems to him impossible. To
solve this odd, transcendental paradox, the thinker plunges into
suppositions which are no more than wild aberrations.

[65]

Such a misguided scholar has to recover his humanity. But he cannot do so except by retracing his steps along the same highway of knowledge on which he went astray. Knowledge, or what is usually called knowledge, is a sorceress with the power to turn human beings into animals, into various types of monsters and even into demons, and then to turn them back into men but with much greater stature than before. The enchantress undertook these two conflicting operations in the Ancient World, first by means of the sophists and second by means of their philosophical heirs, as we have already seen. The sophists boldly shattered the heavenly spheres of the mind as though they were made of crystal, entered higher regions of thought and, for a brief while, rode roughshod over knowledge; their philosophical successors drove them from the field which they had unjustly occupied. Thus, German philosophy really did accede to a higher level of thought than the one at which the current philosophy operated. German philosophy considered reality in complete isolation from the idea and realised, as a result of such isolation, that reality remained an unknown factor and an impossibility. Then, like the sophists and with the enthusiasm characteristic of vain enterprises, it hastily concluded that the real, and consequently the subjective had to be sought at all costs in the very heart of the idea, that is, of the objective. Immediately there emerges the theory of *absolute identity* and *Hegelian* logic which devours metaphysics, like Saturn and his sons. This was the cause of the collapse of philosophy and of all that was true and holy. However, the different orders of reflection do not determine either truth or error; they are indifferent to both. As a result both truth and error find room enough to settle at any level. The higher the reflection, the more room there is. When true philosophers approached the same sphere through the open gateway, they fought with error which had preceded them, and took possession of that new heavenly zone on behalf of truth. This is philosophy's response: it is true that what is real is unknown when completely separated from the idea and, if you wish, is impossible in such a state. However, it does not follow that the real belongs to the idea, that the idea contains the real, sends it forth and later re-absorbs it. All this can be shown as directly contrary to fact, and as absurd. Another consequence, however, does follow: the

[65]

real is never without the idea from which it is divided only by an arbitrary mental abstraction; it is with the idea, but not in the idea as a moment of the idea; the real and the idea are indivisible, though not identical. What is real cannot stand without the idea, but it is never one and the same as the idea. On the other hand, the idea can to a certain extent stand without what is real. It is one thing to say that the real is *intrinsically related* to the idea, an ontological synthesis; it is quite another thing to say that one should or could suppress the dual status, and concentrate them into a single unit. As I have already mentioned, the real is indivisible from the idea and, at the same time, utterly distinct, because the same being is in both but not in the same form nor under the same conditions. The eternal nature of being is such that in its most perfect unity it appears in two perfectly distinct and totally inconfusable forms.

66. This explains the duality of the wise person, so different from the merely learned person. The wise person is born from complete conformity of the real man with ideas, and through ideas with the whole order of real things. This conformity can come about only from within, through his own activity, not from without. It depends on his own activity, that is, his free power of will which alone renders thought practical, that is, operative. And the whole of this activity of the will, although communicated to thought, is distinct from theoretical thought, which remains confined within ideas and information. It is action intimately linked to thought, but not confused with it; an action of the subject on the subject, who uses thought as his means and instrument. This action modifies and ennobles the real subject — the human person — who participates in the divine excellence of ideas themselves without ever being able to be transformed into them.

67. When mankind was still in its infancy, as it were, and had not as yet ventured far in its exploration of the realms of abstract thought — vast, perilous regions like the immense deserts traversed by explorers — people encountered this *image of wisdom* in all her natural simplicity and truthfulness. Mankind attempted to reach out to her and, in doing so, realised how difficult the enterprise was, as wisdom seemed to become increasingly remote. The closer they got to her, the more apparent her divine origin (just as the astronaut ascending ever higher

realises how far away the stars are, or the mountaineer on the first ridges sees the peak, which at first appeared so close, receding from him). This dynamic quest was most appositely called *philosophy*, that is, 'love and study of wisdom'. However, this was not yet philosophy in the later, restricted meaning of *systematic body of knowledge*, in which I take it. Ancient philosophy is more than a science and is distinct from science. It is more than systematic knowledge, whose only mission is, and can only be, to enlighten the mind. This does indeed bring powerful support to good will, whose task it is to round off the operation by imparting wisdom to mankind. But such support, bestowed on the will without aggression or compulsion, leaves it free. It even increases freedom of will either to direct or transform the human subject and all its powers in the way shown by knowledge, or to do the opposite when the will, by an error of judgment, considers its greatness and happiness to lie in other things. This can involve it in a struggle for supremacy over genuine science and the truth contained therein. The will, though not expecting victory, pursues that greater glory which corresponds to the dignity and nobility of the enemy against whom it fights to the death without surrendering.

Philosophy, therefore , taken as 'a practical disposition to wisdom', is more than philosophy as systematic knowledge which, compared to wisdom, has a far more humble status. This rightful humiliation, revealed here below by the gospel, which made humility the highest and most reasonable of the virtues, gives rise to annoyance which, at times, amounts to fury in the thinker devoted purely to systematic knowledge, who considers himself as pure thought, and as such wishes to be all that is. His inferior powers are in disarray; he allows them to act as though they were no part of him, and they end by dragging him along behind them. They disrupt his very thought by diverting it from the truth, but this does not worry him. Perfect thought, according to him, does not lie in the *mode* but the *power* of thought. So for him, thought is powerful because it struggles with truth, and the violence of the struggle brings into play even the minor powers of such weak constitutions. Nevertheless, thought, which considers itself so powerful in the midst of violence, is actually the slave of a corrupt will. It impels the thinker to justify his own disorder, and to find a philosophical

[67]

basis for it. Thought then rejects moral laws and invents others; it decrees that this is the real basis of freedom. Finally, thought presents itself as object-man, the new god Pan, absorbing morality and the world. The worship of man is the new cult appearing on earth.

68. But philosophy, understood as 'a practical disposition to wisdom', is not only more than systematic knowledge; it is quite distinct from it. If we now ask what it is, truth, the former of the two elements composing wisdom, will be amply illustrated. Seneca notes that philosophy, unlike mathematics, physics and similar studies which borrow their principles from other, higher branches of science, 'does not derive any principles from other sources but erects the whole edifice from the ground up'.[77] I have already explained this statement by defining philosophy as the study of the ultimate causes, which are ultimate relative to their discovery by man but primary relative to the tree of knowledge, which has its roots in them. This explains why an ancient author called them *mothers*. Thus philosophy is the only systematic knowledge which can say in a way entirely its own: *Sed summa sequar vestigia rerum* [But I always seek the very essence of things].[78]

Philosophy as I understand it is a body of systematic knowledge and, occupying first place, does not derive any of its principles from other sciences, although all other sciences derive their principles from philosophy. However, precisely because it is a body of systematic knowledge, it cannot be first chronologically in the intellectual order because every *science* is the

[77] 'Philosophy takes nothing from any other source; it builds its entire structure upon its own efforts. Mathematics, I may say, is a building erected on another's land, it takes its principles from an outside source and passes the benefits on to dependent disciplines'* (Sen., *Ep.* 88).

[78] *Aeneid* 1: 345 — Servius takes *fastigia* as *primordia* — Bacon (*The Advancement of Learning*, 3, 1) proposes the compilation of a universal science dealing with *fastigia rerum tantummodo*, the proper role of philosophy. However, the inadequacy of Bacon, who was so influential — or is thought to be — in reviving correct method in natural sciences, can be gauged by this alone: although the study he proposed involved collecting axioms 'not proper to the sciences, but applicable in common to many sciences — many axioms in a genus',* in fact these axioms, which are always few in number, cannot constitute a body of knowledge unless they are reduced to perfect unity.

[68]

product of reflection which is not the first mode of knowledge that we have; we possess and use other modes before embarking upon philosophy. I have already said somewhere that philosophy could not exist unless it derived its *postulates*, not its principles, from outside itself. These postulates, which human nature bestows on philosophy as a condition of its existence, are two: the natural and immediate apprehension of being, and feeling;[79] the *idea* and the *primal reality*, which subsequently become objects of reflection. Out of such materials — never out of nothing — thought constructs philosophical teaching. The act which imparts information about being I call *intuition*; this is the primary mode of knowledge, and is clearly prior to philosophical thinking. The faculty of intuition is the *intellect* in the true sense of the word. Feeling as such does not belong to the intellective order (although there are intellectual, rational and ethical feelings which accompany it or follow it closely) but does supply the intellect with *matter*. The first feeling is that which constitutes the human subject because man (intuiting being and perceiving his own body with the immanent perception which makes him simultaneously an animal and a rational being)[80] is an individual, substantial feeling which receives accidental alterations and is active in various ways. *Primal perception*, in which the union of soul and body consists, is a mode of knowing which operates concurrently with *first intuition* and is only logically posterior. This *first act* constitutes the faculty called reason. Intuition and primal perception pertain to *direct knowledge* to which many other cognitive acts such as all subsequent, accidental perceptions, are reduced.[81] Direct knowledge is not reflection but substantially prior to philosophical reflection. The occurrence of reflection represents a second way of knowing, and many reflections precede the higher level generated by philosophy. The complex of these reflections, or more exactly a part of them, constitutes what I have called *popular knowledge*.[82] All these modes of knowledge precede philosophical knowledge.

[79] *Anthropology as an Aid to Moral Science*, 10–21.

[80] *Psychology*, vol. 1, 247–287.

[81] See *A New Essay concerning the Origin of Ideas*, vol. 2.

[82] *Ibid.*

68a. To determine more precisely the point in the series of various reflections which divides human knowledge into two main parts or stages, pre-philosophical and philosophical, it is sufficient to make use of our definition of philosophy as a science. If philosophy deals with ultimate causes, its formation obviously occurs when man, either implicitly or explicitly, asks himself the question: 'What are the ultimate causes of all that can be known?' This second-order question marks the beginning of the philosophical undertaking by the human mind. It is true that this is still not philosophy; it is still not the science of ultimate causes, but it is the question which leads to inquiry and as such is the highway leading to the discovery of philosophy. Consequently, one may say that it is at this stage that man begins to philosophise.

Now, clearly, it is unthinkable that the human mind was entirely void of cognitions before we felt the need for philosophy. In fact, it contains a great many which not only dispose faculties by exercising them, but presents the mind with abundant material for the construction of the new philosophical edifice which it will start in due time. And what role does reflection play in the construction of this system? Actually, nothing more than clothing previously known truth in new forms which offer this noble advantage: through them we see truth from many and more radiant viewpoints and can use it in new and very useful ways. We need to distinguish truth carefully and the forms which make it more accessible, more visible and easier for us to use. We also have to distinguish ideas from the forms they take in the human mind and in which they are then expressed in human language. When ideas and facts are broken up in various ways by analysis, brought together again in a synthesis and arranged in their essential relationships, they can be used in countless arguments; they can be grouped together and arranged in formulae in accordance with the requirements of the mind, which they provide with untrammelled conclusions allowing it to operate swiftly. As a result, the spirit feels strengthened, enriched and endowed with new and greater powers. Gold bars are not of great use as such, but if you send them to the mint, you can have them back as coins which can easily be exchanged for anything you wish. The mint here stands for the philosophical mind, which develops ideas

[68a]

and extracts their inner content. They then appear to be new truths although, I repeat, when all is said and done, they have merely been given new forms. The ideas which your mind has examined were already present, and contained what you then extracted. What was implicit has been made explicit. Thus a principle may be enunciated in a brief statement, but if you deduce it to its consequences, an entire world of knowledge is yours. This is an inestimable gain. However, you have to admit that you have not created anything; all that knowledge was already contained in the principle. You could not have extracted it if it had not already been present. The mind sees a large number of facts individually; philosophical thought considers them together, organises their relationship, integrates them and arranges them into a wonderful *system*. This is fine work, but the information was already present with its own perhaps complex and complete relationships, which required abstraction and analysis, just as rocks need to be broken by the hammer and dressed before they can fit into their proper place in a building. Nonetheless, in the last resort, philosophical thought acts and always works upon what is put before it. It cannot create, that is, it cannot find anything completely new. The function of integration merely consists in passing from the term given by an essential relationship to the other term by virtue of a known law.[83]

The difference, therefore, between the ordinary person and the philosopher does not mean that the former lacks cognitions which the latter has, but that the ordinary person applies his mind to his many cognitions, not exactly at random, but as he requires them. The philosopher on the other hand undertakes the examination of the whole complex of such cognitions, not because he needs to use them all at once, but for the joy of contemplating such wealth which he wants to evaluate and order properly. In both cases the cognitions are the same. It is their use which differs.

69. Because the first element of wisdom is TRUTH, whatever form it may take, I said that wisdom (and consequently philosophy as defined in antiquity as the practical study of wisdom) contains a first cognitional element, distinct from systematic

[83] See *Psychology*, vol. 3, 1324.

knowledge. The difference lies in this: the element of wisdom is truth, without regard to its forms, and consequently under all forms whether they exist prior to or at the philosophical stage. Philosophy, however, as systematic knowledge, examines a special kind of forms with which philosophical reflection clothes the truth. From this it follows that wisdom can both precede and follow philosophy. Although philosophy is of great assistance to wisdom by making truth accessible to mankind from a number of more conspicuous viewpoints, it is in no way indispensable or necessary to wisdom.

I would not like to incur the indignation of philosophers for what I have said, although in the case of sophists I am resigned to it. Rather, I hope to avert or in some way calm it. No one should better understand the nature of noble and genuine love for mankind than philosophers, who should therefore welcome any teaching which demonstrates that all are capable of wisdom which, as gift, is not confined to the single class of philosophers. Consequently, all those merit the title 'wise' who, besides receiving the same truth — albeit implicitly — from their first existence in the light of reason, live to a certain age and nurture to varying degrees the truth they have received in germ. This, of course, will depend upon their needs and opportunities. They must also be favourably disposed towards the truth which they know, while freely acknowledging her supreme authority and her unchangeable beauty. Thus their wills will be united and as it were welded effectively to truth, which they take as the guide of their other faculties. All these wise people will have managed to order and harmonise their human faculties in this way, and to align their mortal and finite nature with the infinite and the eternal, that is, with truth, whose favour they seek.

As truth is the first element and foundation of wisdom, we have to conclude that because she is variously developed in human beings, even though in herself she is always one and the same, she is immeasurably fruitful and manifold in her manifestations as she presents herself to different understandings in many more or less magnificent and ornate forms. The same can be said about the *forms of wisdom* which are as numerous and rich as the forms of truth. Thus, starting with some unknown sage who should be called *abnormis sapiens crasseque minerva* [a philosopher of no distinct school and an artless genius] all the

[69]

way up to an Augustine or a Thomas Aquinas or any other learned sage, we shall have a really long series not only of famous men, but also of people unknown to their fellows, or even despised by them, although they are not despicable and justly deserve the title 'wise'.

This conclusion can only hearten those who, observing human ignorance and realising the sheer difficulty of *systematic knowledge* accessible only to the few, may confuse it with *wisdom* or think it is the only path to wisdom. The temptation in this case is to show too little trust in human nature which is then spurned as quite incapable of attaining the good.

On the contrary, all persons, philosophers or not, who care about the dignity and happiness of men, should both wish our conclusion to be true and rejoice when they acknowledge it as true. This message is the good news announced to little ones, and coincides with the message which, in the perfect and supernatural order, the Wisdom of God himself gave to mankind when He said: 'He who comes to me I shall not cast out.'[84]

70. This implies no discredit to philosophy which, however it is conceived, always has truth as its object and aim, and is therefore akin to wisdom. If it is taken as systematic knowledge, it teaches the most sublime truths (and I have already said that the person who teaches error instead of the truth is no true philosopher). If it is taken as the study of wisdom, it not only seeks truth but embodies it in action. Thus, Plato, in his description of the philosopher, includes both meanings of the term, when he asks:

> Can there be anything closer to wisdom than truth?
> Nothing.
> Is it possible then that the same nature can be both philosophical (*a lover of wisdom*) and false at one and the same time?
> In no way.
> So the person who is desirous of learning is inevitably and exceedingly attached to all manner of truths.[85]

[84] Jn 6: 37.
[85] *Republic*, 6.

This ought to be the attitude of the philosopher even if the term is used to refer solely to someone dedicated to the study of systematic knowledge. Here we discover the relationship and the close link between the two elements which we have found to be integral and even essential parts of wisdom, that is, *truth* and *life lived in conformity with truth*, which is virtue.

The first component is always possessed by the sage whatever form it may take. It is the object of philosophy, not in any random form but in a scientific, universal, comprehensive form, which radiates its splendour to the human consciousness. Can the philosopher gain possession of truth and reach the sublime knowledge of truth unless he loves it? But what if he loves it only when it radiates splendour, and fears it when it reproves?[86] This is tantamount to saying: if man's will is pitted against truth, if he battles with it, if he rejects it as guide and teacher of life, if it is subjected to continual reprimands, his intellect, as it assents to or dissents from statements, under the guidance of the will which dislikes the truth, cannot fully and readily recognise and admit what is true with perfect impartiality and fairness wherever it occurs, whatever it may be. When the will is unjust, truth becomes vexatious, hateful and repugnant to the assenting subject. 'Whenever reason is contrary to man,' said a famous sophist of the last century, 'man will be contrary to reason.'[87]

But reason is contrary to man only when man has willingly set himself up in opposition to reason. Reason never takes the lead in opposing man. Leibniz used to say that even mathematical truths would lead to tremendous disputes between scholars if these truths demanded sacrifices and laid down rules.

70a. *Virtue*, then, or disposition to virtue leads everyone to *truth* just as much as it does philosophers. The connection between the two constituents of Wisdom is very close. At the same time, this is the source of the honour and dignity of

---

[86] 'They love it when it is splendid and hate it when it reproaches'* (St. Augustine).

[87] T. Hobbes. See the dedicatory letter to his *Treatise on Human Nature*. It is said that Hobbes' aversion to mathematics arose from the fact that his attempt at a solution of the problem of squaring the circle had been shown to be false by Wallis, who knew more about mathematics than he did.

[70a]

philosophy. It shows that this discipline, unlike all others, although it is not itself wisdom nor a special form of wisdom, can nonetheless be fully undertaken only by a wise person. Thus Plato's Socrates, whilst commending this study, asks Glaucon: 'And must not that be a blameless study which he only can pursue adequately who has the gift of a good memory, and is quick to learn — noble, gracious, the friend of truth, justice, courage, temperance, who are his kindred?'[88]

This statement is rightly qualified by the word: 'adequately'. It is a fact that those whose will (in which the whole person is involved) and therefore whose lives are not in harmony with truth may utter part of the truth (and so appear to be philosophers) but never the whole truth. Otherwise, it would not have been possible to launch a common, justified attack upon the pagan philosophers and others who imitate them, on the grounds that *magna loquuntur sed modica faciunt* [they say impressive things but do very little].[89]

But perhaps we should consider it bold and praiseworthy of them to refrain from carrying out all they said and taught. As one of their own number said: 'They come out with a lot of strange, mistaken and reprehensible remarks'. The writer in question, after mentioning some of them, goes on: 'Philosophers express a lot of views like these, but would never dare to put them into practice unless they lived in the republic of the Cyclops and the Laestrygones.'[90] They not only do not carry out the whole truth; they do not and cannot even speak the integral truth which alone, according to our author, constitutes that *element of wisdom* and *object of philosophical science* of which I was speaking.

71. Readers who remember where I have located the seat of this integrity of truth will be aware that I am not using a vague, indeterminate argument to disparage many who deserve praise for the vigorous way they devote themselves to philosophy. I

---

[88] *Republic*, 6. There is no ancient work in which philosophy and the philosopher are more admirably described than in this Platonic dialogue, both before and after this quotation.

[89] John Chrysostom, *sup. Matt. Opera imperfecta*, Hom. 10; *Sup. Jo.*, Hom. 65.

[90] Sextus Empiricus, *Hypotuposis*, 3, 24 and 25.

have not the slightest intention, as they know perfectly well, of maintaining that philosophers worthy of the name have to know every individual truth. If so, not only would some devotees of philosophy be excluded from the ranks of philosophers; it would be impossible to find a single philosopher in the whole world. Every man, however clever, and however long he may have devoted himself to thinking, is ignorant of many things and indeed of many more than he knows. Thus, it is not material integrity of truth to which I am referring but formal integrity of which, as I said earlier, philosophy is the system, 'the systematic knowledge of truth',[91] as Aristotle also had defined it. We should bear in mind the way in which the Creator gave human nature a share in the light of truth.

As we have seen, God wished human nature to be intelligent, and ordained that truth should be visible to human beings from the very beginning of their lives. They were to see it not partly but wholly, as something unitary and very simple and therefore incapable of division. This is why no individual part of truth, separate from the whole body, can be seen by the first intuition. Indeed, there is no such part, although the mind, when it sees the whole, can then limit its reflection within the whole, and focus it on a part which it determines for itself.

71a. This truth, which is *being, intelligible per se* and which, though lacking nothing (if 'being' lacked anything, it would cease to be 'being') is continually present to the mind, contains all truths in itself, but in an implicit and virtual mode. Consequently, these truths are not seen initially as distinct or separate from each other, and in the act proper to them. This happens only when the human spirit itself, with the aid of bodily feelings and different cognitive activity, actuates what it sees in potential form, makes explicit what it already possesses implicitly, and makes distinct what is indistinct. At this point, it brings to the surface what is submerged and hidden in the power of being as though in a boundless sea. As Socrates would say, the human mind goes fishing and puts its catch in the storeroom of its memory.

If we did not need to do all this, and nature presented us with

[91] *Metaphysics*, 2: 1.

[71a]

particular, ready-made items of information, there would be no cause for any rational activity on our part. We would be truly wonderful beings through the precious truths we could contain, like the golden gods inserted in the breasts of the Sileni. Nevertheless, we would be devoid of that noteworthy action whereby we become our own master, as it were. *Being*, therefore, which is the object of the intuition granted to human nature is truth in its formal integrity. This integrity has to be transferred by human activity, to which God has assigned it, into the systematic work of philosophy. This is achieved, as I have already said, by means of elevated reflection. The first object, and therefore the principle of philosophy, can only be the first light in nature, the first principle of the inexhaustible knowledge with which mankind can enrich itself. All other information is enkindled from it as from an everlasting, sacred flame preserved in the temple of nature. If this is indeed the first light, it alone must contain within itself the first and ultimate reasons for whatever we seek to discover which, when they are found, philosophy professes to teach.

There is no doubt that from antiquity to the present day, there have been numerous, brilliant and sublime investigations into this science. Strictly speaking, however, it cannot be said that it has been found, or has even existed, except at the point of discovery of the principle which was the object of such investigations. This is the sole basis upon which we can build in an ordered and truly scientific manner.

71b. This *intelligible being* is as it were the seal of human nature which it renders intelligent. It is then grasped by reflection and transferred into the field of systematic knowledge where it becomes the foundation stone of the building and contains the truth in its formal integrity, although still implicitly. This integrity is never lost as the philosopher's mind labours to build on that foundation; the walls gradually rise above ground and although the process may not get as far as the roof, we can truly say, from that stage onwards, that philosophy has been founded, although not fully completed.

In such a building the architect has first to think about fitting the stones together perfectly to ensure there are no gaps or cracks, and that each stone is dressed and levelled precisely to provide support for the next. By this I mean that the special truths which need to be put in order and structured to form an intellectual discipline should pass from one to another without any break, as a continuation of the one idea which we intuit naturally. The first order of such truths is based on that idea and the following orders upon each other, so that the entire structure stands firm upon the single initial foundation. Moreover, not all types of stone are suitable for such a construction but only those which, derived from the original idea as from the depths of a rich quarry, retain the same nature and character of hard, firm, resistant stone.

This needs some explanation, and I can find none better than that offered by Plato at the end of the fifth dialogue in the *Republic* where Socrates wants Glaucon to realise that no one can be truthfully said to love something unless he loved it in its entirety — not loving one part of the thing and detesting another. He concludes from this that when a philosopher is said to love wisdom, he is eager for all wisdom, not for some species or part of wisdom. At this point, Plato refers *en passant* to the formal integrity of truth which I mentioned earlier as a necessary condition of the object of philosophy. He then adds that true philosophers, that is, those who love wisdom, are those who desire to see the truth. People who want to see something else he says — with his usual attic salt —should not be called philosophers but *would-be philosophers*, because they do at least resemble philosophers in their desire to see. Then, as soon as Plato asks about the nature of the truth on which the true philosopher desires to fix his gaze, he makes us understand how firm and hard those stones must be which alone are suitable for raising the edifice of philosophical science.

71c. The truth of which the great man speaks is *being*: hence philosophy should be seen as the *systematic knowledge of being*. But here Plato distinguishes three things: what is, what is not, and what is at one moment in part and at another moment not in part. 'What is' constitutes being; 'what is not' constitutes non-being; 'what partly is now, and now partly is not', is something half-way between being and nothing. Of this, it cannot be said simply and absolutely either that it is or that it is not; it has to be qualified by some distinction, or condition or limitation. Being is the object of *systematic knowledge* and cognition; nothing — that which is nothing in every sense — provides only ignorance because it offers the mind no object; what is in part and is not in part presents itself cognitively as mid-way between systematic knowledge and ignorance. It cannot be termed systematic knowledge (ἐπιστήμη) nor complete ignorance but *opinion* (δόξα).

Philosophy therefore contemplates that which simply and absolutely is, being without qualification, and its relationships with non-being, or with anything that *is* merely in part. Thus it is distinguished from ignorance and opinion. Whatever merely is can never not be and is consequently eternal; it is always in the same mode and is therefore immutable. By essence it is, that is, its essence as such lies in being; it is therefore necessary, totally firm, enduring, insurmountable, totally equal to itself. Such is the firmness and hardness of those stones with which — when all other more unreliable stones have been rejected — the walls of the palace of philosophy were to be built.

To explain the difference between knowledge of these eternal things and opinion concerning contingent and mutable things, Plato uses an example. He distinguishes *beautiful things* from *the beautiful* seen in its idea. Beautiful things, which are many and various, may become, or may have been, ugly. The beautiful itself, however, as the idea makes it known to the mind, is perfectly one and can never have been, nor can ever become ugly, because its essence is precisely to be beautiful, and no essence can be thought different from what it is and how it unchangeably appears to the intellect. Things which may at one moment be beautiful, and ugly at another, are not purely and simply the beautiful, but are now partly such and now partly not such. They share in beauty and as a result Plato calls them *likenesses* of the beautiful. He says that anyone who takes the *likeness* of things for *things themselves* resembles a person who takes his dreams for real things. The majority of mankind dream in this way because in thinking they do not go beyond the things which share in being; they either persuade themselves that there is nothing beyond these things, or think about it no further. Very few people succeed in reflecting about these unchangeable essences in a simple and absolute way; they alone are wide awake. The faculty which the mind has to remain awake to consider things as they really are is the prerequisite of the philosopher. What Plato says about beauty, then, should be

[71c]

applied also to justice and other essences.[92] These in the last resort are the only materials suitable for constructing the edifice of philosophy.

72. As I said, philosophy is the study of the ultimate reasons. Now the ultimate reasons of all contingent and mutable things, which are and are not, are to be found in their essences. These appear in ideas which are necessary and unchangeable, which simply are, not which are at one moment and are not at the next. Such stones are necessary, and to find them, says Plato, we must detach ourselves from bodily and corruptible things and turn completely to eternal, divine things; thus, he calls this study περιαγογήν, that is, a revolution[93] and a kind of death, 'a dissolution or tearing away of the spirit from the body when we turn to invisible things and those that are true.'*[94] The link between virtue, which as we said is the second constituent of wisdom, and philosophy is such that no one is fitted for philosophy unless virtue has made him noble and sublime in soul.

But the stones, when found, have to be assembled carefully to fit the design for the temple which is to be built. And as these stones are everlasting and much harder than diamond, so the design, too, is eternal and unique. This, too, is sufficiently clear to the human mind from the stones themselves. Once dug from the quarry, and cleansed of extraneous materials, they can be identified by a number and the indication of the place in the

---

[92] Plato's work lacks exact classification of these essences and their gradual reduction to the three ultimate categories which, although reciprocally impenetrable, manifest from within the perfect unity of being. Plato touched upon this unity when speaking of the idea of the good but, as I go on to point out, he did not realise that this idea was only one of three forms. Even this philosopher, without any doubt the greatest prior to Christianity — at least of those whose works have come down to us — was unable to ascend with sufficient constancy from *ideas* to the *reality* of absolute being. He frequently admits that this cannot be done without some extraordinary assistance given to mankind by God. This is the final and greatest statement uttered in the field of ancient philosophy. In the light of this, it is no wonder that Clement of Alexandria spoke of philosophy as a special legacy given by God to the Greeks in particular, and as a foundation for or rather an introduction to, Christian doctrine. See *Stromata*, 6 and 7.

[93] *Republic*, 6.

[94] See Alcinous, Chap. 1, and the fine commentary of Carpentarius that accompanies it. See also Ammonius in *Porphyry*.

building where they have to be inserted. The builder needs only to locate them faithfully and place them, with extreme exactness, in the order indicated upon them. As he labours, the design manifests itself and falls into place perfectly without any need for drawings.

72a. In my view, Plato — it is difficult to abandon such a great man once he has been mentioned — who was able to tell us which were the proper stones to use in constructing philosophy, had neither seen the whole building nor the entire design. He deserves full and everlasting credit for having worked out what the summit and, I would almost say, the pinnacle are, although he is rather fearful (which I find the best proof of his greatness of soul) of not speaking of it adequately. Hence his excessive brevity. He takes the idea of good as the pinnacle of the building and calls it the greatest *branch of learning*; he wants the city guardians to be imbued with it above any other type of knowledge. 'Because it would be of no use to possess something without the good. So, if we are unaware of that idea, and even if we know other things perfectly well, though without that idea, none of this knowledge can be of any use to us.' He then adds: 'Our whole soul desires the good and acts entirely to that end in the hope that the good really is something. The soul, however, has doubts and cannot properly grasp what good is, nor can it reach any firm persuasion as it can in other things. As a result, it falls into error over other things when it persists in judging which things are useful.' With these words, having whetted the listeners' desire to know such a wonderful and mysterious truth, namely the nature of Good, Glaucon earnestly begs Socrates to discuss the matter. Socrates, however, says: 'I am afraid I cannot do this. I would appear inept and give listeners cause for laughter were I to go beyond my capacity.' Consequently, declining the invitation just then to enter into the question of the essence of good, he promises to say which of its offspring looks most like it. Even so, he warns his listeners that such a restriction may still cause him to lead them astray. They should be careful, in such an important discussion, to be sure that he is not offering them an empty concept. What Socrates calls the *offspring of the good* is the light of human reason, which is so like its begetter. No other thinker in the whole of pagan antiquity rose to such a height and uttered a more stupendous statement than this. He says that in

[72a]

the order of corporeal things, we need more than eyesight and
visible things in order to see. We also need *light* which brings the
eye into operation by making things colourful and visible. The
same is true in the order of intelligible things. As the light of the
visible world emanates from the sun, so the light that forms the
intelligence and makes things intelligible is the direct offspring
of *essential good* which Plato often calls the idea of good because
the essence lies in the idea.[95] This light, therefore, is according to
Plato the source of the knowledge and truth which the intellect
apprehends. From their perfection, Plato wishes the mind to
ascend even higher and come to know the perfection and the

---

[95] The fundamental equivocation in Plato's philosophy which prevented
him from achieving perfection and gaining universal assent, the equivocation
which made his work the source of errors and heresies and eventually
alienated the Christian schools, arose from his continual confusion between
idea and *reality*. This distinction is obvious when it presents itself directly to
the spirit, but becomes difficult to see in the midst of philosophical
speculation. The thinker then finds it very hard not to unify concepts which
he had previously held as quite distinct. Plato, for example, frequently uses
indiscriminately the terms *good, the idea of good, the essence of good* as
though they were synonymous. He does occasionally distinguish between
them in practice, but he is not constant and faithful to such use. For example,
when he maintains in chapter 6 of the Republic, that possession of everything
is of no avail without the idea of the good, the two orders of ideality and
reality appear distinct. But immediately after asserting that *the idea of good* is
the cause of truth and knowledge, he also says that it is the cause of
contingent things, and speaks indifferently of the idea and of the good itself
because he posits the true and permanent being of anything in the idea. This
is perfectly true if the reference is to the *being* of anything; this being is not
contingent. But, if the reference is to the *contingent element* of the thing
itself, it is false. What is true is that the contingent element would not and
could not be known without being with which it has an essential, causal
relationship, but not identity. The idea is the condition of the existence and
knowability of the contingent element, but is not itself the contingent
element, nor can it be; it is necessary. It is true that we see the essence of
anything in the idea, but the essence of a thing is an appurtenance of the
objective mode of existence of contingent things which, however, also have a
subjective or *extrasubjective* mode of existence. Contingency consists
exclusively in the second mode, though this second mode depends on the
first as creatures depend on the Creator. As a rule, ordinary people's
intelligence does not distinguish between these two modes and consequently
avoids the difficulty philosophers have when distinguishing and comparing
them. Seeing that the two modes never stand one without the other,
philosophers finally come to confuse them.

even greater eminence of that Sun which not only generates the light, but also causes all mutable things and in causing them gives them the power to generate, develop and feed themselves. Nevertheless, the Sun is not itself any one of these.

72b. I would express the matter as follows, according to the mind of the great philosopher: real, mutable and contingent things (Plato calls them *generabilia*, that is, subject to generation) are neither known by us nor are knowable except in their essences, which are everlasting and *per se* knowable and, when communicated to the mind, are called ideas. All such essences are reduced to one original light, the light of reason. This is simply *being*, manifest to the mind as soon as the mind begins to exist, or — and this is the same thing — the unlimited, totally undetermined *essence of being* intuited by us is the first idea which produces all others, just as bodily light produces colours. The other ideas and essences found in it are merely the *idea of being* variously determined and limited just as colours are the refracted, not united light, divided into luminous sheaves, that is, limited. Now, truth, the permanent being of things which always retains the same mode, and does not waver between being and non-being — it simply *is* — is found in their essences, of which contingent and mutable things are simply the imperfect expressions and, as Plato puts it, *likenesses*. Thus, as a likeness is caused by an original of which it is an imitation, so the essences are the causes of the realities. The light of the essences, which contain the true being of the realities, is the Sun. And the Sun is the essential good of all these things together. This doctrine is, as it happens, so wonderful and reverent especially on the lips of a Gentile, that I do not think the reader will mind if at this point I quote the very words of this extraordinary man.

> Socrates: You know that when a man turns his eyes not to things on whose colours the light of day is shining, but to those where the moon and stars shine, his eyes grow dim and appear almost blind, as though pure sight were not in them?
> Glaucon: Yes, certainly.
> Socrates: But when they look at things on which the sun is shining, I fancy that these same eyes see distinctly, and are obviously sightful?
> Glaucon: Correct.

[72b]

Socrates: Now consider the spirit in the same way. When it is resting on that in which truth and ens itself are shining, it understands and knows, and shows that it has understood. But when it is applied to that which is mingled with darkness, which passes from generation to corruption, its sight is dulled, it suggests various opinions, and appears mindless.

Glaucon: I think you're right.

Socrates: This, then, which imparts truth to the things that are understood, and the power of understanding to the one who understands, you should call the idea of good, the cause of the knowledge and truth apprehended by the intellect. But because knowledge and truth are both beautiful, you will be right in thinking that good itself is different from and more beautiful than either. And as it is right to think light and sight sun-like, but not right to think that they are the sun, so here it is right to think that both knowledge and truth are like the good, but never that either of them is the good itself. The majesty of the good is higher still.

Glaucon: You speak of an incalculable beauty, if it gives knowledge and truth, and itself excels them in beauty. Surely you do not mean that this is pleasure?

Socrates: Not at all! Rather consider the image in this further aspect.

Glaucon: How?

Socrates: I fancy that you will say that the sun gives to visible objects not only the power of being seen, but also their generation and growth and nourishment, although the sun itself is not generation.

Glaucon: So?

Socrates: Similarly you may say that what is *good*, relative to things known, not only enables them to be known, but also provides them with being and essence. In other words, it surpasses these things in dignity and power.

Glaucon: This is indeed wonderful!"[96]

73. No other Gentile mind before Christ's time reached such intellectual heights. The pinnacle of philosophy is clearly shown here to be in God, the author of the light of human reason, the seat of the essences, the author of all things.

---

[96] *Republic*, 6.

[73]

Moreover, God is presented most perceptively as the *essence of good* because only the nature of good is of itself diffusive. It is through this 'instinct for diffusion' that God keeps the universe in subsistence. However, as I said, Plato, despite depicting the summit of the great philosophical edifice so accurately, was unable to depict the entire structure so carefully and distinctly. While it is certain that only the idea of the good contains the intentional principle and real end of the world, the idea of a final cause is not the only *ultimate cause*; we must add the *exemplary cause*, which is an idea in itself or (to express it more clearly) that to which the idea is analogous, and the *efficient cause*. These three causes provide philosophical meditation with the three ultimate reasons for everything. None of these causes is greater than another, nor can one be fused in another as Plato seems to imagine when he subjects the others to the nature of good or confuses them with it. Here too, the great philosopher was prevented from making the necessary distinction between them by his disregard of the law of *synthesis*, of which I speak continually. According to this law, even if several things are to be taken together and each can be eliminated by argument simply on the supposition that what should accompany it is actually lacking, these things can still be distinct in the extreme from one another.

Consequently, when Plato realised that the *idea of the good* could not be unless it contained *intelligibility* and *potency*, he took them as elements of the idea of good, not as ideas distinct from the idea of good. If he had also considered that the idea of potency is unthinkable unless it contains the concepts of intelligibility and good, or that the exemplar (which, as I said, is *per se* idea, or word of which the idea is analogous) cannot be without the exemplified potency and good, he would easily have realised that none of these three can be reduced to the other, although each of them requires and supports the others. To devise a clear plan of philosophical knowledge, he would also have had to observe 1. that the concept of efficient cause derives from and is included in that of *real being* and subject; 2. that the exemplary cause is *ideal being* (which is reduced to the divine Word to which it is analogous), *being per se* manifest or *per se* object; 3. and finally that the idea of the final cause arises from the idea of the good, which is *moral being*, a kind of marriage bed for subject-being and objective-being. These are three forms each of which contains within itself one and the same *being*, whole and entire, in such a way that this trinity is consumed in the simple unity of being itself. I am not implying by this that Plato mistakenly deduces the light of human reason, the essence of mutable things and these things themselves, from the essential good, as from an immediate cause. Indeed, what is ultimate for God according to the logical order of our mind, is first in respect of the world; it is the first reason explaining the creative movement. The great thinker, however, who had only the natural light of reason, was too hasty in viewing divine things in the order which they have in relation to the world without first considering, as he should have done, the other, prior and absolute order which exists among divine things. Thus, although his outstanding intellect is a matter for amazement (he called the light of reason the *offspring of essential good who closely resembles his father*), nevertheless, his great and noble attempt to reach the very heights is clear proof of the limitations of the human mind which, although it reached out to heaven, could never attain it. Nevertheless, through analogy with natural light, it was able to point from a distance to a Word or an eternal light, the offspring of essential good, although even here it probably needed the help of ancient traditions. Only God's word is able to guide human intelligence without error along the path of heavenly reason, and make it fit for the most sublime philosophy of all.

74. Philosophy begins and ends with *being* and its *intrinsic order,* that is, its three forms which are reflected in the world and constitute the basis of the *categories* to which all things are reduced. These three forms become the final causes which are the focus of philosophical thinking. In fact, when dealing with *being* under a first, real form, it is necessary to investigate the first reason for all realities which go to make up the real world. In dealing with *being* under a first, objective form, it is necessary to investigate the first reason for all the ideas and cognitions which constitute the ideal, intelligible world. In dealing with *being* under a first form of good, it is necessary to investigate the first reason for all exigencies and laws, for all moral activity with its effects which constitute the moral world. The interlacing of these three worlds is the creation which

hangs from its Creator, whom it resembles, as fruit hangs from a tree.

75. These three marks can be easily recognised in the nature of things, and in the very structure of the universe. They are like three highways along which the thinker journeys to discover the final causes of things, which is the philosopher's role. It is shown also in the threefold division of ancient philosophy, accepted by the greatest philosophers, into *natural, rational* and *moral*.[97] And although the tremendous subsequent development of these three primal members gave rise to so many subdivisions that the three trunks sharing the common root of being were lost sight of, nevertheless, if we retrace our steps and synthesise what analysis has multiplied and, one might say, dispersed, the three primal parts on which my writings are focused once more would come into their own.[98]

St. Augustine points out that this division was not instituted by philosophers but discovered by them in the very nature of things.[99] He detects in it traces of the divine Trinity and discerns in it the *three problems* of human knowledge which, although posited, had never been solved by the Gentile philosophers. In fact, the answers could be found only in the context of the Christian doctrine of the three divine Persons. He says: "Although there is wide divergence of opinion (on each of the

---

[97] 'The MAJORITY and the GREATEST of philosophers proclaim that philosophy has three forms: moral, natural and rational'* (Seneca., *Ep.* 89). It is noteworthy how sensual thinkers in every age have attempted to exclude areas of knowledge, thereby impoverishing mankind. This uncivilised approach is always found in licentious, impious scholars who, nevertheless, covet the titles 'master', 'enlightened' and 'cultured', and so on. In the letter quoted above, Seneca observes that the Epicureans restricted philosophy to two parts, eliminating the rational part. The Cyrenaics restricted it to one by excluding rational and natural philosophy. They acted in the same way as Protestants: if they come across any inspired book which too openly condemns their errors, they remove it from the canon of Scripture.

[98] *Ideological and logical sciences* form the rational part; *metaphysical sciences*, which can be reduced to two (psychology and theosophy) pertain to the natural part; the sciences which deal with *human activity* form the moral part.

[99] 'Hence philosophers desired a threefold discipline in wisdom. Indeed, they are able to note that it was threefold. However, they only discovered that this was so; they did not invent it'* (*The City of God*, 11: 25).

three important, general questions), everyone admits that there is some cause of nature, some form of knowledge, some great synthesis of life.'[100]

This is how the very summit of philosophy, like the peak of a high mountain lost in majestic clouds, is perpetuated by the heavenly light preserved in Christian belief which places a sacred, heavenly crown upon the head of philosophy. It is thus quite clear that VIRTUE , which I have called the second element of wisdom, and religion, which is the perfection of virtue, leads the way to TRUTH, the first element, which philosophy, as an activity, investigates and of which philosophy, as science, is the system.

76. This *science* then gives a new and more sublime form to *wisdom* which has as its basis the knowledge of truth. But because truth can be known in its essential form in two ways — one which is common to all human beings, the other as the fruit of reflection and awareness specific to philosophers — it follows that there are two forms of wisdom. One form, based on everyday, direct and ordinary knowledge, is common to all, and operates whenever human freedom of action, unaffected by the darkness produced by feelings and undisturbed by fits of blind passion, walks in the light of truth which it knows and loves above all else. As a result, the human subject, who dwells in the will, is shaped and tuned to the object. They are like two strings on the same lyre. The other form of wisdom, peculiar to the philosopher, is not based solely on systematic knowledge, which is rarely perfect and complete, but upon systematic knowledge together with the stock of cognitions which he already possesses and from which systematic knowledge stands out as a kind of base relief. But when people love everything they know to be true, whatever the form in which they know it, they seek to implement it fully and to render it subsistent and alive within them. It is true that the mind, on its journey to the higher sphere of knowledge, has to face new dangers and hitherto unknown struggles against new forms of error. Our often ambiguous reason, ascending to a higher level of reflection and operating in an infinitely wider field, delights in testing its powers both by discovering and concealing the truth, and by

[100] *Ibid.*

[76]

struggling with itself, as though it were on the high seas where winds are fiercer than on a narrow lake. Nevertheless, we can overcome such tempests if we are guided by an unbounded love of truth. When we have finally attained systematic knowledge, we can more profoundly honour and witness to the truth which we possess in this way and see clearly from so many viewpoints. We can also devote ourselves more perfectly to this truth through our *reflective* and *conscious will* which wells up like a new power from within systematic knowledge and finds in the truth it enjoys a special joy which is also knowledge and love and new respect for truth. Philosophy thus offers new contributions to an increase of wisdom, and gives new stimulus to the love of wisdom. In a word, wisdom first goes ahead of us to guide us to philosophy with which it dwells; philosophy for its part then restores us to this higher wisdom. Such are the close and estimable relations between philosophy and wisdom.

77. All attempts to loosen such natural, sacred bonds have failed. Whenever philosophers have determined to separate *systematic knowledge* from *moral virtue* and pretended that *knowledge* should stand on its own feet as self-sufficient, the result has been disastrous. Knowledge, like a human body from which the blood is removed and replaced by, say, the blood of a goat, has languished and perished at the reckless hands of those who subjected it to such treatment. It is in fact easier to create a living, intelligent being by chemically tossing together physical components than to create philosophy without love of truth and virtue. Such an aim is the delusion of the materialist, and the everlasting dream of the rationalist. Philosophy is simply a faithful representative and draughtsman, as it were, of *being* (anything else is sophistry, not philosophy). Being, in turn, is essentially ordered with a beginning, middle and end, that is, subsistence, intelligibility and lovableness which give rise to virtue and its attendant happiness. So philosophy, after portraying ens as the beginning and middle, inevitably ends and comes to rest in the knowledge of virtue and happiness where ens, as in its final perfection, comes to rest and achieves fulfilment. But knowledge dependent on virtue does not reveal itself to its adversaries. Indeed, just as in the case of feelings, which nobody could invent or imagine unless they had experienced them, so finally the only valid observation and experience is that which

reveals in a positive and intimate manner the moral phenomena unfolded and exhibited by the nature and excellence of virtue. This cannot be said, at least to the same extent, of vice, which has a negative and privative character and is adequately understood through knowledge of the positive, which is its contrary. Once more, therefore, we should remember that the essential intention in the study of philosophy is the practice of virtue. As it is written, but on a higher plane of study and wisdom: 'My son, if you desire wisdom, observe justice and God will give it to you.'[101]

78. Separating the intellectual from the active, moral part, as the German School wants to do, means destroying man. It amounts to absorbing morality in pure, systematic knowledge. Kant and Fichte, the first founders of this school, were unable to explain how the mind could know things other than man; they were too imbued with the subjectivist prejudice which their age had swallowed whole but never digested. Upon their ignorance, they erected the new system and declared that reason was totally incapable of perceiving the external world, and thus incapable of doing what it does continually. Nevertheless, they were afraid that people would be unduly terrified of the absurdities of a doctrine which, like an irate goddess criticising *reason*, berated reason and reduced it to impotence. They therefore resorted characteristically to *action* where they recognised real communication between man and the external world. Using the term *practical reasoning* (but within a subjective context) they restored to the human intellect what they had taken from it under the term *theoretical reason*. This makeshift arrangement could not last because inconsistencies do not last. Consequently, Schelling, Hegel and their disciples abolished the dualism that remained in man; they were more faithful to the principle that man cannot go outside himself. The outstanding proof they gave for this was their own intellects' incapacity for stepping outside itself. Rather than admit their own ignorance — a University professor's dignity implied that he should know everything — they barefacedly denied the most obvious, everyday facts of nature. They said that action persisted in the form of phenomena in man until he attained *systematic*

[101] Eccles 1: 33.

[78]

knowledge and, more specifically, the *idea* which alone exists and becomes man, action, object, subject, concept, nature, God, everything. Man does not master the great truth that the *idea* is all, as long as his own consciousness is immersed in the profound struggle to reach it. This is successively creation and annihilation (there can be no rest but only never-ending motion as Heraclitus said). Through this struggle, man never just 'is', but is always *becoming*. Either he becomes pure idea, or nothing, or re-emerges from nothingness as someone 'who eats and drinks and sleeps and puts on clothes'. In a word he re-enters material nature, either to be deified or idealised or to fall back once again into the great nothingness. According to this philosophy, every act and consequently all morality is merely the fleeting transformation of the idea. The Man-Idea is superior to everything else; he is all, and is not subject to any external laws. Moreover, although it vanishes into nothing, *self-consciousness* is alone truthful because it does not step outside itself. It must indeed conquer the knowledge of other things which in Germany is known *tout court* as consciousness. According to German philosophy, *self-consciousness* and *consciousness* (knowledge of other things) are like cannibals locked in combat and, with the victory going to self-consciousness, consciousness is voraciously devoured. Thus *consciousness*, that is, knowledge of God and of one's fellows is devoured by the ravenous hunger of self-consciousness which alone remains dominant. Moral obligations to God and men are also devoured; even the knowledge of these antiquated notions has disappeared. At this point man, pure self-consciousness, which constitutes the peak of his greatness, is freed from every obligation. All that remains is the pleasure — not the duty of course — of worshipping himself; *nothingness* also remains, into which he will soon tumble to emerge later as though from some primeval egg. These are not my conclusions; the credit for having deduced them goes partly to Hegel himself and partly to his disciples who so far are not sufficiently eminent to be mentioned.

Under the guise of systematic knowledge and philosophy, the German sophists set out to disparage man, tossing him endlessly back and forth between *nothingness* and the *all*. Along with man, systematic knowledge, philosophy and wisdom were

[78]

held in derision; all of them continuously emerge from the vast sea of nothingness to which they then flow back. No wonder that the voice of philosophy in Germany seems at present silent and confused. Nevertheless, the duality of *knowledge* and *action* which those sophists abhor does not eliminate the unity of being, identical in idea and act, nor does it prevent the unity of wisdom which results from the very close structural, harmonious and living bond between these two elements, just as it is inevitable that 'one' remains when all plurality is stripped away from it. Nor is there any conflict between contemplation and action, as though action prevented the fullness of contemplation, as is so often assumed. The mind contemplates in the person who acts as well as in the person who does nothing. Where there is action, a man's mind contemplates also what he himself is doing. Nothing is excluded from such contemplation although the things contemplated may also have another form of being which places them outside contemplation. It is contemplation itself which informs and assures us of this.

79. Let us sum up. I said that the first element of wisdom lies in the knowledge of truth, of which systematic knowledge is merely a reflection. However, this knowledge does not begin to be an element of wisdom as long as it is purely speculative, that is, not yet accepted and cherished; as long as we have not made our own contribution to it; as long as knowledge has not become a free act. The vision itself of what is true is twofold, necessary on the one hand, voluntary and loving on the other. The latter would sometimes be better called *contemplation*, sometimes *practical knowledge*. There is, therefore, some knowledge and some science which are, psychologically speaking, prior to the point at which wisdom begins.

80. But to complete this argument and to crown the conception of wisdom, I must now pass from the natural order to another order of unparalleled sublimity, that is, to the supernatural order. Let us take up the argument from the beginning.

We attain knowledge in two ways. One is difficult and slow. We are left to our own devices, without education and instruction, or the assistance of a teacher, and we move forward as best we can in the quest for truth. The other is easy and rapid. We learn from teachers not only the few truths which we could have discovered on our own, but an orderly and boundless stock of information gathered by the efforts of countless scholars, efforts which have been amassed, as it were, and handed down over the centuries to successive generations as the common heritage or patrimony of the human family. All are unanimous that this second way of learning is infinitely better than the first. All down the ages, there have been teachers and schools, even in more civilised periods when, given the greater development of individual minds, they might have been considered less essential. In fact, they were seen as more important. There was no limit to the concern to set up universities and high schools, and all types of establishment in which the most distinguished teachers communicated knowledge to their many students. The communication of truth from mind to mind by speech is the quickest and most efficient of all. By this method, we move with least effort from ignorance to knowledge. It initiates, stimulates, directs, enriches, strengthens and, one might say, multiplies human intelligence.

80a. It is obvious, though, that a teacher cannot teach what he does not know; hence, the importance of his being learned. The esteem and confidence of the disciples in their teacher is a positive advantage. Indeed, when numerous, difficult problems of great importance arise, we would want a completely infallible and omniscient teacher. This desire to know the truth with certainty, which makes us picture our ideal teacher as one endowed with the two gifts of infallibility and omniscience, often moves us to extol effusively the doctrine and authority of our teachers. At different times, various teachers have been called 'divine' or celebrated under other exaggerated titles. Often disciples would swear on the words of their teachers, and were pleased to solve all their problems with the solemn formula: *ipse dixit*. But Plato, who also was called 'divine', never claimed for himself any divine knowledge when he came across one of these important and mysterious problems. Rather, he admitted his ignorance despite the universal desire for answers to questions on which human destiny depends — questions cultivated by philosophy as trees are cultivated for their fruit. He wanted God himself to draw near and reveal to us how such things stood, and give us complete assurance about them with his infallible authority.[102]

[102] *Phaedo.*

[80a]

We have an extreme need of both of these things: we need to know the truth about such questions and to know it without any hesitation — hesitation alone is sufficient to leave us unhappy. If Alexander the Great thanked the gods for allowing him to be born when Aristotle was alive, how much more fortunate he would have considered himself if he had had God as his teacher? All who laboured and studied amongst the Gentiles to attain truth; all who sacrificed their time on long journeys, in late nights, in all sorts of privations, to achieve truth, and then managed to come up only with conflicting opinions, or more or less probable conjectures, without any certainty of reaching it; all of them would have been delighted if, even for a single moment, they had been able to confer with God himself and hear from his own mouth the infallible answers and the indubitable teachings for which they longed. Indeed, the ardent, anxious longing to know is common and natural to mankind, and no one can rest until he knows the final outcome for virtue and vice, or what will become of man after this short life if the soul survives the body's decay, or whether the soul which survives remains separated from the body, or what he will do and endure in eternal life, or whether he will be happy or unhappy? We can neither live in uncertainty about such questions nor come to a positive decision free of any uncertainty. This explains why the imagined opinions of philosophers about such issues were vague, conjectural, multiple, contradictory, lacking in authority and without durable consensus. This was especially so under the poets whose fables rendered the answers even more incredible. Consequently, the most powerful minds, in order to attain some positive, less vague concept, clung, like shipwrecked sailors grasping at every straw and every leaf floating in the sea, to certain ancient authorities whose distant message was transmitted to them by means of popular tradition.[103]

What would respond better to the immediate needs and desire of all mankind than the discovery of such an outstanding

---

[103] Thus Plato in *Phaedo* where Socrates says: 'There is a long-established theory, as we recall, that the souls of the dead depart into the other world and return once more to this world from the dead.'* He then launches out into the wonderful dialogue in which he wishes to prove the soul's immortality, and recounts many fables of the poets, thereby showing his need to rely upon some authority, but without finding anything better.

[80a]

teacher who knew all these things infallibly and could, with complete authority, inspire belief and the power to persuade in everyone? Surely this could be done only by God himself? No one, surely, would resent a teacher of such status or regret his coming to earth to teach mankind? No one would be ashamed to become his disciple or stop his ears so as not to hear him. No one, unless he were so insane as to hate the light and so perverted as to stifle within himself the liveliest, immortal instinct in human nature.

81. It is desirable, therefore, that all who love truth and who seek wisdom should want God to become the teacher of mankind. It is also probable, granted that God is perfect and aware of the needs and tendencies of human nature which he created, that he wants to do so. Indeed, it is not only probable but the most luminous of all facts. It has resounded down the ages and has filled the whole world with its power.

There is, consequently, a divine, supernatural knowledge that fulfils the longings of human beings and the requirements of hesitant reason which, after attempting to discover and show man the path to happiness, admitted that it could find no reliable way among the unforeseeable and inevitable vicissitudes of a life whose mystery it could not fathom. Life is like a linked chain of dreams to be broken soon and instantaneously. Reason, brought to this moment, found itself before the iron gates of death, unable to get in and see beyond them to its eternal dwelling place, although intellective souls sensed their immortality. If wisdom is correctly defined as the 'study of happiness',[104] we have to conclude that the supernatural knowledge which God Himself imparted to mankind when he became our teacher — the only knowledge which has revealed to us the mystery of the grave and of the new, everlasting life to which death gives entrance — alone deserves the title of wisdom. Moreover, we learn from such a great teacher not just how to know what good things are being prepared for us in the next world but the

---

[104] 'I hold that the best concept of man is fulfilled if we say that wisdom is simply the science of happiness'* (Leibniz, *Praef. Cod. jur. gentium diplomat.*). —'Wisdom is one. It consists in the living apprehension of the true good'* (Tomasius, *In cautelis ab initio*). — 'I maintain that learning or wisdom consists in a careful and wholesome knowledge of truth or, which amounts to the same thing, the fostering of man's happiness'* (Christ. Wolff).

[81]

conditions we must obey to possess them, the art of going about this, and the means of acquiring it. Thus, in this supernatural school, another problem was solved which had been posed and discussed in the natural order by the sharpest minds: 'Can virtue be taught?' In several places, Plato answered negatively, stating that *virtue* cannot be taught in the way *knowledge* can, that no teachers of virtue can be drawn from the ranks of human beings, and consequently no disciples either. God alone could be both teacher and donor of wisdom.[105] Here was a new and powerful reason, recognised by natural philosophy, which considered a divine teacher not only desirable but necessary. In truth, God has the power to simultaneously communicate truth to man's mind and virtue to his will. Knowing, therefore, as we do now, that we have a teacher whose school is not lodged in some magnificent auditorium or spacious colonnade, or pleasant wood or villa, or town, but is heard throughout the world, I feel obliged to sketch the portrait of wisdom. I want to indicate more clearly what is taught and learned in this school in which both components of wisdom are bestowed, freely and fully, on all those who long for it in a way possible and fitting to a God who does the teaching. I shall first consider the *new knowledge* and immediately afterwards I shall deal with the *new virtue*.

82. I have already distinguished *truth* and the various *forms* in which it appears to mankind. Such forms differ according to the age and the various developments of human intellects in such a way that truth takes on a form peculiar to childhood, youth, adulthood and old age; it has certain forms among ordinary folk, others only among the educated. But lying behind all these forms, there is truth itself which is *ideal being*, in which all entities are knowable. Truth, which precedes all its forms, communicates directly with us and makes us intelligent. But who teaches us pure truth, prior to all forms and receptive to them all? Who utters the first word by means of which we interpret and understand all the rest? No human being teaches the truth in this way and, if there were such a human teacher, where would he have been taught? How could he communicate it? In words? Words are mere sounds which later become signs, not

---

[105] Plato demonstrates the truth of this, one of the most sublime to which human reason has attained, in the two dialogues, *Meno* and *Theaetetus*.

so much through the power and action of the person uttering them as through the efforts of the listener who interprets them, and who could not understand them unless he were able to switch his mind from physical sounds to the truth signified by them. This truth is not found in sounds but within. Every human magisterium therefore implies a prior divine magisterium, offered by him who was called 'the true light which enlightens every one who comes into the world.'[106] We *believe* in this magisterium by *nature*, not as a result of reasoning. Consequently, even in the natural order, not just in the supernatural order, *faith* precedes *reason*. The words: 'If you had not believed, you would not understand' are true in both orders. Here we have the first teacher, the only one who is truly entitled to such a name, the only one who communicates the truth. Others merely advise and encourage those who have already received the truth to think about it, ponder on it and view it under special forms. This teacher justifiably checked the pride of those who are wise according to this world when he told his disciples: 'You are not to seek to be called "Teachers" because you have only one "Teacher" and you are all brothers.'[107]

This precept was given when God appeared as a visible teacher and added to the first word with which he enlightened mankind on the day of creation. He first enabled us to grasp the truth by intuition and then added a second message even more sublime than the first although, like that, it was internal and true, and prior to the forms it took. Like the first word, this too was efficacious and *per se* visible; it required no other light to be seen. The first word was the gate through which mankind could enter the *world of natural knowledge*; the second was the gate admitting him to another, vaster *world of supernatural knowledge*.

82a. I have already sketched the relationship between these two lights and shown how the way in which we are enlightened in the order of natural things is identical with the method used in the supernatural order. As I said (cf. 31–37) teacher and school are the same. More could be said, but it would take too long. I merely remark that God, when he created man,

---

[106] Jn 1: 9.
[107] Mt 23: 8.

instructed him by the light of reason and, at the same time, enabled him to learn under many forms more about the very truth which he saw without forms. God also enabled us to benefit from the teaching of others, to teach others ourselves, and communicate to them the truths and forms we know. As a result, the school of our divine master, the first and only one to communicate the light of truth, is that which renders all other forms of teaching possible. With the aid of that light, we ourselves search for the truth, teach ourselves or are taught by others. The first teacher, therefore, instructs all others, just as he trains the disciples themselves. Both teachers and disciples exist by virtue of our first silent, yet extremely powerful teacher. The same occurs in the supernatural order. The divine master who enlightens the soul equips it to inquire into, to learn and teach, the truths which relate to that order, and thus render possible an external, human magisterium in the supernatural order. Those appointed to exercise this human magisterium in the supernatural order were placed by God himself over the highest truths. To them, and to all nations and ages, it was said: 'You are not to call yourselves teachers, because you have only one teacher and you are all brothers.' Such a warning could come only from the mouth of God, and served as a continual reminder of the origin, clarity and power of their message. It was to resound forever down the ages until the end of the world, and its thunder has been rolling ceaselessly for nineteen centuries above all earthly clamour and petty hubbub. *External* revelation and *preaching* would not be properly understood nor assented to by us, nor rendered operative through the co-operation of the human will, unless it was interpreted, explained and enhanced to each human being by the inner light of *character* and *grace*. Augustine, a scholar whose mind went deeper than most into this truth, came across the words in which Christ calls himself 'the beginning who also speaks to you,' and wrote:

> Thus does he speak in the gospel in human form. It was heard outwardly by us so that we might believe, search within, and find in the eternal truth the good and only teacher who instructs all his disciples. There, Lord, I hear your voice which tells us that he who instructs us is speaking to us. Anyone who does not instruct us, however much he says, has nothing to say to us. Now, who

instructs us except the unchanging truth? For even when we are admonished by a changeable creature, we are led into the unchangeable truth where we really learn if we halt and listen and exult with joy when we hear the voice of the bridegroom who brings us back whence we are.'[108]

Thus, this wisest of men, from the episcopal chair of learning on which he sat as a dispenser of lofty truths, spoke in a new, humble manner unknown in the philosophical schools. He said to one and all, learned and unlearned: 'A safer way is that we who speak and you who listen acknowledge ourselves as fellow disciples of a single teacher. Safest of all, and most beneficial, is that you should listen to us not as teachers but as fellow disciples.'[109]

83. Supernatural teaching is thus made up of two elements: *interior light,* and *external revelation* perpetuated throughout the world by preaching and the Church's magisterium. Our divine teacher indicated both those elements. Asked who he was, he replied: 'The PRINCIPLE WHO (or *therefore*) ALSO SPEAKS TO YOU.'*[110] In saying *principle* he referred to the inner light which is in fact the *principle* of all truth and knowledge. The human voice cannot be the principle, nor communicate to anyone else the principle of intelligence; our voice, to be understood, needs to find the first light already present in us. This first light is the key that opens and interprets the meaning of all sensible signs. When he adds: *who also speaks to you* he refers to that external, audible teaching which corresponds to and develops the internal instruction which he, God made man, wished to exercise in our humanity, and then entrust to his Apostles who would hand on to others the things they had heard and understood from him. At the same time, he would continue to give the interior light so that all could understand. Thus, the term 'principle', clearly refers to the *divine nature* and the divine teaching. The next phrase 'and therefore I am speaking to you' refers to *human nature* and the human teaching which depends on it. Both natures are in the one and identical divine person, both teachings are exercised by the same person, with

---

[108] St. Augustine, *Confessions*, 11: 8.

[109] St. Augustine, *Sermons*, 23: 2.

[110] Jn 8: 25.

the second teaching resulting from the first: 'and therefore I am speaking to you',[111] ὅτι καὶ λαλῶ ὑμῖν: as though he were saying: 'I have the power and the right to talk to you because I am the principle of all things who enlightens you: I could not utter such words to you unless I caused you to understand them within.'

84. As I have said, philosophy, which involves *reflection*, runs the risk of being impoverished if it is confined within the ambit of reflection and rejects everything that is and lives outside itself. As a result, many thinkers, imprisoned in the kind of *special thinking* they adopt as philosophers and confuse with *general thinking*, find it difficult to acknowledge that, prior to reflection itself, there exists a light which touches the soul directly and shines on all human beings. This light does not require philosophy in order to shed its radiance; philosophy however needs it as a lamp needs a flame from which to take its light. Self-enclosed philosophy cannot understand the supernatural magisterium to which I refer, because it does not even understand the nature of the natural magisterium of truth. The German school, having adopted such philosophical ignorance, built upon it a whole system, with all the power and profundity of minds working upon falsehood. Hegel's followers unequivocally waged a furious campaign against anything they called 'direct', meaning by this something divine which raises man's mind above scientific and determined thought. They denied God's existence for the curious reason that 'the concept of God is not self-reflective', as if the concept of God presented to man's mind a non-conscious God. Anything outside the realm of reflection or anything which existed without reflection had simply become invisible to them.

85. As I said earlier, the order in which knowledge of supernatural things occurs is similar, so to speak, and of the same character, as the order in which knowledge of natural things occurs. In the case of natural things, there is a first, interior light; similarly there is a first interior light in our knowledge of supernatural things. The initial light in the natural order is truth,

---

[111] I consider that this passage cannot be rendered by: *Prorsus sum is quem vobis dixi.* Cf. Possinus (*Spicilegium Evangelicum* 5, 59), Floderus who published a short work on this section (Uppsala 1773) and almost all the Protestants. This interpretation does violence to the sacred text.

which takes on the various forms that go to make up all knowledge within the natural ambit, including scientific knowledge and the ultimate speculations of philosophy. The first interior light in the supernatural order is again the truth which takes on the various forms that constitute all supernatural cognitions, including the loftiest theological contemplation. The first light is the criterion of natural certainty which man refers to in any case of doubt[112]; the other first light is the proximate criterion of supernatural certainty. This, too, is consulted by anyone who wishes to know whether a teaching proclaimed in the name of God is true or false.[113] This first light grows brighter both through a person's own meditations and instruction from others. The other first light also develops and multiplies either by a person's own reflection or by listening to the words of others. This is why the spirit of God (and his laws) is said to be multiple.[114] In both orders, then, the same pattern is seen, the same hand, the same maker, the same divine teacher. What is the difference, therefore, between the two original truths, between the two orders of cognitions?

The first light which makes the soul of man intelligent is *ideal* and undetermined *being*. The other first light is also *being*, not purely ideal but rather *subsistent* and living being. God is subsistent being: he himself declares: 'I am BEING.'[115] Having used the personal pronoun, 'I', he revealed himself as *person;*

[112] I refer the reader to St. Augustine's *The Teacher*, in which the learned saint shows how God is the only teacher who reveals to the mind even natural, human truth. The great bishop says in wonderful words: 'In all matters where we have some understanding, we refer not to some person speaking to us from without, but to the truth, presiding from within over the mind itself, although we may indeed be advised by words to make the reference. He who is referred to, teaches. It is Christ, that is, the unchangeable power of God and everlasting wisdom, who is said to dwell within. Every rational soul refers to this everlasting wisdom, but he is open to each only to the extent that the person's GOOD OR BAD WILL allows. If the individual errs, he does so not because of some defect in the truth to which he refers, just as often it is not any defect in the light which prevents our seeing'* (no. 38).

[113] 'All your sons shall be taught by the Lord,'* Isaiah had prophesied (54: 15).

[114] Job 11: 6; Wisdom 7: 22.

[115] Exod 3: 14.

being, as object, is the Word, and this object-being is person, about whom is written: 'In the beginning was the Word, and the Word was with God, and the Word was God.'[116] The same Word elsewhere calls himself *principle*:[117] principle of every intelligence and all knowledge, because the principle of knowledge is the first *object*, and the first and essential object which contains all objects is being. The other objects of thought are objects through being; being is object *per se*. The idea, therefore, is 'being' intuited by us, but it is not the WORD; the latter, not the former, is subsistence. The former is being which conceals its personship and reveals only its undetermined, impersonal objectivity. The human mind which intuits the idea does not grasp the personship of being, nor its subsistence and thus does not see Almighty God. But the one who sees the Word, even as in a mirror darkly, sees God. So, if natural science somehow terminates in what Boethius calls *sola rerum PRIMAEVA RATIO* [*THE SOLE* PRIMAL REASON for things], supernatural knowledge reaches out to that which is at the same time *nullius indigens VIVAX MENS* [the LIVING MIND lacking nothing].*[118]

Man, who is a *real* subject, cannot halt before the idea; he aspires to unite himself with what is real. But the real given to us in nature is finite. The idea, which leads us to know and love this finite reality, at the same time shows it as finite. The idea, however, is infinite, and reveals the possibility, the necessity of another infinite real being which is not given to us as human beings. Because we extend our desire to what we know, we reach out to what is infinite, which the idea of being shows must be. Without what is infinite neither the potency of the idea would be exhausted, nor would the knowledge possible to us be completed; nor would our desire for knowledge, to unity and enjoyment be satisfied. But this infinite real is given to us initially in the supernatural light which God freely bestows on us.

---

[116] Jn 1: 1.

[117] Jn 8: 25.

[118] 'Philosophy is a kind of love and study of Wisdom, and of friendship for Wisdom. I do not mean the wisdom found in certain crafts or in mechanical knowledge and information, but that Wisdom which, lacking nothing, is a living mind and the sole primal reason for things'* (*In Porphyry*, Dial. I Ex. Victorin.).

Perception of this substantial and subsistent light is perception of the divine Word. In that Word, man's desire comes to rest and, in this way, even in this present life, is satiated.

86. The teacher about whom we are speaking is distinguished from all other teachers, none of whom would ever dream, when imparting to their students different sciences and subjects, of lecturing about themselves. Imagine what would happen if a professor, even in a German university, were vain enough to begin a lecture like this: 'Gentlemen, this year I shall talk to you about myself; my subject will be me in person.' His listeners, however high-minded and however enthusiastic they were about supporting their professors, would be carried away not by admiration but by compassion, and would sadly inform the Rector of the University of the misfortune that had befallen such a great intellect. But the unique teacher to whom I was referring aroused neither compassion nor amusement when he specifically said to people that the knowledge he taught was that which made him known to them. One German professor's envy was indeed aroused by such divine words, but in vain.[119]

We acknowledge that the teacher who speaks to us in this way is also the proper and greatest object of knowledge and science, known in the very instant it is communicated as that which is *per se* intelligible. This teacher has merely to say: 'Here I am, look at me!' and we are taught. This is the true art of teaching. But the teacher to whom I refer is God, in whom all things are contained, even those things which are not God but are created by God. These too have a kind of existence in him 'who sustains all things by his powerful word'.[120] Indeed, all things are intelligible in God since God is intelligible by essence and, in so far as he is intelligible, is called the Word. Consequently, the person who knows God, the Word of God, knows the all, because the all is found in the Word. No one can attain to such complete knowledge of things unless he attains to him in whom all things are contained, on whom they are based and joined together in

---

[119] Strauss, in his *Life of Jesus*, remarked that Jesus was always talking about himself, and that his whole teaching was based on knowledge of himself who alone was able to save. Strauss was shocked by this and scornful about it.

[120] Heb 1: 3.

unity. No great philosopher ever attempted to synthesise his own cognitions, without referring them to the Divine Being. No one thought that he had to find elsewhere the fulfilment of what can be humanly known. No one ever considered human knowledge final and absolute until, through speculation, it became a stream flowing into the sea of being and wisdom where it evaporated, as it were, and then condensed into the water of knowledge.

87. The *idea* is an empty form, as I said; it contains not the *fullness of being* but an outline of it. It offers us only the shadow of perfect being. The idea, because it does not contain perfect being within itself, does not offer it to mankind. But the Word, who is supernatural light and fullness of being, contains the fullness of that being, of which a pale sketch is visible in the idea. Sense, that is, the ability to feel corporeal things in the natural order and even finite, incorporeal things such as the soul, comes to the aid of the intellect, that is, the power of intuiting the idea. But how poor such aid is! As Dante says:

> '... behind the senses
> You see how short are reason's wings.'[121]

In fact, we do not possess any organ or other sensory power which can sense God. Relative to divine things, therefore, which alone can fill out the idea, we have an empty, powerless idea. For the work of creation to reach all possible perfection, the human being, provided with understanding by means of the idea, needed the additional boon of a feeling co-extensive with the idea. But since the idea embraces both finite and infinite, it could not be properly aided or as it were counter-balanced except by a feeling of equal breadth. God, however, could not be numbered amongst the beings of nature; he always remains distinct from them, limited as they are by their condition as created beings. Human nature, therefore, could have no feeling of God. On the other hand, God's work cannot remain imperfect. What is not included in nature nor owes its existence to nature is added by God in his operations purely out of his own generosity and infinite holiness. Revelation tells us that God created our first parents in a state of supernatural grace. Even if

[121] *Paradiso*, 2: 56–57.

[87]

we did not know that this revelation were true, what wisdom it would display! How it would harmonise and fit with divine perfections! Who could have devised such a profoundly reasonable and philosophical message given to human beings before they began to philosophise and before systematic knowledge was discovered! Even as late as this, in an age which claims to be urbane and philosophical, there are still a number who have not managed to grasp how fitting and suitable it was to God's attributes that the Creator should add a supernatural light to the natural light. Because they do not see the connection between the idea and natural feeling, and how disproportionate and inadequate the latter is to the former, they still do not realise that the natural light is insufficient for all human beings. If, even today, there are people who rely on natural wisdom to reach this conclusion, who in less cultured times could have conceived such a revelation? This was far beyond human capacity. But once we can see, or are shown this disproportion, we realise how human beings, the sublime work of the perfect being, would be like children born with one leg long, the other short, if God had not endowed them with a supernatural sense. Human beings did have a natural sense, but nothing more in their essential nature, and although what they had was adequate for human nature, it did not satisfy the one who wrote: 'In wisdom, you have made them all.'[122] It is human nature, therefore, not the unknowing and unreflecting individual, which pleads as it were for the gift of the supernatural as a poor man pleads simply because he is poor. It is reason, with its own light, that enables us to be aware of the lack of some other light to complete the first, although we cannot imagine what form this other light will take. It is the human heart which insists on possessing as much reality as it can conceive. Through the idea, the heart conceives a kind of confused infinity and throws itself into the void in an attempt to shatter what it sees as the narrow limits of nature.

88. The Creator, who had made mankind, knew from the beginning the mysterious emptiness which was so inexplicable to man. He himself both enabled man to understand it, and himself filled it. He allowed man's adversary, who wished to destroy human nature by flattering its self-esteem and

122 Ps 104: 24.

[88]

persuading man that he could become like God himself, to ruin God's handiwork. He allowed him to fall. But when we fell through disobedience, spurning God's supernatural graces and becoming incapable and unworthy of them, when all our powers were sorely affected, the Creator healed us and restored us to a more wonderful and more sublime status than before. This was not the work of the first light of natural reason nor of the idea, but of the other first light, the light of supernatural reason. It was the work of the WORD of God.

God, the teacher whom Plato wished would come to earth to reveal to us the essential truths and to provide us with certainty, is at one and the same time light, the sole, essential object of what is knowable, a person, the divine Word who became flesh and appeared among men as true man without ceasing to be true God; his name was JESUS Christ, Saviour, Anointed One of God. He taught us about the Father, having said to those who had faith in him: 'No one has ever seen God. It is the only Son, who is close to the Father's heart, who has made him known.'[123]

Again, to one of his disciples he said: 'Philip, he who has seen me, has seen the Father.'[124] And again, he sent the Spirit of truth as he had promised: 'When the Spirit of truth comes, he will guide you into all truth; for he will not speak on his own, but will speak whatever he hears and he will declare to you the things that are to come. He will glorify me because he will take what is mine and declare it to you.'[125]

89. Thus the Triune God was revealed to human beings: the *Master* revealed himself and fulfilled in them everything knowable. Nature and systematic knowledge had set us on the road to the infinite being by a threefold path so long that God could never be reached. Then, unexpectedly, human beings were transported to the infinitely remote location which implicitly they wished to reach. They found themselves there miraculously, not by any reasoning of their own but by virtue of faith. They believed in this Being:

'As in the primary truth which man believes'.[126]

123 Jn 1: 18.
124 Jn 14: 9.
125 Jn 16: 13.
126 [Dante], *Paradiso* 2: 44–45.

They believed him and in him and confided themselves to him, still unaware of the relationship between the eminent position they already occupied and the threefold path on which they had ventured with their reason. Later, by means of reasoning, they fell back upon faith and acknowledged that the goal they were pursuing and towards which the three paths of knowledge converged — the only point that was unattainable because infinitely remote — was the very point in which faith had so unexpectedly placed them. The fact is that *being* presents itself to us in a threefold form, as *reality*, as *idea*, as *energy*. Each of these forms reduces to infinite being as to its final term of actuation, as though human beings, in some divine dream pursue the *infinite reality*, which they do not find in nature. However, they clearly realise that if there were some infinite reality with all corresponding attributes, it would have to be infinite being itself. They pursue something *infinitely knowable* which exists only potentially in the idea, but they also realise that if an object which is intrinsically intelligible were really and actually infinite, with all the corresponding attributes, it too could only be infinite being. Finally, they pursue the *infinite love* which, in them, is merely an endlessly disappointed capacity to love, always betrayed by the blandishments and unreliability of all natural things. Infinite love, they see clearly, is impossible unless there is an infinite reality, infinitely known and as such a most lovable object. They realise that if there were such a term of love, it could only be infinite being itself, all-being, all-good. Each of the three forms leads thought to the same term, to the identical infinite being. These three paths were signposted by the three divisions of philosophy I have already mentioned. Plato seems to have seen that each of them must inevitably terminate in God, in whom he acknowledged the 'cause of the subsistence of things, the explanation of our understanding, the order of existence.'[127] But who accepted

---

[127] St. Augustine speaks as follows of this interpretation of Plato: 'Perhaps those are praised more highly because they understood Plato (the Alexandrian philosophers who lived in Christian times were able to interpret Plato so that he seemed closer to Christian teaching), the foremost of the Gentile philosophers, and followed him more eagerly and truly. They feel about God in such a way that they find in him the CAUSE OF SUBSISTENCE, the EXPLANATION OF OUR UNDERSTANDING and the ORDER FOR LIVING. Of

what he said? Who believed the unreliable message of a man admitting that he awaited a divine master to reveal to him the truth about such things? Could anyone who believed or understood Plato's lofty conception be satisfied with a good whose existence he knew, but of whose presence he was deprived. This was merely a negative, indicative way of knowing God; it was not knowledge arising from perception, feeling, fruition.

Then, with one problem solved, an even more complicated one arose: 'If those three things are so different, how can they be reduced to one? And if they *do* reduce to one, how do they appear so different?' The doctrine of the TRINITY offers the most complete and most profound solution to this problem confronting the human spirit, which has always considered it as an unconquered enigma. It places before man the doctrine of being in all its forms. The doctrine of the most venerable of mysteries comes down from heaven like a golden dome to cover the edifice of natural knowledge. Were it not in place, the edifice would be open to the wind and rain, and human beings (philosophers included) would be condemned to live ill at ease with themselves, searching for something they never find. This is the *supernatural dimension of knowledge* which is just as necessary as the *supernatural dimension of life.* Just as human existence is not everlasting and blissful but becomes such, thanks to a supernatural gift, so human knowledge, which is not complete and absolute, becomes such as a result of supernatural enlightenment and faith.

90. As I have already said, the foundations of wisdom are built upon knowledge of truth. Consequently, a new apprehension of truth provides the foundation for a new form of wisdom — a fuller apprehension gives rise to a fuller form of wisdom. Whatever form it may take, natural knowledge remains imperfect but, united with supernatural knowledge, achieves its perfect form. Human wisdom, therefore, cannot be other than

these three aspects, the first is taken as referring to the natural order, the second to the rational order, and the third to the moral order'* (*The City of God*, 8: 4). He later speaks of the Platonists who spoke of: 'The CREATOR OF ALL THINGS, the ONE WHO ILLUSTRATES THE TRUTH and THE BOUNTEOUS GIVER OF HAPPINESS'* (*ibid.*, Chapter 5). Again, he says that they knew God as 'the MAKER of all creation, the LIGHT of things to be known and the GOOD of things to be done'* (*ibid.*, Chapter 9).

imperfect, a preliminary draft, a search for wisdom, as the philosophers themselves admitted. The founder himself of the Italian school rejected as arrogant the title 'scholar', calling himself instead a 'student' of wisdom.[128] Only with the advent of supernatural knowledge were the foundations laid of a new and perfect form of wisdom that does not merely pursue truth, but possesses and enjoys it.

90a. We come now to the second and formal constituent of wisdom. This resides in the will when the will, displaying its full vigour, addresses, assents, approves and submits itself, together with all its powers, to known truth. This is the true concept of virtue. We act in a virtuous and orderly way when we direct the desires of our will and the acts to which they give rise so that they conform to the objective order of entia or, as Saint Augustine puts it: 'Perfect justice consists in loving more important things more and less important things less.'*[129] Now, at times, the *subjective, limited order* of human nature clashes with the *objective order*, which is truth. In this conflict, we cannot continue to be just without some sacrifice. We must sacrifice what is, or what we take to be, our own good, in favour of the absolute order, good and venerable in itself, which is devoid of any specifically subjective relationship. If, however, we study man confined within nature's limits, we can see that although the objective order is present to him in the idea, its reality is not given to him. Natural man, as I said earlier, perceives only a part of reality, the finite reality of the world (although not all, or even most of it). In the idea, however, he intuits the whole of ideal being. This imbalance between the *ideal* and the *real* which makes knowledge incomplete is also the imbalance which makes it impossible for us to achieve perfect virtue. On the one hand, the idea reveals to us the entire universal, absolute order of things as a moral necessity from which we cannot dissent without our being unjust or blameworthy; on the other, it does

---

[128] 'Now, although those who, in some way, appear to rise above their fellow men by their praiseworthy life are called men of wisdom, when he was asked what his profession was, he replied that he was a philosopher, in other words a student and lover of wisdom since, in his view, to call oneself wise was a MOST ARROGANT claim'* (St Augustine, *The City of God*, 8: 2).

[129] *On True Religion*, c. 47.

[90a]

not endow us with the power to translate this order into action. Where then do we obtain such power? This comes from the order of real, not ideal things. Reality is concerned with action; ideality simply shows us what is to be done. We must therefore find strength within ourselves or in external reality, that is, in that sphere of real things which is allotted to us. However, this sphere is extremely limited. Neither infinite reality nor the greater part of finite realities find any place in it. It follows that the strength which we can derive from the real entities allotted to us by nature is not commensurate with the greatness of the ideal order which confronts us as an inexorable law. Indeed, the finite things that we perceive conspire at times, as I said, against that law. Instead of helping us to obey it, they tempt us to violate it. This is precisely because the finite order which they reveal is different from and therefore very often opposed to the infinite order of ideality. To make up somehow for this lamentable lack of real strength which prevents us from fulfilling the great moral design in which our eminent dignity consists, what did the most outstanding philosophers do? I am not referring to those who despaired of harmonising the real and the ideal orders. Unwilling and incapable of renouncing the real order, they rejected the ideal and decreed that we should be content to be matter or sense and thus, against our nature, should calmly yield to the pleasures of the moment, spurred on by the thought of death. I am not concerned with such philosophers. I ask how the most outstanding philosophers endeavoured to help us to find the powers denied us by reality, but still necessary for fulfilling the law proper to the ideal order. There is no doubt that these lovers of what is good did all they could. They were aware that human beings sought in vain — in the limited area of reality allotted to them — for the moral strength they required. But instead of providing them with the strength to do good, limited reality often came into conflict with the objective order and increased the power of limited, blind subjective instinct. Our philosophers endeavoured therefore to alienate us from real things and to confine us within the order of ideas. They extolled the idea as something infinitely beautiful, and with all their eloquence exhorted us to fix our gaze solely on this divine light, to be satisfied with her wonderful countenance, and consider ourselves happy. And in order to ensure that such a lofty precept

[90a]

would not intimidate us, causing us to feel that an even more onerous duty might be imposed upon us instead of an increase of strength to fulfil our duty, these philosophers extolled the power of the human will, which previously they had held as weak and in need of strengthening. They now claimed that the only thing over which we had power was the energy which they prescribed. The best philosophers considered actual beings and goods — which are the sole sources enabling us to act effectively — to be inadequate for providing us with the moral vigour we required. On the contrary, these things were seen as the reason for moral weakness and as obstacles to virtue. The philosophers' only recourse was to require, from the very idea which imposed the obligation, the power to implement it. In Plato's *Phaedo*, Socrates is at pains to show why the philosopher must withdraw completely from *sensible things* and find a safe haven in *ideas*. This implied resorting to philosophic abstraction and abandoning the body and bodily things, whilst awaiting the blessed moment of total alienation from them at death.

> Since the body places countless obstacles (to wisdom) because it naturally needs to be fed, and in addition the diseases from which it suffers prevent the search for truth, it fills us with amorous desires, greed, fear, numerous fantasies, in short, with numerous empty promises which produce nothing important or true. The body alone, with its multiple, covetous desires, urges us on to warfare, to sedition, to armed conflict. Everything is done out of love for money which we are driven to pursue thanks to the body which makes use of it. Thus, all these things deter us from the study of philosophy. Finally, even if it gives us some respite and we manage to apply ourselves to anything whatsoever, the body once more thwarts us completely by disturbing our spirit as we pursue our inquiries. We are stunned as though by a series of blows and, as a result of such an obstacle, cannot attain the clarity of truth. Moreover, we have already clearly established that if we wish to understand anything in its pure state, we have to abandon the body and see things from the spirit's point of view. It is clear, therefore, that we shall take possession of what we long for, and which we profess to cherish, that is, wisdom, when we are dead, as reason shows, but not while

[90a]

> we are still alive. In other words, if we cannot through our
> bodily powers grasp anything in its pure state, then either
> we are quite unable to attain knowledge, or we reach it
> solely after death. In death, the spirit itself will be sep-
> arated from the body, but not before. Thus, while we live,
> we shall draw near to knowledge if we have as little truck
> with the body as possible. We shall have nothing to do
> with the body unless impelled by urgent necessity. We
> shall not allow ourselves to be satisfied by it but keep aloof
> from its contagion until God himself releases us.[130]

The greatest non-Christian philosophers were deeply mistrustful of the sinister influence exerted on us by the limited
span of reality which nature allows us to perceive. Consequently, they neither expected any help in their attempt to be
virtuous and to acquire wisdom, nor found it possible (until a
portion of real ens had been lost to them) to acquire the wisdom
which they so much longed for. And this was only *natural
wisdom*; they knew no other. They provided no other hope, and
even this was conditioned by the need to abandon reality as
though it were poison, communicating with it as rarely as possible and only in dire necessity, seeking a haven in ideas alone,
some secret habitation in which to hide away, isolated and dead,
as it were, to the world.

91. And this was considered the most wonderful endeavour
of human reason! Reason could ascend no further, nor express
any truer or profounder truths. This was the only possible solution to the great problem. Ideas are certainly divine, the only
divine element to be found in nature even after the whole
universe has been scanned inch by inch. Moreover, divine things
do not defer to anything. There is nothing comparable to them.
They determine what is of value; anything that runs counter to
them becomes contemptible. This is what the understanding
reads in ideas, admiring the authority emanating from them,
and gazing upon their incomparable beauty.

What risks and suffering have been undergone by lovers of
these ideas, as I said. Archimedes, for example, was unaware of
the Romans' entry into Syracuse; this is one demonstration of
vigour of mind which withdraws momentarily from any

---

[130] *Phaedo.*

[91]

sense-experience. Other examples are the travels and poverty of Anacharsis; the vigils and labours of Aristotle;[131] Carneades' forgetting to eat.[132] The privations and sufferings of so many others, all prove that the love of knowledge may acquire, like any other passion, an almost infinite power over man's soul. But they do not prove that we ever find complete satisfaction either in other unworthy passions or in this most noble passion for knowledge. We cannot sustain continuous mental contemplation; on the contrary, how short is the time we can give to such absorption in thought! How few there are who, disregarding sensible things, wish to live or can live devoted solely to intangible ideas and as it were suspended in them, or have the leisure to pursue and develop such fatiguing, natural delight! Does it follow perhaps that even the few who, by their laudable endeavours, ascend to the realms of pure ideas and remain there for a few moments, only to fall back subsequently into the natural and ordinary realm of reality,[133] order and arrange all the real actions in their life in accordance with the ideas they contemplate? Rather the world of finite sense-experience is lying in wait to engage them in battle. It allows them to travel freely to the world of ideas knowing perfectly well that they will not thereby escape and, after a brief absence, will be back. Just as an angler, who has caught an enormous fish, slackens and pays out the line so that the fish can move about in the water for a while, but carefully reels it in when it is exhausted, so too often the

---

[131] See Diogenes Laertius. in *Aristotle*.

[132] 'He so marvellously devoted himself to study that when he sat down to eat, he reflected so deeply that he forgot to reach out to the table. But with Melissa, who took the place of a wife, — her duty limited to not interrupting his studies, but helping when he was hungry — he used his right hand as necessary. So he enjoyed life with his spirit, while surrounded by a body which he treated as alien and redundant'* (Valerius Maximus, bk. 8, c. 7, n. 5). However, in this very passage from Valerius Maximus there is enough to remind readers that this most studious of men did not always have his spirit surrounded by a body that was like someone else's useless garment. This exaggerated praise involves a blatant contradiction.

[133] Speaking of pure ideas, St. Augustine says: 'Few are privileged to attain the cutting-edge of the mind; and even when they get as far as they can, they are driven back. All that we have is transient knowledge of what is intransient'* (*On the Trinity*, 12, no. 23).

blandishment of the sensible world works upon us. This happens because, from birth, we bear within ourselves the seeds of evil and the tinder of concupiscence. We feel that we escape the seduction of the world when we manage to detach our mind from it by pure abstractions, which we then pursue wildly and arrogantly. But at the same time our many evil and shameful acts give bad example to others. They get the impression that, from the truths we have pondered, we have derived only the pride which causes us to sin all the more gravely. Plato was right to admit that, in our present life, natural wisdom might certainly be conceived, but is never fully achieved. This explains why he thought that good people should expect it only after death. Even the Stoics, who greatly exaggerated the power of free-will, doubted or completely denied that there was any time or place where wise men, whom they conceived mentally and described so wonderfully, would be found.[134]

92. Natural philosophy is thus convinced and admits its incapacity for making men wise, even if we are speaking only about wisdom seen as an idea in the light proper to nature. But God, the teacher of men, made both things simultaneously, that is, he extended infinitely the concept of wisdom and endowed us with the strength to actuate it in ourselves. Thus, one Father of the Church rightly remarks that those assisted by faith could accomplish much more by their deeds than philosophers could conceive and desire, or teach with words.[135] God achieved this by creating a balance between idea and reality which is not present in human nature.

As I said, the idea can reach out freely to infinity, revealing universal being. It thereby reveals the full order of being to which the will, a faculty which naturally follows the intellect must unite. On the other hand, *natural reality* offers us only a tiny crumb of being which cannot contain the full and absolute order revealed by the idea, but a minimal order which can be

---

[134] See Justus Lipsius, *Manuductio ad Stoicam Philosophiam.*

[135] St. Ambrose says of Abraham: 'Abraham was clearly a great man, and famous for his many virtues which philosophy, however much it wished, was powerless to match. Moreover, what philosophy imagined was less than Abraham's actual achievement, just as the simple faith of truth is greater than the boastful deceit of eloquence'* (*On the Patriarch Abraham*, bk. 1, c. 2).

[92]

enclosed in such a tiny portion of being. I also said that man, as a real being, can only be moved to act by a real being — not by an idea, therefore, but by his own activity and his own instincts or by the stimulus of external reality. As a result of will power, he can, to a certain extent, actuate his mind in the idea and be delighted with it, but for a brief period, and only then by leaving his other powers inactive and making an almost superhuman effort that few can achieve. But the lesser powers immediately come into play oppressed by the very idleness which has afflicted them and longing, as it were, for revenge. At this point, sensible reality appears to become a more zealous fomenter of disorder than before.

Let us suppose that just as we *intuit* the whole of ideal being in an implicit, simple mode, which can then be indefinitely unfolded, so we *perceive* the whole of real being in an equally implicit, simple mode, which also is capable of unfolding indefinitely. In this case it is clear that the great, immense exigency of the idea, which imposed moral duty, would find a correspondence in us in a fount of equally great, immense power, suitable for carrying out the imposed duty. If this were to happen, all finite realities would be known, or could be known and considered as parts, or rather as minuscule, transient particles of the whole of real being in which they would be lost, like drops in the ocean. And the identical order would be present in this reality as in the idea. Moreover, this real order would give us sufficient stimulus and strength to actuate the *ideal* with the efficacy of the will. There would no longer be any discrepancy or invincible contrast between the ideal and the real orders. One would call forth the other; they would kiss, as it were. The will, no longer divided between two contenders, would be able to devote itself with a single act to both as united in the *identity of being*. The consequence would be perfect justice, and wisdom possessed in peace.

Our supposition, however, is no longer a dream; it is not something we might desire God to do; it is no longer something that we presume God would do in intimate accord with his divine attributes. The gospel has been proclaimed to show us that this is what God, the Creator and sustainer of mankind, has in fact done, and what the gospel does in all those who freely receive it: 'And he gave them the power to become sons of

[92]

God.'[136] The Word is 'the character of the substance of the Father',[137] that is, the Word through whom God is rendered perceptible. That is the force of the Greek word *character*.

Christianity, therefore, has taught that the Word is the character, or face of God as he is often called in the Scriptures, and is imprinted on the souls of those who accept Christ's baptism with faith. Their wills, directed to him and clinging to him, are sanctified and justified. As a result, those who have received the impress of the Word and consequently perceive him are thereby given a communication with being in its full, infinite reality, albeit in an implicit and extremely simple mode. It is like a tiny, fertile seed, entrusted to the soul to cultivate and develop with its own acts and co-operation. Thus we have been granted not only full knowledge but also the necessary energy to conform with the demands of knowledge. We now possess the two elements of perfect knowledge. So, consistent with this sublime doctrine, we find written in the sacred books: 'THE FOUNT OF WISDOM, THE WORD OF GOD IN THE HIGHEST.'*[138]

93. In the present life, it is true, we have been given this full, absolute and infinite reality in an implicit and potential manner. On the other hand, the finite reality of the world acts upon us explicitly and immediately and, through its *mode of action*, with greater efficiency than the infinite reality. We still have to struggle, therefore, against the poverty and limitations of finite reality which would seek to make us exclusively its own, preventing us from devoting ourselves to the all. Here the clash and the struggle is not directly between reality and idea but between

---

[136] Jn 1: 12–13.

[137] χαρακτὴρ ὑποστάσεως τοῦ πατρός (Hebrews 1: 3). The character is what allows us to know something or, as Euripides' annotator explains (Hecuba 1. 379) σφραγὶς καὶ σημεῖον [the imprint and distinguishing mark]. Consequently, what we call the Word is the one who reveals the Father. However, because he cannot reveal the Father by some 'accident' of his — there are no accidents in the Word — he does so by his substance, according to Chrysostom's explanation of the passage in St. Paul: τὸ ὅμοιον εἶναι κατὰ πάντα, κατ' οὐσίαν [the very same being in all things, and in substance]. The Word, therefore, or the character imprinted on the souls of the faithful, according to Christian doctrines, is the real (infinite) being manifest in himself whom we later know to be a person, the second person of the Trinity.

[138] Eccles 1: 5.

finite reality with its greater urgency, and infinite reality which strengthens and draws us by means of its greater dignity and grandeur. Providence, which provides for our good from on high, left us this difficulty to overcome so that virtue and wisdom might be won by our generous efforts and not be attributed to us without our consent and co-operation. It is precisely here that we find the summit of man's excellence and glory: as far as possible, we are the authors of our own wisdom and our own virtue. God made this possible for those who were linked to him. He then left us the duty of actuating the potentiality he had conferred upon us. Perception of that infinite reality, that is, of the Word of God, may be converted to an even greater actuality by the grace he imparts. The Word can unfold without limit and bestow upon us all the moral force we need. This incomparable strength can overcome any suffering, any pleasure by which the finite, thriving reality of the world attempts to lead us astray. All this is made fully available to man when he is united to, and assisted by God. That is why the apostle says: 'I can do all things in him who strengthens me.'[139]

94. Christianity derived from God's divine assistance a new and profound teaching which was completely original and inaccessible to philosophers. It was, nonetheless, so compatible with God's nature on the one hand and with man's on the other, so coherent with all rational and revealed truths, that reason itself could do no other than approve it and wonder how something not its own — which it did not possess and could never have discerned — could be bestowed upon it as though it were its own. But according to Christ's teaching, the Word, when conjoined to human beings, imparts his Spirit which, by sanctifying the human will also sanctifies the human being, provided we remain free and do not oppose it. This is the first sanctification which both requires and makes possible human co-operation. It is *sanctity*, but it cannot yet be called *wisdom* since the meaning of this word would seem restricted to something acquired by us through our positive, open co-operation. Nevertheless, the seeds of wisdom are found in such sanctity. From now on, God and humans always work together provided we do not willingly flee from such blessed companionship. God,

[139] Phil 4: 13.

[94]

for his part, has instituted positive, external means called *sacraments* to which he has allotted some determined grace. We also have the faculty of carrying out numerous acts of virtue. These include internal and external acts of worship, all of which produce an increase of inner grace. The exercise of all this activity on the human and divine planes leads to continuous growth in us of the Spirit of the Word which is the Spirit of holiness and of perfection. The word *spirit* expresses most aptly not only that which impels, but the impulse itself and the operating instinct of an intellectual nature which derives its activity from the vitality and reality of the light which illuminates the depths of its understanding. In our case, this light is the Word which dwells in the very intellective essence of the soul and invests the will with its Spirit without our needing to resort to any act of reflection. Now I have already stated that this Spirit of the Word is Being, just as the Word is, but under another form. The Spirit is Being as lovable and *loved per se*, and hence operative and perfective *per se*. Its dwelling place, therefore, is the will, and its effect and condition in us is holy activity to a greater or lesser degree. Moreover, it has been revealed that the Spirit has a *personal subsistence* which is not confused with the other two persons from whom this third person proceeds.

95. When the two constituents of *wisdom*, which, as I said, are *knowledge* and *virtue*, are transferred from the natural to the supernatural order, they are verified and realised so sublimely that both are found to consist in a kind of contact and interchange with God himself. Perception of the Word holds the place of knowledge; the Holy Spirit, living and working in the human soul, holds the place of virtue.[140] This explains why Scripture says of Wisdom, which has virtue as its formal part: 'He himself (the Creator) created it in the Holy Spirit.'[141] It is this Spirit which fights on behalf of man, in man and with man

---

[140] 'But he who is united to the Lord becomes one Spirit with him'* ([1] Cor 6: 17). 'But if by the Spirit you put to death the deeds of the body you will live. For all who are led by the Spirit of God are sons of God'* (Rom 8: 13–14). 'The Spirit himself intercedes for us with sighs too deep for words'* (Rom 8: 26).

[141] Eccles 1: 9.

against the flesh, that is, against that portion of finite reality which, in its exclusiveness, threatens to disrupt the order of full and infinite reality.[142]

95a. Now the divine Spirit, through his effects and gifts, unfolds in us contemporaneously with the unfolding of knowledge or supernatural light, which in the baptised is the divine Word. Such unfolding divides the just in the Church into four classes. First are uneducated people who work manually. These are guided and kept far from evil by reverence and *fear* of God, whose majesty, which they fear and reverence, they know intimately. This first mode of *wisdom* is of much more worth than any *body of knowledge* possessed by those who do not use it to live a good life. As Scripture says: 'Better the God-fearing man who knows less and is less clever, than the intelligent person who transgresses the law of the Most High.'[143] In the uneducated, there is no conscious, theoretical knowledge distinct from action. There is only one form of knowledge, which is both light and moral instinct and, I would say, contains only the *art* of right acting. However, when an unlearned person applies his mind to learning, theory is separated out and ideal *knowledge* appears distinct from *piety*; the former is pure speculation, the latter action. Although this piety is derived from ideal knowledge and is conditioned by it, nevertheless knowledge is not the proximate cause of the action, which is based directly on a practical recognition of truth in the body of knowledge.

95b. These people who possess *knowledge* and *piety* constitute a second category of the just, whose mode of *wisdom* is more highly developed than that of the unlettered. But being learned and pious does not guarantee prudence in spiritual government or in achieving great things on behalf of those governed. To attain this higher stage, acute *counsel* and ardent *fortitude* are required. Such counsel implies speed and firmness of judgment in arriving at rules for judging and ordering

[142] 'Walk by the Spirit and do not gratify the desires of the flesh. For the desires of the flesh are against the Spirit, and the desires of the Spirit are against the flesh, for these are opposed to each other'* (Gal 5: 16–17).

[143] 'Better the God-fearing man who lacks intelligence, than the highly prudent man who transgresses the law of the Almighty'* (Eccles 19: 24).

[95a–95b]

matters[144] and in finding the most suitable means for reaching a goal. Such means include the countless, factual circumstances which escape ordinary sight and are already taken into account and incorporated into the solution. The fortitude of which I am speaking consists in a disposition enabling us to overcome all obstacles, to feel no fear of obstacles, to be sure that we can overcome them by heavenly piety, by constancy of spirit, and especially by trust in the arbiter of all the facts that move us to act and reproduce his very own thought and constancy. After this third category of just souls, in whom there shines a much more developed mode of wisdom[145] than in the previous two, the fourth category is made up of those rare souls who, exalted above all finite things, live enveloped in the infinity of God. In this mental contemplation, they communicate reflectively with God, re-immersing in him themselves and the things that make up the universe, while God re-immerses himself in them, and through them in the things that make up the universe. From this source, they also derive, by a process of abstraction, a lofty, noble and ideal knowledge of divine things which pertains to the most perfect form of *Wisdom*, from which they draw what is called 'understanding'.

95c. Something analogous to these four classes of wise people exists even in the natural order. Plato,[146] showing great

---

[144] To this category belongs the wisdom whose function it was, according to the ancients, to *judge*, to *order* and *govern rightly*. 'In common parlance... it has generally been the case that those who order things rightly and govern them well are called wise'* (*Summa contra Gentiles*, bk. 1, chap. 1). — (Aristotle, *Metaphysics*., bk. 1) —'He judges and orders everything'* (*S.T.*, I-II, q. 57, art. 2).

[145] This type of wisdom may be designated by the special term *prudence*, which distinguishes it from the more perfect form characteristic of the fourth category. In this connection, St. Thomas writes: 'Wisdom and Prudence differ. Wisdom is knowledge of divine things and pertains therefore to CONTEMPLATION: (Jn 28: 28). "The fear of the Lord is Wisdom": prudence, in the proper sense, is knowledge of human things. That is why Scripture says (Prov 10: 23): "Wisdom is prudence for man" because the science of human things is called prudence'* (*In Ep. 1 ad Cor.*, chap. 1). It is always the same wisdom, but is given different names according to how it unfolds. When completely unfolded, it retains its own name.

[146] At the end of the 6th book of the *Republic*, Plato distinguishes *what is sensible* from *what is intelligible*. He divides each of them into two genera.

[95c]

perspicacity, and followed substantially by Aristotle,[147] rightly
wanted the term *knowledge* to be given to the science of mathematical and similar truths which are deduced from certain

The sensible is divided into images and representations, called *shadows*, and
into corporeal things themselves, which Plato calls *likenesses* of intelligible
things. The intelligible is then divided into the genus found by the mind
when it starts from sensible things which it presumes to be true, and into the
genus found when the mind moves from the same sensible things, but does
not suppose them to be true. Rather, it considers them as they are: mere
suppositions, shadows, likenesses. In this way, the mind arrives at eternal,
divine things and at God, the principle of all things. 'And when I speak of the
other division of the intelligible,' Socrates says to Glaucon, 'you will
understand me to speak of that other sort of knowledge which reason herself
attains by the power of demonstration, no longer using *suppositions* as
principles, but only as presuppositions — that is, as steps and points of
departure into a world which is above presuppositions, in order that she may
soar beyond them to the principle of the universe. Then, clinging to those
things which are inherent in the principle, by successive steps she goes
forward right to the end without the aid of any sensible object, but by means
of ideas, moving to ideas, and through ideas.' Plato wants only the
knowledge of this divine principle of the universe to be called *understanding*;
the knowledge of geometrical and similar propositions, which start from
certain presuppositions, are to be called *cogitation*. Between them both lie
opinion which has sensible things as its object and embraces *faith* and
imagination in so far as sensible things are those called *likenesses* or *shadows*.

[147] In book 6 of *Ethics*, Aristotle posits five things which always stand in
relationship to truth (*quae se habent ad verum*). He calls them *art, science,
wisdom, prudence* and *understanding*. If we take wisdom and put it together
with *understanding*, we find a classification corresponding to that made
much earlier of the gifts of the Holy Spirit by Isaiah. What a wonderful
conjunction there is between the natural and supernatural orders of
intelligence! *Art*, in fact, corresponds to the *fear of God*, which is reduced to
the simple art of virtue; knowledge corresponds to Isaiah's *knowledge*,
which has piety as its practical part; prudence, whose second act according to
Aristotle is counsel ('It seems that the work of the prudent person is to give
good counsel about good things themselves'*), corresponds to Isaiah's
counsel whose practical action pertains to fortitude; finally, the *wisdom* and
understanding in Isaiah's list correspond to the the *wisdom* and
understanding of Aristotle.

   The difference between Plato and Aristotle is this: Plato posits the
understanding alone as the information about the principle of the universe.
In understanding, he includes ideas, and rational principles, and the efficient
and final cause. Aristotle distinguishes the rational principles from the causes
and says that ideas and rational principles pertain to the *understanding*, and
the highest causes to *wisdom*.

[95c]

assumptions. *Understanding*, however, was to be reserved for information about the principle of the universe which is not presupposed but absolutely 'is'. In this principle, all things have their objective being.

96. All these different forms of Wisdom are bestowed upon us by one and the same Spirit, the Spirit of the Word. In this Word, which is the eternal archetype of infinite wisdom and indeed both objective and personal wisdom, God wanted us to see and touch, sensibly as it were, in an individual of our own species, the realised ideal of the wisdom of which man is capable. Thus, God satisfied that which fittingness required. He bestowed on human nature the additional, uncreated gift to which we had no claim, but which we needed if we were to attain fully the final end of the wisdom and satisfaction adumbrated by the idea. The incarnation of the Word, therefore, far excelled the longing of human nature which could not take in even the thought of so great a mystery. In fact, any assumption of ours that our Creator would make up for the void in our idea, which could not be filled by what is finite, would be fully justified. But, when the God-man appeared, the idea itself became the good measure, pressed down, shaken about and running over of which the gospel speaks.[148] On the man, therefore, whose personhood God himself wished to form, there was to 'rest the Spirit of the Lord, the spirit of wisdom and understanding, the spirit of counsel and might, the spirit of knowledge and piety and fear of the Lord.'[149] In these words, uttered more than seven centuries before the birth of JESUS Christ, the statement that the Spirit of the Lord would rest upon that man finds its obvious explanation and fulfilment in the hypostatic union. If the Word became indivisible from the humanity he assumed, the Spirit of the Word inevitably came to rest in its fullness upon that humanity. In him, the Spirit could not come and go, increase or diminish his gifts, as can happen with other human beings who remain human persons, whether they are joined to the Word or not, whether they share in the Spirit or not. In others, to whom the communication of the Word is the diffusion of the Spirit, there is a rising scale of gifts and perfections which begins with

[148] Lk 4: 38.
[149] Is 11: 2–3.

[96]

the fear of the Lord — called by Scripture the beginning of Wisdom[150] because it is the first mode of wisdom[151] — and ascends to knowledge and piety, then to counsel and fortitude, and finally to wisdom and understanding. In Christ (a word which refers specifically to *anointing* with the Holy Spirit[152]), all these gifts, shared by humans, are united, but in an inverse logical order. Thus the most perfect and ultimate wisdom is first conceived in him. From wisdom is derived understanding, as a result of the faculty of Christ's human mind, which enables him to intuit in that wisdom, at will, the order of essences and ideas. Counsel and fortitude can next be derived from wisdom and understanding by means of the faculty, also possessed by Christ's soul, to apply wisdom and understanding to the functions of judging, ordering, governing and acting in a spirit of magnanimity. From these four gifts can issue knowledge and piety by means of the faculty for knowing general and particular things and applying them to the honour and worship of God. Finally, from all these things together, we have that tremendous, respectful fear of Christ's human nature which, though so limited and restricted, was accompanied, filled, possessed, taken over by a guest of such majesty who directed, sanctified and completely ordered it as his very own person.

This is God's wise man who easily conquers with his reality the ideal wise man whom we conjure up for ourselves. Only God could and did conceive and realise him at the same time, and place him in the world for us to see. God's wise man was incarnate wisdom in whose mouth, nine hundred years before

---

[150] Ps 110: 10; Prov 1: 7; 9: 10; Eccles 1: 16.

[151] 'For the fear of the Lord is wisdom and instruction'* (Eccles 1: 27). Because it is a first seed containing a multiplicity of other forms of Wisdom, it is called 'fullness of Wisdom' relative to the fruits it produces: 'To fear God is the fullness of wisdom: and fullness is from the FRUITS thereof'* (Eccles 1: 20). And on the same lines: 'The root of wisdom is to fear the Lord: and the branches thereof are long-lived'* (Eccles 1: 25).

[152] Sacred doctrine teaches that JESUS was conceived as man by the working of the Holy Spirit (Mt 1: 20; Lk 1: 35). He was therefore sanctified at the very moment of his conception and hypostatic union. This is referred to in the words: 'whom the Father consecrated and sent into the world'* (Jn 10: 36). Hence the title *Anointed* or Christ is proper to him in a sense which cannot be applied to any other man.

[96]

his birth, were put the following words: 'I was set up from eternity and of old before the earth was made. The depths were not as yet and I was already conceived, neither had the fountains of water as yet sprung out. The mountains with their huge bulk had not as yet been established: before the hills I was brought forth. I was with him forming all things and was delighted every day, playing before him at all times, playing in the world and my delights were to be with the children of men. Now, therefore, children, hear me: Blessed are they that keep my ways.'[153]

97. Thus Almighty God, as teacher of men, spoke several centuries before Plato was born at Athens, to express the longing for such a teacher and to show how much mankind needed him. This teacher, this God-man, the living, palpable archetype of the Wise man 'in whom are hidden all the treasures of wisdom and knowledge',[154] this wisdom incarnate, this just and holy one from his twofold eternal and temporal origin, has by his very nature and condition clearly occupied for nineteen centuries first place among human beings. And he acquired it through a new title by the merits of his perfect sacrifice. He is of necessity the *head* of mankind, the *prince* of humankind. But even as prince, he came to serve and minister to mankind, whose ingratitude he overcame by giving up his life, which he laid down and took up of his own volition, to ascend to God the Father and act on high as the *advocate* of his enemies.[155] Thus mankind, divided and scattered by death, the effect of sin, and deprived of its father by nature, was brought back to *unity* by the conqueror of death who gave us as father his own, unique Father, Almighty God. We were re-established under the rule of one 'to whom all power in heaven and earth was given';[156] we were reunited with a head so outstanding that he could never be reached by our thought and desire, which was also unable to conceive or guess how this could come about. This mode of union — one of God's many creations on man's behalf[157] — was

153 Prov 8.

154 Col 2: 3.

155 1 Jn 2: 1.

156 Mt 28: 8.

157 'Praise the Lord and call upon his name: make known all his doings among the nations'* (1 Chron 16: 8; Ps 76: 13).

[97]

not merely human friendship, companionship, submission or beneficence, of which we can form some idea. It was completely different: unimaginable, divine, an embrace of perception by which the Word is sealed in the soul, an indwelling embrace by which the Spirit is poured into the soul, a physical embrace through Christ's manhood mysteriously at work in the sacraments and itself hidden by a sacrament in the Eucharist food. Thus, if we wish, we can become true and living members of the body that has Christ as its head and of which, as head, he could say in all truth: 'I am the vine, you the branches; he who abides in me and I in him, he it is that bears much fruit.'[158] These are the foundations, holy mountains as it were, on which Christ built his Church. However, because God respects our freedom and wants our assent and acceptance so that his gifts become the object, as it were, of a freely bestowed contract, we still have a choice between the offer of a noble place as sons in his divine family, or of remaining as outsiders or base slaves.

98. Let me recapitulate in part what I have said. The intellect conceives, more or less perfectly, an ideal concept of perfection for everything artistic or moral. However, no human work of art expresses the concept fully although anyone who gets close to it is highly praised. So the fulfilment of every ideal always constitutes, for us, a painful, unfulfilled longing. This is further proof that, in us, the idea far outreaches our powers. But the ideal that we desire most of all is that of ourselves and the *greatest art* is that by which we plan to attain it. But it is precisely the art of self-perfection in which we are most deficient. Then, out of his own greatness, the Creator, as a result of his own greatness, came to the aid of us, his creatures who were in such great need. Holding as exemplar of all his works an ideal unparalleled in its perfection and more perfect than the human mind can conceive, he never fails to attain it. The *ideal human being* is the ideal *wise human being*. The Stoics and other philosophers introduced the concept of such a human being, but no one ever realised it. Indeed, in accordance with the well-known interpretation Socrates gave to the Delphic oracle, the wise man was he who knew only 'that he did not know'. But the ideal of the wise man in God's mind was brought about on earth. The human

[158] Jn 15: 5.

type was effected in a wise-type man. Mankind found its own ideal divinized in JESUS Christ. Moreover, this divinized ideal had become real. The Word and the Holy Spirit took the place in this wise man of the two constituents of wisdom, *knowledge* and *virtue*. Both of these were communicated to us. JESUS Christ said: 'For this I was born (as man) and for this I have come into the world (as God at the incarnation), to bear witness to the truth.'[159] This truth was the same divine Word who said: 'I am the way, the truth and the life: no one comes to the Father except through me.'[160] As man, he bore witness before us to the divine Word: as Word incarnate, he also bore witness to himself because the words he uttered when he taught us were related to the inner light, which they unfolded and made accessible to reflection. It was the *voice of the Word* which rang out to bear witness to that Word who enlightened without need of words.[161] This inner Word to whom the proclamations and the spoken words of the Word ran in parallel, was the mirror, the confirmation of such spoken words, which everyone who was given this light bore within himself. After saying that he had come to bear witness to the truth, Christ immediately added: 'Everyone who IS OF THE TRUTH, hears my voice.'*[162] However imperfect, perception of the Word endows us with a new and more sublime being. It is a second birth in which we 'are not born of blood or the will of the flesh or the will of man, but of God.'[163] Those who are born again in this way 'have the power to become sons of God'[164] by listening to the voice of Christ. The *external words* uttered by Christ bear witness, therefore, to

[159] Jn 18: 37.

[160] Jn 14: 6.

[161] St. Augustine says of Mary, the sister of Lazarus, taken as the model of the contemplative life: 'She (Mary) lived by the word, but a spoken word. There will be life by the word but without the sound of a word. The Word himself is life. We shall be like him since we shall see him as he is.'* But even here on earth, the Christian's life begins; he lives by the Word, *nullo sonante verbo* [without the sound of a word]. Hence it is said: 'Blessed are those who have not seen, yet believed.'

[162] Jn 18: 37.

[163] Jn 1: 13.

[164] Jn 1: 12.

the inner Word, while the *inner Word*, which is light in itself, demonstrates and confirms the truth of those words. Since the Word, wherever he is sent, is sent by the Father, even into souls, the Father, whose subsistence is perceived in the Word, bears witness to him by sending him into this world and into souls. Christ said: 'I am, who (preaching to the world) bear witness to myself (who dwells in human souls) and the Father who sent me bears witness to me.'[165] Because 'the Son cannot do anything of his own accord but only what he sees the Father doing.'[166] Thus the external and internal works that I do, I do not do alone, but with the Father. This expresses the perfect correspondence and unity of being between *what is divinely intelligible* and *what is divinely real*. Analogously, our human mind conceives and desires the idea relative to what is real. It is to this perfect correspondence between forms and identity of being that Christ attributes the wholly satisfactory witness which he bears to the truth.[167]

99. However, Christ brings to our attention a similar correspondence between the first two divine persons in an absolute and universal mode. He witnesses to its presence in himself in the moral order when he says: 'I am the way, the truth and the life.' The *way* is knowledge, the idea, to which all laws and commands are reduced; moral duties lay down for us the path by

---

[165] Jn 8: 18.

[166] Jn 5: 19.

[167] Elsewhere, he states that if he, the Word, were not identical in substance and activity with the Father, his witness would not be true. Therefore he says: 'If I bear witness to myself, my witness is not true; there is another who bears witness to me and I know that the testimony he bears to me is true'* (Jn 5: 31–32). For evidence or an affirmation to be true, the thing affirmed as real should truly be, with a reality which corresponds fully to its idea. *Reality*, therefore, when adequate to the *idea*, is true, and the witness which it bears is true. The divine Word therefore bears witness to himself, because he is *intelligible*, divine substance (whose analogue in us is the idea), and because there is perfect correspondence between what is divinely intelligible and what is divinely subsistent. In the form of subsistence what is divine is the Father. But this substance, pronounced from eternity, is the generated Word. This utterance or generation (which comprises in itself every mission of the Word) is the Father's witness; the Word on his part knows by his own condition that this is true witness because the divine substance, as uttered, is thereby intelligible *per se*.

which we attain our end. Now the Word contains all ideas, laws
and moral obligations; these are the *understanding* which, as I
said above, lies in *wisdom*, and is separated from wisdom by
reflection and by the limitation enjoined on wisdom. *Truth,*
then, is here taken to be the *realisation* of the moral idea or law
as in: 'The law was given through Moses ... truth was made
through JESUS Christ,'[168] that is, the complete fulfilment of the
Law. Since JESUS Christ did not come to abolish the Law but to
fulfil it,[169] he accomplished what human beings had previously
been unable to achieve: he equalled and surpassed by the holiness of his actions the ideal of virtue which the law of Moses had
outlined for the Hebrews to realise. Thus, relative to the moral
order, we see the balance restored in Christ within the idea (not
the Mosaic idea, but his own). He did not say 'The Law of
Moses is the way' but: 'I am the way' and I am the truth of the
actions which correspond fully to that idea. This balance is also
restored in all those who were to believe in him and in what he
said. Having within themselves the IMMANENT WORD,[170] they are
transformed, so to speak, into other Christs. The Word is also
the *way* in them, indicating what must be done, and the *truth*,
endowing them with power to implement it. In addition, he is
life which, because it consists in the production of a substantial
feeling or in the act of such a feeling, is produced when the
Word communicates his Spirit and arouses in the soul an efficacious feeling. This elevates the soul to a deiform life, allowing it
to recognise the Word and enjoy him. This feeling, although
eternal of its nature, grows and becomes perfect in time, and is
revealed in the bliss of eternity.

No other master has ever exercised this kind of teaching
before human beings. Everything that Christianity teaches on
this issue is worthy of God, and so worthy that the human
mind, whatever ideal it fashioned of the wise human being,
could never have come anywhere near it. If anyone had thought
or proposed it, it would have seemed to be absurd and not
understood. We did not know God and ourselves sufficiently to

[168] Jn 1: 17.

[169] Mt 5: 17.

[170] Christ said to the Jews: 'You do not have his (the Father's) word abiding
in you for you do not believe in him whom he has sent'* (Jn 5: 38).

be able to imagine what our mutual relation could be. However, when JESUS Christ exercised this teaching,[171] human beings

[171] Modern German sophists attribute to popular imagination this divine ideal of the wise human being, which was unattainable by the greatest minds of the ancient world despite their efforts to outline and portray it. Their arguments are based on analogy and hypothesis but on what kind of analogy and hypothesis? According to them, popular imagination invented different mythologies by altering history when the world was in its infancy. This was due mainly to the poets. The hypothesis is this. The gospel was invented at the height of the Graeco-Roman culture of Greece and Rome — though without any help from the poets! Then some obscure group of people — so it is said — made this new mythology their own and persuaded one and all, learned and ignorant, weak and powerful, that it was true! Moreover, they sealed the truth of the mythology by shedding rivers of their own blood for it. The new mythology must have been more unfortunate than the old, which arose when there was as yet no science, and progressed without opposition either from science or the powers of this world. This would explain why neither the populace who invented the mythology nor their poets had to shed the tiniest drop of blood to make it known! A pity that such an analogy which appears so convincing to certain German philosophers allows of one tiny difference. The mythologies of the ancient world show through internal evidence that they are dreams and wild, contradicting imaginations, a confused and sorry medley of vices and virtues like the human beings who created them, a mass of impossibilities and ridiculous absurdities, a multiplicity of unconnected fables with neither head nor tail, a series of senseless superstitions unworthy of the profaned, divided, humanised divinity to which are attributed every crime, the foulest passions, ignorance and human frenzy. In other words, the effect corresponds exactly to the cause, the work to popular imagination, its author. According to Strauss and all those who support this *mythical system*, the analogy is such that popular imagination can now do exactly the contrary of what it has always done. In other words, it can suddenly change nature and become a unique, sublimely wise mind capable of inventing the gospel and in it the personage of Christ. This was done secretly, over few years, without anyone realising it. Popular imagination invented a unique religious system, internally consistent, that could never be convicted of any contradiction or of any impossibility, that was consistent with all human sciences whatever new developments they might exhibit, consistent with all truths of nature however deeply they were investigated. In fact, the more nature revealed its secrets to men, the more consistent this mythology was with history. Moreover, it was worthy of God, sublime in its teaching, and contained all the sublime truths that philosophy could proclaim or even surmise. Most pure and most holy in its morals, it was extremely generous in its actions, most humane in its inclinations, and truly beneficial to mankind. It had the power to imprint itself on the noblest and loftiest minds and hearts; it conquered all human knowledge and power, reformed mankind and all human societies, founded

[99]

believed the fact before seeing and believing its possibility. It was easier to believe in its existence than in its possibility.

100. When great changes occur, there is a transformation not only in what we think, but even in the way we think. In addition, old words are used in new ways and acquire new meanings. Languages change, and perhaps Jesus Christ was referring to this when he promised that the faithful would speak 'new tongues',[172] an expression which would seem to mean much more than to speak in languages other than one's own. Thus, in using ordinary, human language, we said so far that theoretically known *truth* is an element of any possible, natural wisdom. But in speaking a 'new tongue', we are now obliged to say that such truth is no longer an *element* of supernatural wisdom but the *way* that leads to it. I therefore reserve the term *Truth* for a new and nobler meaning; it is the *idea as realised* — if I can express it in such terms — in its vital, fully perfected state. It is no longer impersonal, but a divine person in whom however it retains its character as object and as intelligible. This is the basis of the analogy between the *idea* and the *divine Word*. As a result, it is impossible in God's Wisdom transmitted to human beings by God himself in his capacity as teacher of mankind, to separate the first element, truth, from the second, virtue, although they can be mentally distinguished. When the two are separated, the first element changes nature. It is no longer what it was, it does not form part of that wisdom. Certainly, the idea remains when truth is separated from its realisation. But it is the divine Word, not the idea, who pertains to man's supernatural wisdom. In this Word, we can distinguish only mentally between the *way* and the *truth*. Nevertheless, although this new wisdom is one and indivisible, it has a twofold aspect; it is biform in its supremely perfect unity (and we might even say triniform if it were possible to explain the meaning of the word here). When seen from one viewpoint, this wisdom is totally

civilisation; capable of responding to all that mankind wanted to know about its future destiny, it satisfied all the most hidden and mysterious wishes of the human heart. For eighteen centuries, during which it has always grown in numbers in the midst of the fiercest struggles, it has ruled the world through the greatest, the most compact, most orderly and gentle society which has ever existed on the earth!

[172] Mk 16: 17.

[100]

resolved in the new meaning given to the word *truth*; when seen from the other, it is totally resolved in and comprehended by the meaning of the new word *charity*. Thus, the two distinct persons of the Word and his Spirit are indivisible and one in being and nature. So while this new meaning of T*ruth* expresses God in the person of the Word, as the Word himself said, the new word *Charity* expresses the same God in the person of the Spirit, as the Scriptures say: 'God is charity and he who remains in charity remains in God and God in him.'[173] Used in this sublime sense, *Truth* and *Charity* are reciprocal witnesses because one is in the other and neither of the two is found outside the other. Anyone possessing such Truth possesses the Charity which fulfils it, and anyone possessing this Charity possesses the fulfilled Truth. And as this Truth is not given to human beings without good works, so Charity is not bestowed without good works. 'He who says "I know him" (JESUS Christ) but disobeys his commands is a liar and the TRUTH is not in him; but whoever keeps his word, in him truly CHARITY is perfect. By this we may be sure that we are in him.'[174] So the one who does good, has charity and also knows truth. But the one who does not do good cannot know truth fully. He cannot feel it, therefore, and consequently does not have the Spirit which alone makes him know this substantial and supersubstantial truth. As we know, it is the Spirit who testifies that Christ is TRUTH.[175] Charity, therefore, is in truth which it fulfils, and Christ was able to ask his Father: 'Sanctify them in the Truth; your word is Truth.'[176] But the fulfilled truth is then in charity: 'Let us not love in word and speech but in deed and in truth: by this we know that our being is drawn from TRUTH.'[177]

101. Two words, therefore, sum up the school of God become teacher of mankind, TRUTH and CHARITY. These two words mean different things, but each includes the other. The 'all' is in each, but charity is in truth as something other, and truth is in

---

[173] Jn 4: 6.

[174] Jn 2: 5.

[175] 1 Jn 5: 6.

[176] Jn 18: 17.

[177] 1 Jn 3: 18–19.

charity as something other. If either did not have the other, it would not be itself. Truth is the teacher himself, JESUS Christ, who unfolds himself to the intellective essence of the soul both externally and internally; externally by revelation and preaching of the gospel down the ages, and in the diversity of ministries; inwardly, through all those divine cognitions which produce knowledge. Similarly, Charity, which is the Holy Spirit, is unfolded in the gifts which I have enumerated, in the extraordinarily rich effects of love, in the fruits of the Spirit, in graces and in holy activity. Consequently, all a disciple's undertakings, all his powers and actions, are accompanied by the Word and his Spirit, who are found in them all. This explains not only why Christian wisdom is reduced to the imitation of Christ, but also how this imitation is possible for human beings in such an original and wonderful way. On the one hand, the *Teacher* of whom we are speaking is so different in nature from mankind that he is able to enter and take his place, as it were, in the very soul of the *disciples* and there direct and even stimulate by his own Spirit all the disciples' powers. On the other hand, and consequently, the disciples' wisdom is simply a share in divine wisdom itself, a share in the Teacher himself who comes into them and, with their consent and approval, dwells in them, enabling them to live with his life. It is not difficult, therefore, to understand the three things of which I have spoken. It becomes perfectly clear that the supernatural wisdom of other men consists merely of the *imitation of Christ*, that this imitation is possible, and that it is possible in a truly wonderful way. What we have is a kind of identity of wisdom. What human mind could ever conceive such an amazing and noble way of effecting the precept which philosophy itself put forward: 'Imitate God'?[178]

102. Eternal wisdom, which is one, utterly simple, subsistent and living, God and Word of God, really does dwell, always identical, in all his followers (and we are all called to this) and lives and reigns in them with their consent. There are two especially joyful consequences from this. First, mankind is truly organised into a single body, with a single divine head. This satisfies our deep, mysterious longing to ensure, without knowing quite how, that the multitude of human beings imitate and

[178] Plato, *Theaetetus*.

[102]

emulate, in their unification, the perfect unity of the species. Secondly, each individual who has Christ within him is ennobled as a kind of end of the universe and becomes, as it were, a centre of his own to which all other things are referred. The disciple is like a star in the immensity of space, exerting its pull, as astronomers believe, on every other heavenly body.

103. This explains the stability and continuous increase of the school of Christ throughout the world. He said to his disciples before departing from them outwardly: 'Behold I am with you all days — even to the consummation of the world.'[179] The spread of the school of Christ, that is, of the Church from age to age, from country to country is the work of the Holy Spirit, the work of charity. This love began with God the Father: 'God so loved the world that he gave his only begotten Son so that everyone who believes in him may not perish but may have eternal life.'[180] The Word who entered mankind when he took flesh, fulfilled God's charity: 'By this we know God's love that he laid down his life for us; and we ought to lay down our lives for the brethren.'[181] Those who became disciples of the Word incarnate received him within themselves and at the same time received the principle of charity itself. Each of them, in whom the Word dwells and who dwell in the Word, lives out this charity continuously here below: 'A new commandment I give to you that you also love one another. By this all men will know that you are my disciples if you have love for one another.'[182] As St. John says: 'If we love one another, God abides in us and his love is perfected in us. By this we know that we abide in him and he in us because he has given us of his own Spirit.'[183]

The Word, therefore, though invisible, dwells on the earth in the souls of his disciples, leaving the mark of his presence in them from generation to generation. He imparts his Spirit to them so that the work of his Church is fresh and new in every age. It can never grow old as it renews its work in every human

[179] Mt 28: 20.
[180] Jn 3: 16; 1 Jn 4: 9–10.
[181] 1 Jn 3: 16.
[182] Jn 13: 34–35.
[183] 1 Jn 4: 12–13.

[103]

being who in some way becomes Christ. This explains why the teaching is always *good news*, or gospel, the name which it has borne from the beginning. In the struggle which the Church wages against the spirit of evil and human weakness, she seems at times to suffer as periods of triumph are followed by periods of bitterness and humiliation. This, however, is merely moment-ary and transitory. As a society, the Church is so constituted that she retains the power of self-restoration and rejuvenation through the governance of pastors with whom Christ promised to be present down the ages and through the charity which he instils in the souls of his faithful and by which he established the Church in the beginning. This explains also the Church's capacity for endless progress. Thus, all Christ's disciples are wise and regularly do what Christ has done and continues to do in them: that is, they carry out the work of the Church and hence the unification of mankind and are, as St. John puts it, 'co-operators of Truth.'[184]

104. The work of *Christian wisdom* consists in such *charity* being exercised in *truth*. All are called to take part; to those who respond, the different ministries are allocated; some are given a major role, others a smaller part in the common undertaking. In charge of the whole work are those to whom Christ had said: 'Peace be with you: as the Father has sent me, so I send you.'[185] These are the wise who teach other wise people, the teachers of those who know. In fact, all Christians have interior know-ledge. This is why an apostle wrote to them: 'As for you, the anointing which you received from him abides in you, and you have no need that anyone should teach you; as his anointing teaches you about everything, and is true, and is no lie, just as it has taught you, abide in him.'[186] Nevertheless, the same apostle taught and admonished because, although all Christians know from within, not everyone knows from without, and the inner Word needs to be unfolded from without. Moreover, while even someone who knows can be seduced by error, the wise are pro-tected when they rely on those whom Christ has sent for the very purpose of teaching and ministering him from without.

[184] 3 Jn 8.
[185] Jn 20: 21.
[186] 1 Jn 2: 27.

[104]

105. This charity of Christian wisdom extends in a truly wonderful way because it extends as far as Truth. As we have seen, the truth of this wisdom knows no bounds. The Master tells his disciples: 'No longer do I call you servants, for the servant does not know what his master is doing; but I have called you friends, for all that I have heard from my Father I have made known to you.'[187] In addition, he promises them his Spirit who will remind them of all that he said to them, and he will instruct them once more 'in all truth.'[188] I have already explained how human beings, although so limited, can bear such an enormous corpus of truth when I pointed out that all truth is bestowed on us in an implicit and potential manner. St. John says as much when he says that the Christian has dwelling in him 'the seed of the Word,'[189] the seed whereby a man is reborn. The unfolding of this seed in different human beings, however, is always limited (although it may vary from person to person) to whatever is necessary to human nature and required by it, that is, to our moral perfection and happiness. The same argument needs to be applied to *charity*. By its nature, charity in each disciple is universal and infinite, although limited in its unfolding and actuation. This must be the case if charity is to respond perfectly to the truth of which I am speaking and from which, as I said, charity is inseparable. Charity is nothing more than the implementation and substantiation of Truth. That is why the Scriptures say: 'because they refused to love the truth and so be saved'[190] and exhorts Christians to 'do the truth in charity'.[191] This truth is not only known; it is done, and it is done through charity. In this sense, it is not like natural truth.

106. The distinction I have made between *natural*, incomplete *truth* and subsistent *supernatural truth* also applies in the case of *charity* which, corresponding to supernatural truth, is distinct from *natural love*. I am not referring here to *subjective*

---

[187] Jn 15: 15.

[188] 'He shall teach you all truth'* (Jn 16: 13).

[189] 'His seed abides in him'* (1 Jn 3: 9).

[190] 'Because they receive not the LOVE OF THE TRUTH that they may be saved'* (2 Thess 2: 10).

[191] 'But DOING THE TRUTH IN CHARITY, we may in all things grow up in him who is the head, even Christ'* (Eph 4: 15).

natural love which varies in kind, in form and in custom, but does not of itself belong to the ethical order. I am referring to *objective natural love* which constitutes natural virtue. This love inherits all the limitations and imperfections to be found in natural and purely ideal truth and moreover is assailed and often destroyed by subjective love which becomes evil as a result of such an assault. Finally, even if objective, natural love, weak and insubstantial as it is, could stand firm when confronted by such a violent and disordered enemy, it would not satisfy the need for love felt by the human heart, which extends as far as the idea, that is, to the infinite, but finds no infinitely lovable object in nature. Nor could such love be the origin of infinite beneficence to which the human spirit tends. Love means willing the good, but lovers cannot wish their beloved an infinite good if they either do not know or do not have any infinite good to communicate. The human heart and mind, therefore, can find no resting place except in the infinite. Its final destiny can only be found in something real and infinite, outside the range of natural love. The *capacity* for affection, which the Creator has planted in human nature, can never be fully and peacefully satisfied in natural love.

Charity, on the other hand, finds and possesses the *final end* of love, that is, the Triune God. And as God loves this end in himself, where he knows it practically and immediately, so he loves it in the people in whom he dwells and, in a different way, in those too in whom he can dwell, that is, in all who live on earth. Consequently, the love of Christ takes on the two forms of *brotherhood* and *humanity*. The first is 'love of the brethren' which was so highly recommended to the earliest disciples by the Apostles,[192] whereby all those in whom Christ already dwells love one another with an ineffable, almost beatifying love, and vie with each other with all respect and assistance in every form of sacrifice so that Christ who dwells in them may continue to increase in the brethren and in the whole

---

[192] 'Love one another with brotherly affection, outdo one another in showing honour'* (Rom 12: 10). 'But, concerning love of the brethren, you have no need of anyone to write to you, as you yourselves have been taught by God to love one another'* (1 Thess 4: 9). 'Let the love of the brotherhood abide in you'* (Heb 13: 1; 1 Pet 2; 1 Pet 1: 22; 2: 17; 3: 8; 5: 9; 2 Pet 1: 7).

community. *Humanity,* then, is that form of charity by which human beings love one another, not because they have Christ within them, but because they are capable of having him. This is the source of that tireless zeal for souls whereby Christians desire and do whatever they can so that outsiders may be brought into Christ's Church, and sinners converted. Thus justified, Christ may pour into their hearts his Spirit, whom they have treated so scornfully. This is Christian philanthropy which aims at serving human beings in all ways so that they may come to possess the true, final, absolute, infinite good. Only possession of this good enables human nature to proclaim its full satisfaction; without this good, no other is ever fully satisfying. Thus Christian philanthropy is reasonable and genuine. It offers human beings the true good they long for in a confused, human way; it offers other goods purely in relation to this supreme good. Other goods in opposition to this relationship would be evil, even if they retained the appearance of good. It is the philanthropy or humanity of Christ of which St. Paul says that 'when the goodness and kindness of God our Saviour (Ἡ φιλανθρωπία τοῦ σωτῆρος ἡμῶν Θεοῦ) intervened, he saved us not because of deeds done by us in righteousness but in virtue of his own mercy.'[193] St. John, too, speaks of it when he says: 'In this is love, not that we loved God but that he loved us and sent his Son to be the expiation of our sins.'[194] In turn, the disciples who know that Christ loved them when they were unworthy and in order to make them worthy, love those who are not yet worthy to be so loved. The disciples love so that others, too, may become worthy of supernatural life by acquiring dignity as members of Christ's body living with the very Spirit of Christ.

107. Charity therefore necessarily contains the spirit of proselytism or, in other words, the principle of association. St. John wrote to the faithful: 'That which we have seen and heard we proclaim also to you, so that you may have fellowship; and our fellowship is with the Father and with his Son JESUS Christ.'[195] And further: 'If we walk in the light as he is in the light, we have fellowship with one another and the blood of JESUS Christ, his

[193] Tit 3: 4–5.
[194] 1 Jn 4: 10.
[195] 1 Jn 1: 3.

Son, cleanses us from all sin.'[196] Charity is always in the *light*, because the light is truth, and Charity is truth put into practice. I said earlier that subsistent *truth*, that is, the divine Word, of his very nature, associated human beings with himself. One identical, real and life-giving principle is shared by all those who are in him. Thus, those who are joined to the Word are like a bunch of grapes, as it were, in which all the grapes together belong to the same bunch and absorb the life-giving sap. The same can be said of *charity*. By its nature charity is union, the most perfect and sublime union which, in some way, can be called 'unification'. It is no wonder, then, that mankind should feel, as soon as charity was brought into the world, an unusual need to associate. Within humanity, a movement arose, tending constantly to produce new, more or less perfect associations. The great society, the Catholic (universal) Church, had been formed by the Teacher himself who had laid down the two principles of truth and charity. Relative to the truth, the Church, as I said, is made up of *teachers* and *disciples*. Relative to charity, it is made up 1. of *ministers* who communicate the Word and his Spirit through certain means, instituted by the Saviour and strengthened by his omnipotence, and who regulate the whole body externally, and 2. of *those to whom they minister*, those who receive such grace and government. And because truth and charity are two forms of the same divine good, so those who as teachers preserve and hand down the truth are bishops and priests who offer sacrifice, administer the sacraments and govern; they are the same people with two powers.

108. But, I said, the Word dwells in every disciple and there pours out his Spirit so that each one is a kind of centre and end of the whole, although he is also a member — more or less important, playing a more or less important role — of the body of which Christ is the head. Each, therefore, possesses his own light of truth and each has his own fire of charity. Even the least of Christians who remains in a state of grace has it. As a result, each one adheres ever more closely to the great, essential and fundamental association which is the Church, and has within himself the principle of, and inclination to, other charitable associations. He is drawn to them in the degree to which he

[196] *Ibid.* 7.

[108]

co-operates with charity, and charity itself, through external cognitions and gifts, unfolds in him. This explains all those *religious associations* which aim to practise charity and beneficence to their neighbour with greater, more extensive and more organised zeal. These associations, clearly, are merely shoots of truth and charity, the burgeoning of ever-productive roots, the natural and inevitable results of the School of God, the teacher and redeemer of mankind. This School is his Church.

Charity can clearly be exercised by any individual but is more productive when undertaken by a group of associated individuals working together in harmony like a kind of peace-loving, well-organised, well-informed and disciplined army engaged in the same campaign. Indeed, anyone who loves something, loves it in its entirety, not in part. So, as the truth to which I am referring has no limits, charity is by its very nature infinite and can never say 'Enough' without self-contradiction. It reaches out for the heights in order to do as much good as it can. The limits of charity are merely subjective. By this, I mean that charity, as long as it remains implicit and hidden in man, cannot expand in external works, and remains implicit to the extent that truth is implicit within us. This ignorance, which can be found even in the Christian relative to reflective knowledge, and the inadequate co-operation afforded by free will to the unfolding of truth itself, are the two limits which the work of charity encounters in different people. These limits, however, may always be expanded and enlarged. Hence the indefinite and ever-new development of charity in Christianity; charity reaches to everything, and with total sacrifice. Now, all goods, including temporal goods, can serve the end for which goods exist, that is, the end of man. This end was a subject much debated by pre-Christian philosophers, who worked by conjecture or on the basis of unreliable arguments without ever seeing the light or coming to agreement. After Christ, however, no one can be in doubt or in the dark over the nature of our final end. It follows that charity is love whereby we forget ourselves in favour of our fellows and seek no pleasure other than that of procuring their total well-being, by undertaking any study, toil and suffering for the sake of their physical, intellectual and moral good. Physical and intellectual good, however, are related to moral good, which is the end of the others.

[108]

These three supreme genera of charity, when carefully considered, recall the three forms of being, real, ideal and moral, and they belong to the three supreme categories which reassume all that the mind can conceive. These three categories are founded on the three primal forms of being. It is thus obvious that the final aim of charity is to enable all to share to the utmost degree in being, and in all three forms of being. And as in this being, which is one and three, truth is resolved, so we perceive once again how charity terminates in truth, and truth is transfused in charity. Truth in its fullness is ordered because being is ordered so that, in the order of generation, real being precedes ideal being and both precede moral being which conjoins to itself and perfects all being. Charity is ordered in the same way. Consequently, any other love which strays from this order is opposed to the *order of truth*, and must be called false and harmful rather than beneficent. Christ, therefore, brought true love into the world, love which could not be true unless it were also totally sublime and divine, just as he brought true, noble and divine wisdom into the world. He was fully justified in saying that this was *his* commandment.[197]

109. Charity, therefore, is exercised by the disciples either as individuals or as united in societies. It is also exercised on behalf of individuals and societies, although its ultimate human term is always the individual. Societies are means and not ends; they cannot have any end other than the good of their associated individuals, or other individuals. Thus, charity contains the immortal principle of the restoration and reform not only of the Church, as I have mentioned when speaking of truth, but of domestic society (education especially is very pleasing to charity) and of civil society. Members of civil society, when animated by charity, are stimulated to ensure that society is based on justice, whose rigour is tempered by the reconciliation of opinions and interests through mutual esteem, reciprocal concessions, and reasonable dealings among the citizens. Above all, the pride and despotism that are so familiar, and almost inseparable from such a powerful society, are mitigated by education about its nature. In other words, it becomes clear that

---

[197] 'This is my command that you love one another as I have loved you'* (Jn 15: 12).

[109]

civil society is the servant, not the master of either the Church or the family, both of which by their very concept take precedence over it. Civil society, therefore, must revere them as its very own end, and respect and serve them. It follows also that family and nation share in that immortality which Christian wisdom transmits to everything it touches or affects and which, before anything else, it imparted in its own words to the universal Church, the great school it founded.

110. Charity, however, as I said, does not terminate in man but in God. It loves human beings either because they share in the divine nature or because they are capable of sharing in it. God, master of the world, is Truth itself which, in moving communicatively amongst men, terminates in Truth. Thus, Truth is at one and the same time, the *origin* and also the *term* of divine teaching which incessantly revolves and abides not in a vicious circle, but in a powerful and living circle. Similarly, God, the Spirit of truth, is Charity which, in bestowing itself upon human beings, continuously returns to itself. As St. Augustine says, love finally loves itself[198] and all is love; God-love is principle and God-love is end. When the ultimate *end of all goods* was unveiled or rather communicated to human beings, they were assured of the two supreme goods, *virtue* and the *blessed life* in its fullness for which they are always groping in the dark. A way of life and behaviour which stops on the way and does not tend to Almighty God as the absolute end of all things may well exhibit some likeness or rather analogy to the virtue to which it is directed. This likeness, analogy or movement, may then be mistaken for virtue by human beings, but virtue it cannot be, 'nor', as St. Augustine says, 'is it true wisdom which, relative to matters viewed prudently, acts with fortitude, restrains with temperance, distributes with justice, but does not direct its attention to the end where God will be all in all in assured eternity and perfect peace.'*[199] In such complete virtue, man already finds the *blessed life* even here on this earth where all is incipient, nothing is fulfilled, where subsistent truth is perceived, but in enigmatic fashion, and charity is exercised, but not without effort. This blessed life is indeed still enfolded in

---

[198] *The City of God*, bk. 12, c. 23; *On Different Questions,* 88 q. 35.

[199] *The City of God*, bk. 19, c. 20.

the veils of truth and in the sufferings of charity, but it is none-theless the truest life. Those experiencing it know they possess inner contentment, and express this in all sincerity. They know they possess the infinite, and they rest in the will of the one whose infinite lovability and majesty are perceived as a place of total safety and the source of a hope which cannot lead them astray. Schooled by God himself to magnanimity, they do not even decide to prefer eternal bliss to temporary merit. They are two equally infinite treasures to be left poised in the balance. As one woman put it: 'Either suffering or death'. The Apostle himself hesitates over which of the two is to be preferred.[200] Or preference is given to merit over vision itself as another woman said: 'Not death but suffering,' and as the Apostle Paul himself says in another passage: 'I wished myself to be an anathema from Christ (that is, separated from his vision) for my brethren.'[201] Nevertheless although, as St. Augustine says, 'the hope of contemplating God, which comes with a delightful and certain understanding of truth'*[202] is sufficient to make us happy in this life where we learn, exercise and merit, there is more to come. When time has run its course, the subsistent truth, which is now in us as *principle*, will show itself as *term*. It opens before us all the eternal treasures hidden in the depth of real being. Thus Christ, in the wonderful words of Scripture, restores to the Father the Kingdom already revealed to men,[203] and Charity, accompanying the Truth from which it is exhaled and to which it corresponds, breaks open, so to speak, the furnace entrapping its flames. It raises and extends the tip of the non-consuming fire, and sweeps toward revealed all-Being. There, it enables us

[200] 'For to me, to live is Christ and to die is gain. If it is to be life in the flesh, that means fruitful labour for me. Yet which I shall choose I cannot tell. I am hard pressed between the two. My desire is to depart and be with Christ for that is far better. But to remain in the flesh is more necessary on your account'* (Phil 1: 21–24).

[201] Rom 9: 3. See S. Th, 4: 1.

[202] *Contra Faustum*, bk. 22.

[203] St. Paul's words: 'when he has handed over the kingdom to God the Father'* (1 Cor 15: 24) are explained by St. Augustine: 'when he leads the believers and those whose faith is a living reality on whose behalf a mediator now intervenes, into the contemplation for which we sigh and groan'* (*On the Trinity*, bk. 1, c. 21).

to live a life of divine, immortal fire. Clearly, the promise is worthy of the Teacher, and in accordance with the sublimity of his school. All is attained if the Teacher is God who, one and entire, has to be 1. truth, the object of the teaching; 2. the source and object of charity and 3. the eternal object of bliss. Any other knowledge apart from this would have been unworthy of such a teacher and such teaching, just as any other end for the world would have been inferior to the greatness of the Creator.

111. St. Augustine points out that having certain things is the same as knowing them, and that they be can ousted from our love by human beings.[204] At the same time, some of them, which cannot be fully known, cannot be possessed by anyone who does not enjoy them (enjoyment is an act of love). Thus, they cannot be possessed unless they are known, nor known unless they are loved and enjoyed. The same conditions apply to the good: 'No one can perfectly possess or know a good which he does not love. For who can know how great a good it is when he does not enjoy it? But he does not enjoy it if he does not love. So the unloving person does not possess what is to be loved.'*[205]
This teaching applied to the life of bliss confirms what I said:

1. Charity is included in *knowledge of truth*, because charity as something good cannot be fully known unless it is loved and enjoyed. Likewise, *knowledge of truth* is included in *charity*, because possession of the lovable object is the same as knowing it. This does not imply any vicious circle, but rather the proviso that Truth and Love dwell in one another, so to speak, so that they can communicate with, and complete each other.

2. These two words, Truth and Charity, which summarise the whole of Christ's teaching, not only contain the *wisdom* proper to man in the present life, but also bliss in the life to come. As a result, the disciple derives from this teaching a wisdom which first of all contents him in his present sufferings, and then affords him eminent dignity and calm

---

[204] 'Consequently, we are not to love anything which can be taken away from abiding and active love. What is to be loved, then, except what cannot fail to be present when it is loved? That is because having and knowing are one and the same thing'* (St. Augustine, *On Different Questions*, qq. 83, 35).

[205] *Ibid.*

amid the conflicts that rage around him whether they are caused by nature's perpetual and fatal collisions, or by mankind's endless and self-willed disputes. Finally, with temporal death, wisdom is changed to eternal bliss.

Our divine Teacher's precept: 'You shall love the Lord your God with all your heart, all your soul and all your mind,'[206] is therefore not only a declaration of justice but also a prudent warning given to human beings. It enables them to find the life of eternal bliss that is their final wish and the sum total of their needs. All this is so because the fullness of truth is contained in perfect charity. In the same way, the life of bliss is revealed and clearly pointed out by the divine Teacher in the perfect knowledge of the truth, which cannot be perfect if we are unaware of the aspect of truth revealed by Love alone. The Master said 'Now this is eternal life that they should know thee, the only true God, and JESUS Christ whom you have sent.'[207]

112. Let me summarise what has been said so far. I have made a distinction between *Philosophy* as a study and *Wisdom*. Philosophy is strictly knowledge, and systematic knowledge which is the product of free reflection. Wisdom is the result of two elements, that is, of *knowledge*, and of *virtue* which converts knowledge into real and moral action. I have also shown that Philosophy has as its object the *fullness of knowledge* contained in the ultimate causes of things. Equally the knowledge which constitutes the first element in wisdom (whatever form it may take) is not any particular knowledge but knowledge of truth in all its completeness and universality although it may exist in human beings as in an unopened seed or in a plant at different stages of development. However, just as the practice of virtue, which is the second component of wisdom, requires the use of human freedom, so the knowledge on which such virtue is based always demands some developed degree of reflection. We have also seen that the knowledge which underpins wisdom is independent of any form. In fact human beings possess knowledge prior to philosophy, and to scientific knowledge which is philosophy itself. There is, therefore, a Wisdom anterior to Philosophy which can be possessed

[206] Mt 22: 17.
[207] Jn 17: 3.

[112]

by all, even the uneducated, and a Wisdom that accompanies Philosophy, a more luminous and advanced Wisdom typical of philosophers whose lives and works correspond to the known truth. We saw, however, that natural knowledge of truth, especially the aspect involving the final destiny of man, despite its unique, incomparable importance, is limited, obscure, uncertain, deceptive, without persuasive force and always disputed. It cannot, therefore, create a solid and adequate foundation for moral virtue, but leads to the inevitable imperfection of human wisdom. We have heard the cries of nature and philosophy which, prior to Christ, by the mouth of Plato, asked God himself to come and solve the enigmas by which even the most learned saw themselves surrounded and confused, and to teach human beings — who despaired of ever finding truth and certainty except from the lips of such a teacher — with certitude about the most important, essential questions. God, as I said, had already seen long beforehand such a need. He heard the prayers of his creature, and deigned to come down as a man among humans to teach them. He did much more than human beings could long for or conceive. He did not act in accordance with human criteria but took the sublime path laid out by his infinite, unfathomable attributes. In all he did, he outdid all human expectations in his actions, his methods and his results. He was not content to communicate systematic knowledge to human beings; he himself, *eternal wisdom,* took flesh and overcame the human perversity and limitation that impeded perfect wisdom in man. He overcame it by the very act of wisdom which allowed him to be killed and thereby redeem humankind; he incorporated us into himself, gave us his own life by which to live and his own light to enlighten us. He invited all human beings to the great feast — sumptuously prepared by him on their behalf — of new, unimaginable wisdom, and fed from his own self all those who accepted his magnanimous invitation.

Plato, as we have seen, pointed out that anyone who loves some thing, loves it in its entirety and wherever it is. If he excludes any part of the thing from that love, or loves it in one place but not in another, he is no longer telling the truth when he says he loves it. Consequently, wisdom too is either loved in its entirety and wherever it is to be found, or it is not really loved.

[112]

What are we to say about those who — without any serious study but rather disdainfully refusing to apply themselves to the study of Christ's teachings in which, millions of Christians claim, is found perfect wisdom taught by God — confine their love and study to some particular natural science, or to wisdom which, as soon as it attains its highest and truest point, admits its own poverty and impotence? Do they speak the truth when they call themselves philosophers in the sense of lovers and seekers of wisdom? Those who truly love wisdom, love it all the more as it reveals and uncovers a superior, more excellent part of itself; they seek it everywhere and embrace it wherever they find it. Those who love it only when they draw it from a muddied stream, or who hate it or pay no heed to it in its limpid and abundant source, do not truly love or seek wisdom. There was indeed general admiration for the saying of Bion when he compared those who neglected Philosophy, and dedicated themselves to the study of other branches of knowledge, to Penelope's suitors who, when rejected by the heroine, married her slave-girls.[208] Nevertheless, after Wisdom, taught by God himself and far superior to Philosophy, was made known among human beings, a new likeness was needed. In it, Abraham's Egyptian servant, Haggar, became the symbol of Philosophy, and her mistress, Sarah, the symbol of Christian Wisdom.[209] If the servant shows insolence, Abraham puts her in the power of Sarah and also rightly discharges her from his household. On the other hand, it is dishonourable, for love of the servant, to dismiss the mistress, from whom alone the promised offspring can be born. No one can call himself a lover of Wisdom if he loves only a branch of knowledge which is handmaid to Wisdom, and commits adultery with the servant girl who so often rebels against her mistress and gives herself airs. Such an attitude is mean and dishonourable.

---

[208] 'There is also a saying of the philosopher Bion who said that just as Penelope's suitors, since they could not lie with Penelope, copulated with her slave girls, so those who cannot lay hold of philosophy pass their time in other disciplines of no worth'* (Plutarch, *On the Education of Children*).

[209] Clement of Alexandria, *Stromata*, 1, 5 ss.; Philo, *De congressu quaerendae eruditionis causa*; Augustine, *Against Fautus*, 22.

Original Language References

The numbers are footnote numbers, except where otherwise indicated

Page 4. *Res ardua, vetustis novitatem dare, novis auctoritatem, obsoletis nitorem, obscuris lucem, fastiditis gratiam, dubiis fidem.*

1. *Multa quidem ad fidem catholicam pertinentia, dum haereticorum calida inquietudine exagitantur, ut adversus eos defendi possint, et considerantur diligentius, et considerantur clarius, et instantius praedicantur.*

   Improbatio quidem haereticorum facit eminere quid Ecclesia sentiat, et quid habeat sana doctrina.

6. *Philosophi, credula gens.*

9. *Est per se ipsa perfecta et nullius indigens doctrina salvatoris: utpote facultas et potestas Dei. Porro graeca philosophia ad eam accedens non potentiorem facit veritatem; sed sophisticam adversus eam impressionem imbecillitatem reddens, propulsansque dolosas contra veritatem insidias, congruens vineae sepimentum et vallum ducit.*

10. *Si autem nullam auctoritatem recipiunt, oportet ad eos convincendos ad naturales rationes confugere.*

    Quaedam vero disputatio est magistralis in scholis , non ad removendum errorem, sed ad instruendum auditores, UT INDUCANTUR AD INTELLECTUM VERITATIS, QUAM INTENDIT, et tunc oportet rationibus inniti investigantibus veritatis radicem, et facientibus scire, quomodo sit verum quod dicitur.

    Alioquin si nudis auctoritatibus Magister quaestionem determinet, certificabitur quidem auditor, quod ita est, SED NIHIL SCIENTIAE VEL INTELLECTUS ACQUIRET.

20. *Cum enim gentes, quae legem non habent,* NATURALITER *ea quae legis sunt faciunt, eiusdem legem non habentes, ipsi sunt sibi leges, qui ostendunt* OPUS LEGIS *scriptum in cordibus suis.*

22. *Proinde in his qui flagrant ingenti amore perspicuae veritatis, non est improbandum studium, sed ad ordinem revocandum, ut a fide incipiat, et bonis moribus nitatur pervenire quo tendit.*

24. *Quod nisi Deus intus adiuverit, omnino non potero.*

25. *Cum etiam credere non possemus, nisi rationales animas haberemus.*

31. *Contrariae opiniones simul eidem esse non possunt.*

32. *Credimus enim Dominum* JESUM *Christum natum de Virgine quae* MARIA *vocabatur. Quid sit aut virgo, et quid sit nasci, et quid sit nomen proprium non credimus sed prorsus novimus.*

33. *Il ne faut pas s'y tromper la raison come l'imagination ne s'élance guère qu'après* L'INCONNU ET L'INFINI.

35. *Idem non esse verum in philosophia et theologia.*

    In theologia verum est: 'Verbum esse carnem factum'; in philosophia simpliciter impossibile est et absurdum.

43. *C'est j'en conviens une ressource un peu désespérée, mais, pour moi, je n'en vois pas d'autre.*

44. *Siccis rustica veritas capillis.*

46. *Loin de l'affaiblir, s'il était en mon pouvoir, je la fortifierais au contraire, je lui donnerais un représentant sérieux et digne d'elle; car elle renferme de grandes vérités, elle doit tenir un rang élevé dans la science, et je regard en conscience comme un véritable malheur l'état déplorable où elle est tombée parmi nous.*

    Quod tibi non vis fieri, alteri ne feceris.

49. *Quis non laudaret barbarorum sapientiam? Si quidem*

nemo eorum in Atheismum nunquam excidit, neque in dubium vocant sint ne Dii an non sint, et curent ne res humanas an non. Nemo igitur neque Indus, neque Celta, neque Aegyptius eam cogitationem in animum induxit, quam vel Evemerus Messenius, vel Diogenes Phryse, vel Hippon, vel Diagoras, vel Sosius, vel Epicurus.

Barbari omnes Deum admittunt.

50. *Quamquam acriter succensebunt nobis, si ita dixerimus.*

51. *Nisi forte tibi Homerum philosophum fuisse persuadent, cum his ipsis, quibus colligunt, negent. Nam modo Stoicum illum faciunt, virtutem solam probantem, et voluptates refugientem, et ab honesto ne immortalitatis quidem pretio recedentem, modo Epicureum, laudantem statum quietae civitatis et interconvivia, cantusque vitam exigentis, modo Peripateticum, bonorum tria genera inducentem, modo Academicum, incerta omnia dicentem.* APPARET NIHIL HORUM ESSE IN ILLO, QUIA OMNIA SUNT: ISTA ENIM INTER SE DISSIDENT.

53. *Philosophiam consequi non potest, qui in verborum pugnis et concertationibus operam suam collocat.*

55. *L'écletisme! Je n'ignore pas que ce nom seul soulève toutes les doctrines exclusives.*

56. *Il n'y a pas un de ces systèmes sur le quel n'ait passé une polémique accablante. Il n'y en a pas un qui ne soit percé à jour en quelque sorte, atteint et convaincu de contenir d'intolérables extravagances.*

57. *L'histoire de la philosophie eût suffit toute seule pour enfanter l'écletisme, c'est-à-dire la tolérance philosophique.*

58. *Je leur proposai un traité de paix sur la base de concessions réciproques.*

62. *Videndum, utrum doceant isti virtutem an non: si docent, philosophi sunt.*

63. *Philosophia — non in verbis, sed in rebus est.*

69. *Maximum hoc est et officium sapientiae et indicium, ut verbis opera concordent, ut et ipse ubique par sibi idemque sit.*

77. *Philosophia nihil ab alio petit, totum opus a solo excitat. Mathematica, ut ita dicam, superficiaria est, il alieno aedificat, aliena accipit principia, quorum beneficio ad ulteriora perveniat.*

78. *Non scientiarum propria, sed quae pluribus earum in commune competant, plurima id genus axiomata.*

86. *Diligunt eam lucentem, oderunt eam redarguentem.*

94. *Solutio atque avulsio animi a corpore, cum ad intelligibilia et ad ea quae vera sunt, convertimur.*

97. *Philosophiae tres partes dixerunt et* MAXIMIS *et* PLURIMI *auctores: moralem, naturalem, et rationalem.*

99. *Hinc philosophi sapientiae disciplinam tripartitam esse voluerunt, imo tripartitam esse animadvertere potuerunt: neque enim ipsi instituterunt, ut ita esset, sed ita esse potius invenerunt.*

103. *Vetus quidem hic extat sermo, cuius memores sumus; abire quidem illuc animas defunctorum rursusque huc reverti fierique ex mortuis.*

104. *Arbitror notioni homini optime satisfieri, si sapientiam nihil aliud esse dicamus, quam ipsam scientiam felicitatis.*

    Una est sapientia. Consistit ea in viva cognitione veri boni.

    Eruditionem sive sapientiam in adcurata et salutari, seu quod idem est, ad promovendam hominis felicitatem adcomodata veritatis cognitione esse positam.

110. PRINCIPIUM QUI ET LOQUOR VOBIS.

112. *De universis autem quae intelligimus, non loquentem qui personat foris, sed intus ipsi menti praesidentem consulimus veritatem, verbis fortasse ut consulamus, admoniti. Ille autem qui consulitur, docet; qui in interiore*

homine habitare dictus est Christus, idest incommutabilis Dei virtus, atque sempiterna sapientia: quam quidem omnis rationalis anima consulit, sed tantum cuique panditur, quantum capere propter propriam SIVE MALAM SIVE BONAM VOLUNTATEM potest. Et si quando fallitur, non fit vitio consultae veritatis, ut neque huius quae foris est lucis vitium est, quod corporei oculi saepe falluntur.

113. *Universos filios tuos doctos a Domino.*

118. *Est enim Philosophia amor et studium, et amicitia quodammodo Sapientiae. Sapientiae vero non huius quae in artibus quibusdam et in aliqua fabrili scientia notitiaque versatur, sed illius sapientiae quae nullius indigens, vivax mens, et sola rerum primaeva ratio est.*

127. *Fortasse enim qui Platonem caeteris philosophis gentium longe lateque praelatum acutius atque veracius intellexisse, atque secuti esse fama celebriore laudantur aliquid tale de Deo sentiunt, ut in illo inveniatur et CAUSA SUBSISTENDI, et RATIO INTELLIGENDI et ORDO VIVENDI. Quorum trium unum ad naturalem, alterum ad rationalem, tertium ad moralem partem intelligitur pertinere.*

Qui verum Deum et RERUM AUCTOREM et VERITATIS ILLUS-TRATOREM, ET BEATITUDINIS LARGITOREM esse dixerunt.

et rerum creatarum sit EFFECTOR, et LUMEN cognoscendarum, et BONUM agendarum.

128. *Cum autem sapientes appellarentur qui modo quodam laudabilis vitae aliis praestare videbantur, iste interrogatus, quid profiteretur, philosophum se esse respondit, idest studiosum et amatorem sapientiae: quoniam sapientem profiteri ARROGANTISSIMUM videbatur.*

129. *Haec est perfecta iustitia quae potius potiora, minus minora diligimus.*

132. *Ita se mirificum doctrinae operibus addixerat, ut cum cibi capessendi causa recubuisset, cogitationibus inhaerens, manum ad mensam porrigere obliviscuntur. Sed cum Melissa, quam uxoris loco habebat, temperato inter studia*

non interpellandi, sed inediae succurrendae officio, dexteram suam necessariis usibus aptabat. Ergo animo tantummodo vita fruebatur; corpore vero quasi alieno et supervacuo circumdatus erat.

133. *Ad quas mentis acie pervenire paucorum est; et cum pervenitur, quantum fieri potest, non in eis manet ipse perventor, sed, veluti acie ipsa reverberata, repellitur, et fit rei non transitoriae transitoria cogitatio.*

135. *Magnus plane vir Abraham, et multarum virtutum clarus insignibus quem votis suis philosophia non potuit aequare. Denique minus est quod ille finxit, quam quod iste gessit, maiorque ambitioso eloquentiae mendacio simplex veritatis fides.*

138. FONS SAPIENTIAE, VERBUM DEI IN EXCELSIS.

140. *Qui autem adhaeret Deo unus Spiritus est.*

 Si autem Spiritu facta carnis mortificaveritis, vivetis. Quicumque enim Spiritu Dei aguntur, hi sunt filii Dei.

 Ipse Spiritus postulat pro nobis gemitibus inenarrabilibus.

142. *Spiritu ambulate et desideria carnis non perficietis: caro enim concupiscit adversus spiritum, spiritus autem adversus carnem; haec enim sibi invicem adversantur.*

143. *Melior est homo qui minuitur sapientia, et deficiens sensu in timore, quam qui abundat sensu, et transgreditur legem Altissimi.*

144. *Multitudinis usus…communiter obtinuit, ut sapientes dicantur qui res directe ordinant, et eas bene gubernant.*

 Iudicat et ordinat de omnibus.

145. *Differunt autem Sapientia et Prudentia. Nam Sapientia est cognitio divinarum rerum, unde pertinet ad contemplationem* (Jn 28: 28). *'Timor Domini ipsa est Sapientia': prudentia vero est cognitio rerum humananrum, unde dicitur* (Prov 10: 23): *'Sapientia est viro prudentia', quia scilicet scientia humanarum rerum prudentia dicitur.*

147. *Videtur autem prudentis esse bene consiliari posse circa ipsa bona.*

151. *Sapientia enim et disciplina timor Domini.*

    plenitudo sapientiae est timere Deum et plenitudo A FRUCTIBUS illius.

    Radix sapientiae est timere Dominum, et rami illius longaevi.

152. *Quem Pater sanctificavit et misit in mundum.*

157. *Confitemini Domino et invocate nomen eius: notas facite in populis adinventiones eius.*

161. *Modo ista (Maria) vivebat de verbo, sed sonante verbo. Erit vita de verbo non sonante verbo. Ipsum verbum vita est. Similes ei erimus quoniam videbimus eum sicuti est.*

162. *Omnis qui EST EX VERITATE audit vocem meam.*

170. *Et verbum eius (Patris) non habetis in vobis manens: quia quem misit ille, huic vos non creditis.*

188. *Docebit vos omnem veritatem.*

189. *Semen ipsius in eo manet.*

190. *Eo quod CARITATEM VERITATIS non receperunt, ut salvi fiant.*

191. *VERITATEM autem FACIENTES IN CARITATE, crescamus in illo per omnia, qui est caput Christus.*

192. *Charitate fraternitatis invicem diligentes: honore invicem praevenientes.*

    De charitate autem fraternitatis non necesse habemus scribere vobis: ipsi enim vos a Deo didicistis, ut diligatis invicem.

    Charitas fraternitatis maneat in vobis.

197. *Hoc est praeceptum meum, ut diligatis invicem, sicut ego dilexi vos.*

199. *Quoniam non est vera sapientia, quae intentionem suam in his quae prudenter discernit, gerit fortiter, cohibet temperanter, iusteque distribuit, non in illum dirigit finem, ubi erit Deus omnia in omnibus, aeternitate certa, et pace perfecta.*

200. *Mihi enim vivere Christus est, et mori lucrum. Quod si vivere in carne, hic mihi fructus operis est, et quid eligam ignoro. Coarctor autem e duobus: desiderium habens dissolvi, et esse cum Christo, multo magis melius: permanere autem in carne, necessarium propter vos.*

202. *Spes vero aeternae contemplationis Dei, habens certam et delectabilem intelligentiam veritatis.*

203. *Cum tradiderit regnum Deo et Patri.*

   Cum credentes et viventes ex fide, pro quibus nunc mediator interpellat, perduxerit ad contemplationem, cui percipiendae suspiramus et gemimus.

204. *Et ideo non amandum est, quod manenti et fruenti amori auferri potest. Cuius ergo rei amor amandus est, nisi eius, quae non potest deesse dum amatur? Id autem est, quod nihil est aliud habere quam nosse.*

205. *Bonum quod non amatur, nemo potest perfecte habere vel nosse: quis enim potest nosse quantum sit bonum, quo non fruitur? Non autem fruitur, si non amat: nec habet igitur quod amandum est, qui non amat.*

208. *Urbanum est etiam Bionis philosophi dictum, qui aiebat, sicut Penelopes proci, cum non possent cum Penelopa concumbere, rem cum eius ancillis habuissent: ita qui Philosophiam nequeunt apprehendere, eos in aliis nullius praecii disciplinis se se conterere.*

Index of Biblical References

Numbers in italic indicate footnote numbers. Bible references are from RSV (Common Bible)

Index of Persons

Numbers in roman indicate paragraphs; numbers in italic indicate footnotes

General Index

Numbers in roman indicate paragraphs; numbers in italic indicate footnotes